Empirical Studies of Translation and Interpreting

This edited book is a collection of the latest empirical studies of translation and interpreting (T&I) from the post-structuralist perspective. The contributors are professors, readers, senior lecturers, lecturers, and research students from an international context. The contributions are characterised by five themes:

- Intervention in T&I
- Process of T&I
- Product of T&I
- T&I and technology
- T&I education

These up-to-date topics are reflective of the shift in attitudes that is being witnessed as a new generation of translation scholars rejects the subjective assertions of previous generations, in favour of an altogether more rigorous approach. The book will notably contribute to the development of T&I and enhance our knowledge of the areas. It will be a useful reference for academics, postgraduate research students, and professional translators and interpreters. The book will also play a role in proposing practical and empirically based ways of training for universities and the industry, so as to overcome traditional barriers to translation and interpreting learning. The book will additionally provide reference material for relevant professional bodies.

Caiwen Wang is Senior Lecturer in Translation and Interpreting Studies at the University of Westminster, UK, and Associate Professor (Teaching) at University College London. Her research interests are in empirical studies of translation and interpreting, and the broad field of linguistics and applied linguistics. She has published in translation studies, interpreting studies, and pragmatic studies, and has had successful research funding bids. She is also a very experienced professional translator and interpreter.

Binghan Zheng is Associate Professor of Translation Studies at Durham University, UK, where he serves as the Director of the Centre for Intercultural Mediation. His research interests include cognitive translation and interpreting studies, neuroscience of translation, and comparative translation and interpreting studies. His recent publications appeared in some of the leading journals in T&I.

Routledge Advances in Translation and Interpreting Studies

For more information about this series, please visit https://www.routledge.com/Routledge-Advances-in-Translation-and-Interpreting-Studies/book-series/RTS

Empirical Studies of Translation and Interpreting

The Post-Structuralist Approach

Edited by Caiwen Wang and
Binghan Zheng

Routledge
Taylor & Francis Group

NEW YORK AND LONDON

First published 2021
by Routledge
605 Third Avenue, New York, NY 10158

and by Routledge
2 Park Square, Milton Park, Abingdon, Oxon, OX14 4RN

Routledge is an imprint of the Taylor & Francis Group, an informa business
© 2021 Taylor & Francis

The right of Caiwen Wang and Binghan Zheng to be identified as the authors of the editorial material, and of the authors for their individual chapters, has been asserted in accordance with sections 77 and 78 of the Copyright, Designs and Patents Act 1988.

Library of Congress Cataloging-in-Publication Data
A catalog record for this title has been requested

ISBN: 9780367856106 (hbk)
ISBN: 9781032005515 (pbk)
ISBN: 9781003017400 (ebk)

Typeset in Sabon
by Deanta Global Publishing Services, Chennai, India

Contents

PART III
Product of T&I   93

PART IV
T&I and Technology   179

PART V
T&I Education   217

Contributors

Yixiao Cui is a PhD candidate (with CSC scholarship) at the School of Modern Languages and Cultures, Durham University. She obtained her MSc in Specialised Translation and Interpreting from UCL. Her research interests include translation and consultation and specialised translation with technology. She has published a research paper in the journal *Perspectives*.

Juntao Deng is an associate professor in translation studies at the School of Foreign Languages, Wuhan Institute of Technology, and was a postdoctoral researcher at Guangdong University of Foreign Studies. His research interests are in computer-assisted interpreter training and he has published a dozen academic papers in Chinese and international journals.

Claudio Fantinuoli is Senior Lecturer and Researcher at the University of Mainz in Germersheim. The focus of his research is computer-assisted interpreting and speech-to-text translation.

Fei Gao is a PhD candidate at the Centre for Translation Studies at the University of Leeds. Her academic interests bring together interpreting studies and corpus linguistics. She is also a freelance interpreter and was a lecturer with Chongqing University of Posts and Telecommunications in China before commencing her PhD project in the UK.

Hailun Huang is a master's candidate at the Department of Linguistics, Zhejiang University, China. Her research interests include interpreting studies and cognitive psychology.

Junying Liang is a full professor in psycholinguistics and interpreting studies at the Department of Linguistics, Zhejiang University, China. She holds a doctorate degree in cognitive psychology, and her current research focuses on psychological approaches to interpreting studies.

Yiguang Liu is a doctoral candidate at the Department of Linguistics, Zhejiang University, China. His research interests include interpreting studies, psycholinguistics, and quantitative linguistics.

Jemina Napier is Professor and Chair of Intercultural Communication and Director of the Centre for Translation and Interpreting Studies in Scotland, in the Department of Languages and Intercultural Studies, School of Social Sciences at Heriot-Watt University in Edinburgh, UK. She is also a Visiting Professor at the Centre for Deaf Studies at Trinity College Dublin, and Adjunct Professor in the Department of Linguistics at Macquarie University, Sydney, Australia. Her research focuses primarily on sign language intercultural communication, conducting linguistic, social, and ethnographic explorations of direct and interpreter-mediated communication to inform intercultural communication, interpreting studies, applied linguistics, and deaf studies theories. Her specialist language is British Sign Language, and she is fluent in Australian and American Sign Languages and International Sign. Jemina was founding editor of the *International Journal of Interpreter Education* and is on the editorial board for the *International Journal of Translation and Interpreting Research* and the *Journal of Deaf Studies and Deaf Education*. She has published over 100 books, edited volumes, and peer-reviewed book chapters and journal articles on studies of interpreting and interpreting pedagogy. Online link: https://www.hw.ac.uk/staff/uk/soss/jemina-nap ier.htm

Elisabetta Pisani holds an MA in Conference Interpreting from the University of Trieste. She is an active conference interpreter.

María del Mar Ogea Pozo holds a BA in Modern Languages and Translation & Interpreting Studies from the University of Salford, UK, as well as an MA in Audiovisual Translation: Dubbing and Subtitling from the University of Seville and an MA in Specialised Translation from the University of Córdoba, Spain. In 2016 she finished a PhD thesis on the subtitling of intercultural documentaries. During the first years after finishing her studies, she worked as an in-house translator and then as a freelance audiovisual translator. Currently, she is a lecturer of Audiovisual Translation and Multimedia Translation at the University of Córdoba (Spain), and also teaches audiovisual translation in the Master's degree in Audiovisual Translation: Localization, Subtitling and Dubbing at the University of Cádiz and the Master's degree in Specialised Translation at the University of Córdoba, Spain. She is the chief editor of *Transletters: International Journal of Translation and Interpreting*, and the coordinator of *TradAV*, a teaching innovation project on audiovisual translation from a multidisciplinary approach.

Raquel de Pedro Ricoy is Professor and holds the Chair of Translation and Interpreting at the University of Stirling, UK. Most of her academic career has centred on the training of translators and interpreters, and she has also worked as a freelance translator, interpreter, and lexicographer. Her research interests lie in the social and cultural dimensions of translation and interpreting, especially in relation to interpreting in public-service settings that involve marginalised communities, and to the translation of multimodal texts. Her most recent projects, which received funding from AHRC/GCRF, relate to the role of translators and interpreters in the mediation of indigenous rights in present-day Peru. She has published extensively and delivered keynote lectures and presentations on these subjects in Europe, America, and Asia. Online link: https://www.stir.ac.uk/people/424068

Claire Y. Shih is Senior Lecturer in Translation Studies at University College London, UK. She publishes widely in the field of translation process research (TPR), eliciting data from think-aloud protocols (TAPs), retrospective interviews, screen recording, and eye-tracking. Her recent publication focuses on translators' online information-seeking behaviours and translation pedagogy. She is currently co-editing the *Routledge Handbook of East Asian Translation*. Her publications can be found here: https://www.ucl.ac.uk/european-languages-culture/people/claire-shih

Rebecca Tipton is Lecturer in Interpreting and Translation Studies at the Centre for Translation and Intercultural Studies, University of Manchester, UK. She has published on interpreting in asylum settings, police interviews, conflict zones, and social work. Her work foregrounds issues of interpreter impartiality, trust, risk, and organisational accountability to limited English–proficient service users. More recent work has focused on interpreter mediation for victims of domestic abuse in statutory and non-statutory services, and on the role of translation and interpreting in Britain's humanitarian history. She is currently Secretary/Treasurer of IATIS. Online link: https://www.research.manchester.ac.uk/portal/en/researchers/rebecca-tipton(0bce078b-32e8-4549-bf1b-154a22a7806f).html

Piero Toto is Senior Lecturer in Languages (Translation) at London Metropolitan University. He is a translation technology trainer and localisation lecturer, as well as an experienced English into Italian translator with a background in linguistics, gender issues, and queer studies. This eclectic mix of interests is at the heart of his academic research and activity, ranging from translations into Italian to published poetry in both English and Italian, to articles on masculinity, queer studies, and translator training. He is also an Associate Lecturer for Italian at the Open University and has run translation/localisation workshops abroad and at other UK universities. He is a member of the Chartered Institute of Linguists, where he acts as ad hoc freelance Italian examiner and assessor on a variety of qualifications and exams.

Natalia Rodríguez Vicente is a postdoctoral research associate working for a project on interpreter-mediated Mental Health Act assessments funded through the UK National Institute for Health Research. She holds a PhD in Interpreting Studies from the Centre for Translation and Interpreting Studies in Scotland at Heriot-Watt University in Edinburgh, UK. Her research focuses on the intersection of interactional pragmatics, clinical communication, and interpreting studies. She has worked for the Evidence and Evaluation for Improvement Team at Healthcare Improvement Scotland (NHS Scotland), where she led a research project on person-centred communication. In addition to her research activities, Natalia has taught several modules at Heriot-Watt University, both at undergraduate and postgraduate level, including lectures and seminars on Public Service Interpreting. She has also delivered continuous professional development courses for practicing interpreters. Prior to her academic career, Natalia worked as a conference interpreter for a public institution in Zaragoza (Spain) and as a project manager at a translation and localisation company in Edinburgh. Natalia is a member of the UK Chartered Institute of Linguists (CIOL) and an associate fellow of the UK Higher Education Academy (HEA).

Binhua Wang is Chair/Professor of Interpreting and Translation Studies and Director of the Centre for Translation Studies at the University of Leeds. He is also Fellow of the Chartered Institute of Linguists (CIoL), vice-chair of the academic committee of the World Interpreter and Translator Training Association (WITTA), and editorial board member of *Babel: International Journal of Translation*. His research has focused on various aspects of interpreting and translation studies, in which he has published over 50 articles including around 40 in refereed CSSCI/Core journals and SSCI/A&HCI journals and over a dozen peer-reviewed book chapters. He has authored the monographs *Theorising Interpreting Studies* (2019, FLTRP) and *A Descriptive Study of Norms in Interpreting* (2013, FLTRP). His research has been funded by some major research grants such as the General Research Fund (GRF) of the Hong Kong Research Grants Council and the China Ministry of Education Research Grant for Humanities and Social Sciences. His textbooks of interpreter training are also widely used in China's MTI and BTI programmes. He is an academic reviewer for some SSCI/A&HCI and CSSCI journals and for some major international publishers such as Routledge, John Benjamins, Palgrave Macmillan, and Springer Nature. Online link: https://ahc.leeds.ac.uk/languages/staff/1223/profe ssor-binhua-wang

Caiwen Wang is Senior Lecturer in Translation and Interpreting Studies at the University of Westminster, UK, and Associate Professor (Teaching) at University College London. Her research interests are in empirical studies of translation and interpreting, and the broad field of linguistics and applied linguistics. She has published in translation studies, interpreting studies, and pragmatic studies, and has had successful research funding bids. She is also a professional translator and interpreter with many

years' experience. Online link: https://www.westminster.ac.uk/about-us/
our-people/directory/wang-caiwen#research

Mianjun Xu is an associate professor at the Faculty of English Language
and Culture/School of Interpreting and Translation Studies/Centre
for Translation Studies, Guangdong University of Foreign Studies,
Guangdong, People's Republic of China. She holds a PhD in translation
and interpreting studies. Her research interests include translation and
interpreting education and intercultural writings and she has published a
dozen academic papers in Chinese and international journals.

Tianyuan Zhao is currently a postdoctoral researcher at the Graduate School
of Translation and Interpreting, Beijing Foreign Studies University,
Beijing, People's Republic of China. Her research interests include interpreting studies and translation education and she has published a number
of academic papers in core Chinese and international journals.

Binghan Zheng is Associate Professor of Translation Studies at Durham
University, where he serves as the Director of the Centre for Intercultural
Mediation. His research interests include cognitive translation and
interpreting studies, neuroscience of translation, and comparative
translation and interpreting studies. His recent publications appeared
in journals such as *Target, Across Languages and Cultures, The
Interpreter and Translator Trainer, Journal of Pragmatics, Brain and
Cognition, Perspectives, LANS-TTS, Babel, Translation and Interpreting
Studies, Foreign Language Teaching and Research*, and *Journal of
Foreign Languages*. He is a guest editor of journals including *Translation
and Interpreting Studies* and *Foreign Language Teaching and Research*.

Xiaojun Zhang is Lecturer and Subject Leader in Translation and
Interpreting Studies at Xi'an Jiaotong-Liverpool University (XJTLU). He
worked at a number of higher education institutes in China, Ireland, and
the UK and was a lecturer in translation and interpreting studies and
a joint programme director at the University of Stirling, UK before he
joined XJTLU. He is the Deputy Chair of the Translation Technology
Education Society affiliated with WITTA (World Interpreting and
Translation Teaching Association) and scientific members for the top
conferences in natural language processing such as LREC, CWMT, CCL,
and AACL. His research interests cover translation technology, natural
language processing, and practical translation.

Bing Zou is a full-time lecturer and a research fellow in the Center for
Translation Studies and School of Interpreting and Translation Studies at
Guangdong University of Foreign Studies. His current research areas of
interest include corpus-based and process-oriented translation and interpreting studies as well as technology-inspired translation pedagogy.

Acknowledgements

We have many people to thank for this exciting edited volume.

Great thanks to Elysse Preposi, Helena Parkinson, and their team at Routledge, who offered their much-appreciated professional assistance from the start of this book and throughout, at a time when COVID-19 hit the world. Thanks to Jayanthi Chander at Deanta Global Publishing for coordinating the production of the book.

We are indebted to the authors for their response when contacted and for their enthusiasm to contribute.

Our heartfelt appreciation also goes to the colleagues who took their time in reading the respective manuscripts and writing extremely detailed and constructive review reports. Our authors were very grateful and often asked us to pass their gratitude on to their anonymous reviewers. The list of our academic reviewers is as below:

Alexa Alfer, Elsa Huertas Barros, Lindsay Bywood, Juntao Deng, Ping Deng, Dezheng Feng, Yi Gu, Xinchao Guan, Chao Han, Séverine Hubscher-Davidson, Zhifeng Kang, Joseph Lambert, Hongjun Lan, Dechao Li, Saihong Li, Junying Liang, Jessica Oppedisano, Feng Pan, Claire Y. Shih, Rebecca Tipton, Piero Toto, Sergey Tyulenev, Natalia Rodríguez Vicente, Caiwen Wang, Haiqing Wang, Yanjing Wu, Mianjun Xu, Xiaojun Zhang, and Binghan Zheng.

Introduction

Caiwen Wang and Binghan Zheng

This edited book showcases some of the latest empirical studies of translation and interpreting (T&I). Some of these studies are the outcomes of funded projects, others are follow-on studies, and still others are PhD researches having been presented at recent T&I conferences. The contributors are professors, senior lecturers, lecturers, and junior researchers from an international context. This combination of well-established and emerging researchers reflects the purpose of this collection as we have just stated.

There are three major motivations behind this volume.

Firstly, according to Pöchhacker (2008), translation studies and interpreting studies have both arrived at an empirical turn now in the twenty-first century, after having undertaken different routes of progress historically. In this era of empirical turn, research in T&I is characterised by a variety of focuses, such as "ethics" (e.g. Van Wyke, 2016; Wang, 2017), "intervention" or "mediation" (e.g. Munday, 2007; Wang, 2017), "risks" (e.g. Slovic & Peters, 2006; Pym, 2015; Pym & Matsushita, 2018), "sociological turn" (e.g. Angelelli, 2012), "technological turn" (e.g. Zhang & Cai, 2015; O'Hagan, 2017), "translation process" (e.g. Hansen, 2017), and "translator and interpreter education" (e.g. Kim, 2017). We believed that an edited book of empirical studies of both T&I in the 2020s would show to readers some, if not all, of the latest developments in T&I studies since the empirical turn. We approached potential researchers without defining any themes before asking them instead what kind of studies they were conducting and whether or not they would be willing to contribute to our edited book. Our collection features intervention/mediation in T&I, the sociological aspect of T&I, the process of T&I, the product of T&I, the technological aspect of T&I, and translator/interpreter education.

Secondly, while approaching potential contributors for empirical studies of T&I that they may have already embarked on, we found that the titles we received share a common feature: the post-structuralist approach, hence, the subtitle for this book. In T&I, the post-structuralist approach is characterised by "a rejection of essentialist claims, traditional positivist concepts, such as equivalence and fidelity, and the stasis of earlier linguistic-based models" (Angellelli & Baer, 2016, p. 3). Schäffner and Bassnett (2010) provided more details on this approach:

> Translation Studies today is no longer concerned with examining whether a translation has been 'faithful' to a source text. Instead, the focus is on social, cultural, and communicative practices, on the cultural and ideological significance of translating and of translations, on the external politics of translation, on the relationship between translation behaviour and socio-cultural factors. In other words, there is a general recognition of the complexity of the phenomenon of translation, an increased concentration on social causation and human agency, and a focus on effects rather than on internal structures.
>
> (p. 10)

The chapters in this volume have reflected these new shifts, therefore providing a snapshot of current T&I empirical studies representing the post-structuralist approach.

Following a stringent peer review process, we have collected 13 chapters in total. These are divided into five thematic parts as below.

Part I has the theme "Intervention in T&I" and explores the social or social-political aspects of T&I. Rebecca Tipton (Chapter 1) identified the ethical challenges faced by interpreters in domestic abuse settings so as to create relevant guidelines for interpreters. The study examined several data sets and concluded that the particularised context of victim support services is in need of setting-specific guidance. Natalia Rodríguez Vicente, Jemina Napier, and Raquel de Pedro Ricoy (Chapter 2) explored the extent to which interpreters' performance can promote or hinder the access of linguistically and culturally diverse patients to the person-centred care principles advocated and promoted by health service providers. By qualitatively analysing the audio-recordings of naturalistic consultation data collected from an outpatient mental healthcare clinic in Scotland, the authors concluded that interpreters may consciously or unconsciously enable or hamper person-centred communication through their interpreting activities.

Part II concentrates on the process of T&I. The two studies reported here have revealed how the activity of translating was carried out by professional translators and student translators, respectively. The chapter contributed by Yixiao Cui and Binghan Zheng (Chapter 3) studied student translators' consultation behaviour in translation, using a combination of quantitative and qualitative methods. The study reported that as perceived translation difficulty increases, translation students spent a longer time on consultation, resorting to more types of online resources and more general-purpose resources, and conducted more transitions between translating and consultation. Combining real-time eye-tracking gaze and retrospective thinking-aloud (RTA), Claire Y. Shih (Chapter 4) studied professional translators' web-navigating behaviour. The author reported ten professional translators' primary actions, secondary actions, and the interplay between the two actions regarding their web-navigating behaviour during the translation process.

Part III investigates the product of T&I and generally departs from a perspective distinguished by the traditional one of equivalence or fidelity. Fei Gao and Binhua Wang (Chapter 5) looked into interpreters' moderations in interpreting political texts by integrating critical discourse analysis (CDA) and corpus linguistics (CL). Their corpus led to the finding that Chinese conference interpreters tend to reconstruct or mediate political discourse in interpreting with a stronger sense of solidarity and obligation than presented in source speeches. The study by María del Mar Ogea Pozo (Chapter 6) examined how humour was subtitled due to sociocultural considerations and the restrictions of subtitling. It showed that a number of mediations were involved, even though equivalence remained a major consideration for translators. Caiwen Wang (Chapter 7) and Bing Zou and Binhua Wang (Chapter 8) are two studies that provide evidence for the existence of translational discourse (Olohan, 2002). Employing the parallel-corpus approach and a retrospective questionnaire combined with interviews, Caiwen Wang explored the extent to which explicitations were implemented in translating figures of speech in political texts, as well as the reasons behind the translator's decisions. The study reported that explicitations happened frequently for the translation of figures of speech, and it was a conscious decision the translator made to facilitate cross-cultural communication. Bing Zou and Binhua Wang, on the other hand, examined the genres and text types of interpreted political discourse. The authors identified the genres and text types from Douglas Biber (1988) that the four types of political discourses under their investigation are closest in comparison, and found that interpreted political discourses are more likely to fall into the genre of professional letters rather than oral speeches.

Part IV concerns the theme "Technology and T&I" and features two innovative studies in the fields. Elisabetta Pisani and Claudio Fantinuoli (Chapter 9) assessed the potentials of automatic speech recognition (ASR) for the rendition of numbers in simultaneous interpreting. They reported that a significant reduction of error rate could be witnessed by applying the ASR technology to the simultaneous interpretation of numbers. Xiaojun Zhang (Chapter 10) introduced some novel discourse-processing methods in statistical machine translation (SMT) and neural machine translation (NMT) architectures. This exploratory study proposed two complementary approaches to integrating cross-sentence context into NMT, and quantitatively as well as qualitatively demonstrated that the two approaches significantly outperform a strong attention-based NMT baseline system.

Part V focuses on the theme "T&I Education" and demonstrates how T&I activities can be aided or enhanced by various pedagogical interventions. By using the Simon task and the digit switch task in their two experiments, Yiguang Liu, Hailun Huang, and Junying Liang (Chapter 11) assessed how interpreter training helped interpreters free themselves from emotional distractions. This study is one of the first attempts at investigation that extends interpreter advantage studies to the psycho-emotional perspective. Piero Toto (Chapter 12) showed us the flipped classroom of translation technology in London Metropolitan University and demonstrated how this approach had enhanced translation students' overall translator competence and satisfaction. Finally, Mianjun Xu, Tianyuan Zhao, and Juntao Deng (Chapter 13) looked into interpreter trainers' perception of massive open online courses as an innovative method for interpreting teaching. This research was originally intended to be a reference document for interpreter training aimed to improve and reform relevant practice in China, but could have global implications for remote interpreting teaching and learning against the backdrop of the COVID-19 pandemic.

As we stated earlier, this edited book intends to present a cross-section of current T&I empirical studies by approaching potential contributors to find out what their ongoing research was like. It happened that among the responses we received, a larger number of studies are related to Chinese and English as the language pair for observations. This brings us to the third of our motivations mentioned at the beginning. Namely, we believe this edited volume reflects, in a timely manner, the internationalising trend in T&I studies as witnessed in Tymoczko (2016):

> Since 2005 translation studies have achieved significant progress in internationalizing the discipline and moving beyond its Eurocentric origins. In turn, this has resulted in the expansion of the concept translation and the redefinition of translational phenomena and practices.
>
> (p. 100)

While the studies collected in our book tend to focus more on the Chinese–English language pair, we contend that the significance of these studies for T&I development is not restricted to this specific language pair. The studies observing Chinese subjects explored particular phenomena in the broad fields of T&I, such as explicitations in translation, web search and consultation behaviour of translators, interpreted discourse, interpreters' mediation, and remote interpreting courses. As such, the significance of these studies is that along with studies of typically European language pairs, they will eventually lead us to discover possible "universals" in T&I (Mauranen & Kujamäki, 2004); they also potentially serve to be pioneers for new lines of inquiry by inspiring studies of the same translation and/or interpreting phenomena among other language pairs. The slight "preponderance" of data collected from the Chinese–English language pair compensates for the scarcity of relevant data in the T&I fields needed for rigid discussions and conclusions, to bridge gaps in T&I theory and practice from one culture to another. Besides, the empirical studies collected in the book contain data from the Arabic, French, German, Italian, Polish, Russian, and Spanish languages, with participants being Asian, European white, black, or of other minority ethnic origins. This, together with the Chinese data, will contribute to our understandings of "the relation between translation practices and how they are conceptualized in various languages in various places in the world" (Van Doorslaer & Flynn, 2013, p. 1).

In the empirical sense, the studies collected in this volume have shown slightly more invested interests in studying some areas of T&I than others, noticeably "Product of T&I." Representing a cross-section of the latest developments in T&I studies, our collection does not intend to suggest that studies of different T&I sections are unbalanced, and neither do we believe this is the case. With more cross-sections revealed by future research, we will be able to capture more characteristics of T&I studies reflecting the post-structuralist approach in the empirical turn.

We hope our readers will appreciate this edited book from the above perspectives and find them useful and beneficial.

References

Angelelli, C. V., (2012). The sociological turn in translation and interpreting studies. *Translation and Interpreting Studies*, 7(2):125–128.

Angelelli, C. V. and Baer, B. J.. (Eds.) (2016). *Researching Translation and Interpreting*. London: Routledge.

Hansen, G., (2017). The translation process as object of research. In: Millán, C. and Batrina, F. (Eds.), *The Routledge Handbook of Translation Studies* (pp. 88–101). London: Routledge.

Kim, M., (2017). Research on translator and interpreter education. In: Millán, C. and Batrina, F. (Eds.), *The Routledge Handbook of Translation Studies*, (pp. 102–116). London: Routledge.

Mauranen, A. and Kujamäki, P., (Eds.) (2004). *Translation Universals: Do They Exist?* Amsterdam: John Benjamins.

Munday, J., (2007). *Translation as Intervention*. London: Continuum.

O'Hagan, M., (2017). The impact of new technologies on translation studies: A technological turn? In: Millán, C. and Batrina, F. (Eds.), *The Routledge Handbook of Translation Studies* (pp. 503–518). London: Routledge.

Olohan, M., (2002). Leave it out! Using a comparable corpus to investigate aspects of explicitation in translation. *Cadernos de Tradução*, 9:153–169.

Pöchhacker, F., (2008). The turns of interpreting studies. In: Hansen, G., Chesterman, A. and Gerzymisch-Arbogast, H. (Eds.), *Efforts and Models in Interpreting and Translation Research* (pp. 25–46). Amsterdam: John Benjamins.

Pym, A., (2015). Translating as risk management. *Journal of Pragmatics*, 85:67–80.

Pym, A. and Matsushita, K., (2018). Risk mitigation in translator decisions. *Across Languages and Cultures*, 19(1):1–18.

Schäffner, C. and Bassnett, S., (2010). *Political Discourse, Media and Translation*. Newcastle: Cambridge Scholars Publishing.

Slovic, P. and Peters, E., (2006). Risk perception and affect. *Current Directions in Psychological Science*, 15(6):322–325.

Tymoczko, M., (2016). Trajectories of research in translation studies: An update with a case study in the neuroscience of translation. *Asia Pacific Translation and Intercultural Studies*, 3(2):99–122, doi:10.1080/23306343.2016.1184833.

Van Doorslaer, L. and Flynn, P., (2013). On constructing continental views on translation studies: An introduction. In: Van Doorslaer, L. and Flynn, P. (Eds.), *Eurocentrism in Translation Studies* (pp. 1–8). Amsterdam: John Benjamins Publishing.

Van Wyke, B., (2016). Translation and ethics. In: Millán, C. and Batrina, F. (Eds.), *The Routledge Handbook of Translation Studies* (pp. 548–560). London: Routledge.

Wang, C., (2017). Interpreters = cultural mediators? *TranslatoLogica*, 1:93–115.

Zhang, C. and Cai, H., (2015). On technological turn of translation studies: Evidences and influences. *Journal of Language Teaching and Research*, 6(4):429–434.

Part I
Intervention in T&I

1 Biopolitics, Complicity, and Community in Domestic Abuse Support Settings

Implications for Interpreter Guidance

Rebecca Tipton

Introduction

> I propose to consider a dimension of political life that has to do with our exposure to violence and our complicity in it, with our vulnerability to loss and the task of mourning that follows, and with finding a basis for community in these conditions.
>
> (Butler, 2004, p. 19)

The lack of attention from policymakers to the specialised support needed by women from black, ethnic minority, and refugee and immigrant backgrounds in Britain has to be considered in the context of growing interest in matters of interpersonal violence at the domestic and international levels (Southall Black Sisters, 2019). Measures designed to respond to violence when it occurs, limit its extent and consequences, and provide care and support for those impacted are outlined in key instruments such as the Istanbul and *Belém do Pará* Conventions, supported by developments in international human rights law that promote the "positive obligations" of the state in this sphere (Rubio-Marín & Estrada-Tanck, 2013; Henn, 2019). However, the translation of such measures into coherent policies at the organisational level is often uneven, especially when it comes to language support provision. In the UK, at least, there is growing recognition of the barriers facing victims who do not have English as a first language (cf. HMIC, 2014; SafeLives, 2017), but a systematic response in terms of interpreter training and the commissioning of provision is lacking.

This chapter reports on the development of guidance for interpreters working in charity support services for victim-survivors of domestic abuse. It draws on underpinning research that has been discussed extensively elsewhere (Tipton, 2017a, 2017b, 2018, 2019b) and presents findings from recent experimental research. The chapter seeks to address the following questions: 1) to what extent can a biopolitical approach to victim support help to theorise "political community" in interpreter-mediated encounters?

2) what evidence of political community can be identified in simulated interpreting practice? and 3) what are the implications of 2) for developing guidance for interpreters in domestic abuse support services?

The chapter starts by situating recent approaches to domestic abuse in the context of human security frameworks and evolving policy formations. This serves as a basis for re-conceptualising victim support and interpreting as biopolitical enterprises, drawing on Butler's (2004) concept of "community" as a response to circumstances in which bodies may be exposed to violence and complicit in it, and Inghilleri's (2008) conceptualisation of a translation ethics that is informed by the ethical encounter itself. The final section presents examples from simulated interpreted encounters and interpreter reflections on both the encounters and the draft guidance to illustrate the affordances of a biopolitical approach in the achievement of political community in this setting.

Background and Theoretical Underpinnings

Developments in International and National Domestic Abuse Policies and Practice

The international response to domestic abuse and violence has been shaped by changing conceptualisations of human security, involving a move away from state-centred (e.g. territorial, military) to person-centred conceptualisations (Rubio-Marín & Estrada-Tanck, 2013, p. 240). This shift has influenced the emergence of "positive obligations" for states to actively take measures to protect human rights, together with due diligence standards, which include "the state's duty to investigate and punish violations of non-state actors and properly redress the victims" (ibid., p. 244). Such developments, however, need to be considered in the wider political context of public management frameworks wherein person-centredness is often articulated in terms of what individuals can do to protect themselves (self-responsibilisation) rather than what protections the state can offer, reflecting neoliberal concerns for self-reliance.

Support for those fleeing abuse and violence in the home has traditionally been provided by the charity sector and funded through a combination of public donations and government funding. In the United Kingdom, austerity policies rolled out since 2010 have led to one in six refuges closing and around 60% of women seeking places being turned away (*The Independent*, October 2019), a situation exacerbated by the COVID-19 pandemic. Despite the consultation in 2019 on enhanced services and legal obligations for local authorities, the Domestic Abuse Bill 2020 only reached its first reading in parliament on 7 July 2020, with many expressing concerns that it does not go far enough in ensuring that immigrant women are able to report safely and are not penalised because of their immigration status (*The Guardian*, March 2020). Though many of the impediments to support experienced by immigrant women are in common with those facing the wider population, such as childcare, housing, and transport, "each of these issues may also carry culturally-specific inflections, exacerbated by racism and class position" (Burman et al., 2004, p. 336); language and communication needs, while often acknowledged, are seldom a focus of political or sector-specific debate.

Difficulties in seeking help are doubtless compounded for those who have been forcibly displaced and who are consequently more likely than others to "lack a secure form of biopolitical personhood" (Parson & Heckert, 2014). This means that the scale of what may be termed the "labour of the self" they face in reconciling and moving on from experiences of abuse can be particularly burdensome, especially if prior experience of interpreter-mediated institutional encounters is perceived as negative (Tipton, 2019a). Regardless of background, the question of how limited English language–proficient individuals can take responsibility for themselves and even hold on to a sense of self when at their most vulnerable (McCormack & Salmenniemi, 2016) has particular resonance in the context of interpreter-mediated encounters, in part due to the high degree of self-reflexivity required, i.e. the ability to reflect on social circumstances and transform them (Green, 2011; Beck et al., 1994). The complex entanglements of the victim–interpreter relation therefore require a lens through which to identify ways in which forms of (structural) violence particular to the victim experience risk being perpetuated and how they can be mitigated. The affordances of an approach grounded in biopolitics are explored in what follows.

Biopolitics and Its Relation to (Interpreter-Mediated) Victim Support Services

The concept of biopolitics has a long history in the academy. Liesen and Walsh (2012) analyse what they term the "competing meanings" of biopolitics in the political sciences, observing a shift from the incorporation of theories and data from life sciences into the study of political behaviour and public policy, to more postmodern orientations that draw on the work of Michel Foucault (e.g. 1978) in an attempt to examine the power of the state on individuals. Through a series of lectures at the Collège de France in the 1970s, Foucault (2007, 2008) addressed "the themes of a peculiarly modern notion of governmental reason and its implications for the bio-political management of populations" (McNay, 2009, p. 55). As McNay observes, the lectures presciently reflected on notions of the self as enterprise, as well as the normalisation of biopower in the techniques of government and governance. Foucault developed the concept of biopower to "capture technologies of power that address the management of, and control over, the life of the population" (Holmer Nadesan, 2008, p. 2), though, as has been observed, the very scant references to the concept in Foucault's *oeuvre* as a whole call into question the extent to which he provides a coherent theory of biopower (Adams, 2017).

In work that offers a reflection on the normalisation of biopower, Green (2011, p. 91) argues that victimisation and vulnerability have been socially constructed to serve political and economic interests in ways that have led to the foregrounding of the "ideal victim" (Christie, 1986), i.e. the type of victim that generates the most sympathy from society. The exclusion of (im)migrant women from much of the public debate on victim protection and victim support underlines the complex process of subjectification such women undergo, especially in relation to prominent social discourses on migration that portray them as potentially dangerous others and therefore less deserving of support.

Green also explores the relationship between the market economy and victimhood, drawing attention to the fact that victims of (all) crime have become a commodity; as such, they have "an exchange value that exists outside of any actual experience of victimisation" (2011, p. 107), leading to the development of a whole economy of victim services. Empirical and anecdotal reports of unevenness in the commissioning of interpreting services in both the statutory (e.g. HMIC, 2014) and voluntary sectors suggest hierarchies of practice are in operation within such an economy. An examination of these hierarchies cannot neglect the complex subjectification processes at play, including those shaped by the belief that (im)migrant victims of abuse have made themselves more socially vulnerable by not having developed command of the majority language.

Relatedly, in becoming a victim, more specifically a victim that actively seeks institutional help, the individual becomes the object of various political strategies within the prevailing political system. Their bodies become subject to what Foucault (1978/2007) terms governmentality, a concept which, according to Pennycook (2002, p. 92), is analytically significant because it makes it possible to move "away from the intentional and centralised strategies of government authorities toward the multiplicity of ways in which the practice of governance may be realised"; in so doing, "much more localised and often contradictory operations of power are highlighted" (ibid.). To understand the hierarchies of practice at play in the wider economy of victim services requires attention to the political strategies in force at a given point in time and the positioning of (im)migrant women within them.

The underpinning research for the interpreter guidance discussed here sought to identify the forms of power that operate in service provision for linguistically and culturally diverse service users and the contradictions that can undermine its effectiveness. This involved investigating the social and political forces at play that can disrupt even the best-intentioned approach to care (including interpreting provision), and the conditions under which such forces are made manifest. Analysing organisational language policy as a technology of biopower and interviews with staff, interpreters, and service users (Tipton, 2017a, 2017b) shed light on the way interpreters (professional and non-professional) are positioned and/or position themselves as technologies of care and control in these settings. When complemented with close analysis of authentic interpreter-mediated interactions (Tipton, 2019b), the findings serve as a reminder that interpreter provisions are never ideologically neutral at the point of policy formation (structure) or service delivery (agency).

For victim-survivors, verbalising experiences of interpersonal violence is at once a release and, when interpreter-mediated, a step into the unknown. Hearing the articulation of one's suffering being communicated through a different voice and different language generates a peculiar form of identity loss and identity (re-)formation. Victimhood can also bring with it new forms of exile and cognitive experience; the spectres of disappearance, uncertainty, and isolation are brought to the fore, particularly for forcibly displaced individuals who are faced with beginning all over again. Being dispossessed of the life a person once led inevitably entails a process of grieving, a process that Butler argues is far from a "privatizing matter" (2004, p. 22) or depoliticising experience. For Butler, grief "furnishes a sense of political community of a complex order...by bringing to the fore the relational ties that have implications for theorizing fundamental dependency and ethical responsibility" (ibid.). It is this concept of political community, borne out of what Butler terms our own political constitution as socially vulnerable bodies, that obliges a new understanding of relationality in interpreter mediation in encounters with victim-survivors, a relationality that to date has received limited attention in interpreting studies.

Interpreters assigned to encounters involving victim-survivors of domestic abuse witness the gamut of individual response to vulnerability and threat to life, responses that can shock in their incongruity and prompt reflection on the socially vulnerable body, leading, for example, to questions about why people often return to the perpetrator. There is a wide body of literature that explores this particular issue (e.g. Gharaibeh & Oweis, 2009; Estrellado & Loh, 2014; Heim et al., 2017) which is beyond the scope of this chapter to discuss, but such moments of incongruity need to be acknowledged in theorising relationality and ethical responsibility in situated practice. Such moments reinforce the unknowability of the victim-survivor, and therefore the unknowability of the grieving process, raising questions as to the extent to which the sense of political community articulated by Butler can and does emerge in interpreter mediation. Whether it *should* emerge is a different question, but one that I argue deserves critical attention in these settings out of concern for promoting anti-discriminatory and person-centred practice.

By conceptualising victim support in general and interpreting in particular as biopolitical enterprises, new light can be shed on the commonly observed tension between interpreting as a means to enable and empower and its potential to dislocate, disrupt, and constrain. Second, it serves as a useful descriptor of interpreting as a whole-person enterprise that requires awareness of both verbal and non-verbal communication *and* a willingness to take decisions that take account of the forms of violence that shape the encounter and may manifest within it.

The Foucauldian approach to biopolitics, though pertinent, is limited in its explanatory power (cf. Lemke, 2011); it cannot easily be operationalised to support a fine-grained analysis of the power relations and hierarchies at play in interpreted encounters. As such, a conceptualisation that foregrounds political advocacy and concern for the welfare of others is proposed here. The following quotation helps to illustrate the relevance of this approach:

> It is very important that...when I say for example, the 'bedroom tax' – I don't need to explain it every time, so this is part of encouraging the client as well when he or she is doing their ESOL classes, 'cos we are not there forever for them. The service is short-lived, even six months or a year, it is a short time and that's it.
>
> (Interview with Professional Interpreter)

Here the interpreter evidences a whole-person approach, making decisions based on knowledge of the service user's trajectory through the supporting organisation. Rather than advocating in the general sense of "speaking on behalf of someone," the extract suggests the interpreter is engaging in a form of political advocacy that takes account of the service user's limited access to interpreting in the charity setting and the likely local contextual (and cognitive) constraints regarding the ability to develop proficiency in the majority language in an expedient manner. The interpreter discursively constructs the victim-survivor as a self-reliant agent and describes taking action to promote that self-reliance, grounded in the political reality of the local context.

Inscribing such practice within common interpreter ethics frameworks is not, however, straightforward, as these frameworks often promote impartiality in ways that preclude the emergence of community in Butler's terms. In being exposed to the violence experienced by another individual, the interpreter quoted above makes an ethical judgement drawing on knowledge and resources that transcend the situation at hand. In short, the action can be described in terms of political advocacy that results in political community with the victim-survivor through showing concern for their longer-term welfare. The achievement of political community, however, does not have to be at the expense of more traditional ethical approaches to interpreting which typically proscribe such interventionist approaches; rather they may work in dialogue.

Translator Ethics

The tension between political community and ethical responsibility is present in Inghilleri's (2008) examination of interpreters in situations of conflict and proposal for an ethics of translation "that takes as its starting point the actual social conditions in which translators operate" (p. 212). Drawing on examples of interpreter decisions taken in the context of the Iraq War and detentions at Guantánamo Bay, Inghilleri complements her reading of Bourdieu's field theory by examining Levinas' conceptualisation of ethical subjectivity and highlighting the difficulties Levinas experienced in "reconciling the idea of the unmediated encounter with the idea of the state, politics and ultimately of justice itself" (2008, p. 218).

In exploring the state as a "third party" in the ethical encounter, Inghilleri writes that Levinas "makes a passage from ethics to politics, which inevitably interferes with the face-to-face relationship" (ibid.), concluding that Levinas' promotion of ethics over politics ultimately becomes unsustainable. This is because, in situations involving multiple others and conflicting loyalties, the individual is faced with the challenge of knowing which individual they are responsible for. Looking to Derrida (e.g. 1978), Inghilleri sees potential to address this tension based on the argument that ethical responsibility "demands the exercise of judgement in the form of political decisions...despite the fact that such decisions necessarily carry the risk of violence" (Inghilleri, 2008, p. 219).

Although interpreters in domestic abuse support settings may not be subject to decision-making in the order of magnitude as in Guantánamo Bay, they are nevertheless frequently confronted with the issue of conflicting loyalties and decisions of a political nature, although they may not recognise them as such. This is partly due to the weight given to skills training in interpreter education, particularly in contexts of learning outside of the academy where most public service training takes place, at least in the United Kingdom. The interpreter's exercise of judgement therefore needs to be underpinned by knowledge of what the risks of violence are and the nature of political decision-making in this setting, two elements that were central to the drafting of the interpreter guidance that I discuss in the remaining sections.

Investigating "Political Community": Methodological Considerations

The domestic violence charity setting presents interpreters with a particularised social context, containing identifiable routines of interpersonal communication, legal requirements, procedures, and discourse practices. For freelance interpreters who may be infrequently assigned to interpret in such settings, the process of socialisation can be challenging. Sensitisation to aspects of organisational life, its protocols, and its scripts is arguably needed to minimise unintended outcomes for service users, but also to help interpreters understand the wider political and ideological structures that govern victim support services.

A multi-method approach was adopted to researching the interactional, attitudinal, and socio-political aspects of victim support across statutory and non-statutory sectors, leading to the creation of draft guidance for interpreters and staff in a domestic abuse support service in 2016. The guidance was subsequently refined based on several workshops with interpreters, feedback from victim support organisations, and a small experiment.

A first stage was to identify commonalities in victim experience and evaluate their implications for interpreter mediation. This was achieved through environmental scans of the literature, analysis of current police interviewing guidelines for domestic abuse victims, and conducting interviews with service providers in statutory (here, police) and charity services, professional interpreters, and former and current service users.

This first dataset highlighted the lack of insight interpreters have into different types of abuse, risk assessment processes, and the rationale behind key risk assessment protocols used in police and other victim support services. It revealed that service providers (police officers and charity staff) frequently observed unwarranted approaches by interpreters that undermine victim-survivor support services and potentially impact on decision-making. Empirical evidence of such approaches was found through analysis of authentic victim interviews with police, though the small amount of data made available precludes generalisation to the interpreter population as a whole (Tipton, 2019b).

Several interpreter workshops based on the draft guidance were followed by a two-stage experiment involving simulated interpreter-mediated encounters with ten professional interpreters at different stages of their career (five Arabic speakers and five Urdu speakers; see Tables 1.1 and 1.2 for participant profiles). While both data sets are drawn on in the analysis presented in the next section, greater weight is given to the experimental data in examining manifestations of violence and interpreter responses to it.

Interpreters were recruited through contact with local interpreter agencies and graduates of MA programmes that include a public-service interpreting component and were paid at the current rates for professional interpreting assignments in the local area. Advance warning was provided that the content of the exercises would include matters of sexual abuse.

A decision was taken to have an all-female team in the experiments and to limit participation to female interpreters in order to minimise discomfort in the simulated encounters, given the content. The roles of service provider and victim in the encounters were played by charity staff to ensure they reflected the discourse practices and content common to support services in the sector.

Six of the ten interpreters in the experiment were given the draft guidance to read in advance of the second simulated encounter, which took place approximately two weeks after the first. All simulated encounters were recorded and transcribed with the support of professional translators. Ethical approval for the study was granted by the University of Manchester.

The experimental approach firstly aimed to document interpreter responses to typical features and content of encounters with victims in the

Table 1.1 Profiles of Arabic-Speaking Interpreters

Gender	Age	Language Background	Highest Interpreting Qualification	Years of Interpreting Experience	Experience of Interpreting in (Domestic) Abuse Encounters	Training in Domestic Abuse?
1. F	40s	Born and lived in Arabic-speaking country until a young adult	MA	1.5	Fewer than 5 assignments	Online training with some focus on safeguarding of victims of abuse No specific training in the values of Women's Aid
2. F	20s	Born and lived in Arabic-speaking country until a young adult	MA	1	0	Online training with some focus on safeguarding of victims of abuse No specific training in the values of Women's Aid
3. F	20s	Brought up in an Arabic-speaking family, born in the UK	MA	0	0	None
4. F	50s	Born and lived in Arabic-speaking country until a young adult	In-house training (City Council)	Over 15 years	Regular assignments over 15 years	None
5. F	40s	Born and lived in Arabic-speaking country until a young adult	In-house training (City Council)	Over 10 years	Regular assignments, estimates 50+	None

Table 1.2 Profiles of Urdu-Speaking Interpreters

Gender	Age	Language Background	Highest Interpreting Qualification	Years of Interpreting Experience	Experience of Interpreting in (Domestic) Abuse Encounters	Training in Domestic Abuse?
1. F	50s	Born and lived in Pakistan until a young adult	In-house training (City Council)	27 years	Regular assignments over 27 years	None
2. F	40s	Born and lived in Pakistan until a young adult	Diploma in public-service interpreting	10 years	Regular assignments over 10 years	None
3. F	40s	Born and lived in the Indian subcontinent until a young adult	In-house training (City Council)	25 years	Regular assignments over 25 years	None
4. F	40s	Born and lived in Pakistan until the age of 29	In-house training (City Council)	10 years	Regular assignments over 10 years	None
5. F	30s	Brought up in an Urdu-speaking family, born in the UK	In-house training (City Council)	5 years	Approx. 10 encounters	None

charity setting. Specifically, it sought to identify how interpreters respond (linguistically) to narratives about sexual and other forms of abuse, evidence of victim-blaming, and whether any salient differences in approach are observed between newly qualified and more experienced interpreters. The *post-hoc* individual interviews yielded insight into experiences of the encounter itself and the wider field, features of interaction such as code-switching, and handling of terminology common to the setting.

The *post-hoc* interviews also shed light on the perceived authenticity of the exercise. One experienced Arabic-speaking interpreter commented: "Everything I saw today, I am familiar with…it put me in the mood, I came out thinking it was a real incident," while another drew attention to the lack of emotion in the simulated encounter compared to her experiences in the field: "I usually prepare myself that my client will feel reluctant to open up." Among the Urdu-speaking interpreters, one commented "it was like a real-life situation even though it was made up," though, importantly, the same interpreter mentioned "if it was a male who was a victim, I would find that embarrassing and challenging and difficult."

The following section presents findings from the experiment relating to matters of risk assessment, victim-blaming, and English language proficiency, showing how the analysis helped to shape and refine the guidance. These topics provide fertile ground for exploring the often hidden potential for violence in the victim experience and contexts of interpreter decision-making. I also discuss the interpreters' reflections on the guidance in relation to its perceived benefits, limitations, and avenues for future research.

Findings and Discussion

Risk Assessment

Standard risk assessments in victim support services include questions on mental wellbeing that were reflected in the simulated encounters. The two extracts below show the handling of this aspect by two interpreters at different stages of their careers (Interpreter 1 had less than two years of experience and Interpreter 5 had over ten years of experience):

Arabic-Speaking Interpreter 1

Caseworker: And, er…how about your mental health and general wellbeing, are you depressed? Or have you ever had any suicidal thoughts?

Interpreter:

حالتك النفسية انتي صايرة يعني داخلة في مرحلة اكتئاب؟ بتفكرين بالانتحار مثلا؟

(*Back translation:* What about your mental health, are you depressed? For example, are you considering suicide?)

Victim:

لا اعوذ بالله هذه الأفكار ما تجي لعندي انا ام وعندي اولاد وانا مسلمة وهذه ال ال الأفكار حرام في الدين عنا ويعني الوحدة بدها تصبر وفوق هيك انا كمان يعني حامل وفي جنين ببطني مسؤولة عنه لذلك انا كثير خايفة على ولادي وخايفة منه.

(*Back translation:* No, I seek refuge in Allah, these thoughts never come to me, I am a mother and I have children and I am Muslim, and these thoughts are forbidden [by my] religion, so any woman should bear that, I am also pregnant and I have a baby I am responsible for, and that is why I am worried about my children and scared of him as well.)

Interpreter: So she says 'no,' obviously, she's a Muslim and these thoughts don't, like, occur to her, and she wants to be the best mum she could be towards her children, er, and also she has a baby, she's carrying a baby and she wants to be there for her newborn baby, so she just, er, wants to try to be the best she could be for her children.

Arabic-Speaking Interpreter 5

Caseworker: And what about your mental wellbeing generally, have you been depressed, or have you had any suicidal thoughts?

Interpreter:

بصورة عامة من الناحية النفسية كيف تحسين؟ هل تحسين بكتابة؟ هل تحسي حالك عندك أفكار للإنتحار

(*Back translation:* In general, how is your mental health? Do you feel depressed or do you want to commit suicide?)

Victim:

أعوذ بالله! شوه الحكي الي بتحكية ؟ هذا حرام أنا ما بفكر بهادا الموضوع.

(*Back translation:* I seek refuge in Allah, what do you say? That is forbidden, I do not think about it.)

Interpreter [overlapping with Victim]: No! That's not forbidden, that's forbidden in Is— I never think about it. That's forbidden in religious-wise.

Interpreter 1 displays an evaluative judgement on the question posed: "So she says 'no,' obviously, she's a Muslim and these thoughts don't, like, occur to her," an approach that is further emphasised through the use of the third person, creating the impression that the interpreter does not think such a question should have been asked. By contrast, Interpreter 5, who is more experienced, maintains the first person, but the overlapping interjection appears to lead to impaired English language output ("that's not forbidden," "in religious-wise"). Further, the forceful "No!" could also be construed as a value judgement on the question, though it arguably conveys the perlocutionary effect of the original. To support understanding of the rationale behind why certain questions are asked in standard risk assessments, a copy of a typical risk assessment form is provided in the guidance, together with a short explanation, grounded in academic research. For example:

Q3. What are you afraid of? Is it further injury or violence?

If a victim is afraid of being killed, for example, they are likely to experience additional violence, threats and emotional abuse (Robinson, 2006).

(Tipton, 2020, p. 11)

However, as I discuss later, the assimilability of this information is in question because of its ethnocentric grounding in the majority culture. In addition, simply having access to the rationale for the risk assessment questions may not be sufficient to support the interpreter's practice, especially in handling culturally inflected victim responses to certain questions. In the examples above, the original question is construed as a face-threatening act by the interpreters and therefore a form of violence that both show a desire not to be complicit in.

Handling Different Levels of English Language Proficiency

The initial data set that shaped the draft guidance included interviews with interpreters and charity staff members in which they reflected on service user English language proficiency and its variability:

> So we get a translator, because you can't say no, but we always find out that their language is far better than what they say, and it's about their lack of confidence....Women whose language is good, we'll often get one translator in and then she'll be fine and she'll soon mix in with the other women [in the refuge].
>
> (Interview with Women's Aid staff member)

Though the simulated encounters in the experiment contained only a very small amount of code-switching by the victim, the *post-hoc* interviews indicated different approaches to the handling of English language proficiency in the field:

> Sometimes when we start interpreting, the clients...say 'we can understand most of the English and we can communicate as well but sometimes we are stuck. Some of the words we don't get it, we don't understand.' In that situation I always inform the [service provider] that's what the client said and I ask the [service provider] what they want me to do. But I respect the [service user] as well and I ask them how they want me to interpret for them and I inform the [service provider] as well. It's the [service provider's] choice.
>
> (Urdu-speaking Interpreter 1, *post-hoc* interview 1)

> Sometimes the client would say 'I've got a good English background so that I would answer questions but step in when I need you.' If the

officer agrees to that, then we let it be. I don't wait to be prompted to
step in if my client doesn't understand the nature of the question.

(Arabic-speaking Interpreter 4, post-hoc interview 2)

Of the ten interpreters interviewed as part of the experiment, five articulated
a clear, if *ad hoc*, personal policy for handling English-language usage by
victim-survivors in encounters. The extracts show the interpreters' concern
for balancing the right to the service user's autonomy to speak English when
desired, but also deference to the service provider out of concern to manage
risk and maximise comprehension. These observations have resonance with
the grieving process (i.e. coming to terms with a new reality) and show how
interpreters grapple with decisions that tread a fine line between safety and
autonomy. For interpreters to acknowledge the potential for the established
participatory framework in which the interpreter takes every other turn to
be a source of violence is likely to be a radical departure from the ortho-
doxies of professional practice; however, when couched in terms of political advocacy and an understanding of how complicity in violence operates
within the encounter, a more nuanced approach to practice can emerge.

The guidance includes a section on English language use by victims to
highlight the potential for victim empowerment, but, based on the findings
from the experiment, it was adjusted to urge caution and interpreter intervention in case of any doubt:

> [empower] survivors to communicate directly in English if they express
> a desire to do so, but remain alert to potential problems arising from the
> pace of the conversation and/or the challenges in expressing emotions,
> stepping in to interpret to mitigate against risk and/or misunderstanding.
>
> (Tipton, 2020, p. 13)

Victim-Blaming

The first dataset of interviews revealed that victim-blaming is frequently
observed in statutory and non-statutory services, despite many of the interpreters being accredited and members of the National Register of Public
Service Interpreters (NRPSI). The reasons for such an approach were not
explicitly investigated as part of this study (and it is unlikely that individuals
would admit to adopting it if asked), but the experimental approach made
it possible to identify examples that shaped the guidance.

Victim-blaming takes many forms, from verbal expressions of impatience
with victim-survivors to ostensibly empathic interjections which, while well-
intended, can have a damaging effect on subsequent decision-making. In
the simulated encounters, three instances were observed. Arabic-speaking
Interpreter 1 used empathic signs (such as exclaiming "wow" at certain
points in the victim's narrative) as did Arabic-speaking Interpreter 5. Urdu-
speaking Interpreter 5's transcript contains an interjection of "Oh God"

when sensitive information on sexual abuse was narrated by the victim, suggesting that such responses may not necessarily be attributed to the level of experience in the field.

Reference to this type of interjection was included in the guidance as an example of approaches that are evaluative of victim experience and therefore not conducive to achieving the organisation's stated goal of helping women "to articulate their needs, access their rights and entitlements and take charge of decision-making about their own lives" (Women's Aid National Quality Standards, 2020, p. 10). The guidance lists the following examples of victim-blaming based on reported experience and analysis of interactions:

- rolling eyes to show boredom when interpreting for the same service user who has decided to return to the family home and suffered further abuse
- showing impatience with tone of voice
- tutting audibly at certain responses
- saying 'wow' (or similar) when difficult elements of a person's experience are recounted
- saying phrases like 'I cannot believe s/he did that to you' / 'I don't know how you have put up with it.'

(Tipton, 2020, p. 14)

By sensitising interpreters to the various manifestations of victim-blaming and its potential impact on service users, the aim is to support the achievement of "political community" in the encounter, i.e. for the interpreter to indicate believability in the victim-survivor's story in unobtrusive ways.

Interpreter Reflections on the Guidance

Six of the ten interpreters (three in each group) were given copies of the guidance prior to the second simulated encounter and prompted to reflect on the content in the second *post-hoc* interview. The data analysis revealed a tendency on the part of the interpreters to talk about the need for training in general terms or conflate this guidance with interpreter codes of ethics, suggesting that they found it difficult to make the connection between the content and its implications for practice. Of the Urdu-speaking interpreters, one did not have time to read the guidance in full and a second commented "I forgot most of it. It's hard to remember to be honest with you," which raises important questions about its assimilability. Arabic-speaking Interpreter 2 commented "maybe I understood more the role of the Women's Aid organisation," but did not elaborate on the connection between understanding the organisation and its values and the impact (if any) on her approach to interpreting. Given the very limited interpreting experience of this interpreter prior to participation in the experiment, this is perhaps not unexpected.

Urdu-speaking Interpreter 3 commented: "[The guidance] was so complete and concise." For this interpreter, the guidance had led to conscious reflection on decisions taken in relation to the concept of "consent": "I gave my opinion on religion and culture. Now I will definitely avoid giving my opinion unless I'm asked." However, these concerns were not fully borne out by this interpreter's performance, highlighting a gap often observed in interpreting studies research between what interpreters say they do and what they do in practice. As the extract below shows, the interpreter adds the words "because obviously I am same culture" (sic), while the key component of the message is couched in terms of reported speech, reflecting the actual words of the victim:

> When I arrived into this country, as I really wanted to be a good wife, and she was giving some reference to, because obviously I am same culture, so she says, 'as you are aware that it is to do with like a bit of like religion and erm, culturally, these things as a husband he has a right over me.'

The guidance prompted this same interpreter to reflect on the standard set of risk assessment questions, although no connection was made to the questions on mental health and suicide that were included in the simulated encounter:

> There's like a set kind of questions, in English, when they ask about, 'has he hurt an animal before?' Those kind of things. There are set questions they ask and sometimes it's difficult to interpret those. The officer says you can't simplify it. And it's just not possible because it doesn't make sense. They need to be rephrased if they are being used for other cultures, other languages. Maybe they make sense in English and only English speakers would understand it.
>
> (Urdu-speaking Interpreter 3)

As mentioned earlier, the guidance provides information on the full list of questions that make up a standard risk assessment, together with supporting information about why certain questions are asked. It is unclear from this interpreter's interview whether they had fully internalised the guidance, as no additional comment is provided on what was meant by "rephrasing" some of the questions. Nevertheless, despite the apparent disconnect between the simulated encounter and real-world experience, the reflection is an important finding and suggests enhancements to intercultural competence would be useful for service providers conducting the standard risk assessment to mitigate the face-threatening nature of some questions as perceived by the interpreters.

The *post-hoc* interviews also draw attention to possible misreadings of the guidance, as identified in Arabic-speaking Interpreter 2's comments in relation to managing a service user's desire to communicate in English, which can be compared to the extract from the guidance given earlier: "Yeah, one of the guidelines that I read to encourage the client to speak English. I agree with this." Later in the interview, the same interpreter comments that "the examples that have been mentioned in the guidelines should be done in workshops or groups of interpreters sharing ideas of what to do." These comments, together with Urdu-speaking Interpreter 3's statement about finding it difficult to remember the guidance, raise an important point about the potential limitations of guidance in the written form and accessed by individuals without additional contextualisation.

A final issue raised by Urdu-speaking Interpreter 3 highlights issues of lack of continuity in interpreter mediation and the need for consistency of practice across these settings, thereby drawing attention to the potential for disruptions in the degree of political community achieved across the victim experience:

> And their expectations get raised because they were so comfortable with their interpreter. Next time round, the person interpreting might not be as sympathetic or understanding. They're already going through trauma and they have expectations and there's no continuity. If we get trained and follow the same guidelines, we don't raise the expectations of the victims. There should be a unified approach.
>
> (Urdu-speaking Interpreter 3)

Conclusion

This chapter has discussed the development of guidance for interpreters working in domestic abuse support services. It proposes a conceptualisation of victim support and interpreter mediation as biopolitical enterprises to support investigation of the interpreter's exposure to violence in its various forms in victim encounters and their potential to mitigate or perpetuate it.

The achievement of political community is underpinned by the recognition that new forms of relationality in interpreter-mediated encounters with victim-survivors need to be considered, a relationality premised on "political advocacy" and supported by advanced knowledge of the forms of violence that inhere in social and organisational structures and the ways in which they can be transcended in interpreter practice.

The analysis of the experimental data did not reveal significant differences in approach by experienced and less experienced interpreters in relation to the features selected for analysis, though the sample size was small. The interpreter reflections on the guidance show difficulties relating to its internalisation and application in these settings, and scope for enhanced intercultural training for service providers, particularly in handling standard risk assessments. The comments suggest that the guidance would be more effective if accompanied by in-person training that can provide contextualisation and mitigate misreadings of prescriptivism.

More research is needed to develop a broader empirical basis for understanding the interactional and affective consequences of interpreter decision-making in these settings, research that also needs to explore the impact of gender on interactions. Several male interpreters came forward to be interviewed as part of the first data set, but the decision to limit the experiments to female participants necessarily impacted on the representativeness of the sample. The importance of male and other gendered perspectives needs to be stressed in the lived experience of support services for (im)migrant women, given the anecdotal reports of shortages of female interpreters for certain language combinations, both in the area in which the study took place and elsewhere.

Acknowledgement of Funding

The author gratefully acknowledges the support of ESRC IAA grant number R118571 and the University of Manchester Impact Case Study support fund, and would like to thank the anonymous reviewers for their constructive comments on the earlier versions of this chapter.

References

Adams, R. (2017). Michel Foucault: Biopolitics and biopower. Key concepts, critical legal thinking. Retrieved from: https://criticallegalthinking.com/2017/05/10/michel-foucault-biopolitics-biopower/ (Accessed 20 May 2020).

Beck, U., Lash, S., & Giddens, A. (1994). *Reflexive Modernization: Tradition and Aesthetics in Modern Social Order.* Cambridge: Polity Press.

Burman, E., Smailes, S. L., & Chantler, K. (2004). Culture as a barrier to service provision and delivery: Domestic violence services for minoritized women. *Critical Social Policy,* 24(3), 332–357. https://doi.org/10.1177/0261018304044363

Butler, J. (2004). *Precarious Life: The Powers of Mourning and Violence.* New York: Verso.

Christie, N. (1986). The ideal victim. In: E. A. Fattah (Ed.), *From Crime Policy to Victim Policy: Reorienting the Justice System* (pp. 17–30). London: Palgrave Macmillan.

Derrida, J. (1978). *Writing and Difference* (A. Bass, Trans.) (pp. 97–192). London: Routledge.

Estrellado, A. F., & Loh, J. (2014). Factors associated with battered Filipino women's decision to stay in or leave an abusive relationship. *Journal of Interpersonal Violence,* 29(4), 575–592. https://doi.org/10.1177/0886260513505709

Foucault, M. (1978). *The History of Sexuality Volume 1: An Introduction* (R. Hurley, Trans.). New York: Pantheon Books.

Foucault, M. (2007). *Security, Territory, Population: Lectures at the Collège de France 1977–1978* (M. Senellart, & G. Burchell, Trans.). London: Palgrave Macmillan.

Foucault, M. (2008). *The Birth of Biopolitics: Lectures at the Collège de France, 1978–1979* (M. Senellart, & G. Burchell, Trans.). London: Palgrave Macmillan.

Gharaibeh, M., & Oweis, A. (2009). Why do Jordanian women stay in an abusive relationship: Implications for health and social well-being. *Journal of Nursing Scholarship : An Official Publication of Sigma Theta Tau International Honor Society of Nursing*, 41(4), 376–384. https://doi.org/10.1111/j.1547-5069.2009.01305.x

Green, S. (2011). Crime, victimisation and vulnerability. In: S. Walklate (Ed.), *Handbook of Victims and Victimology* (pp. 91–118). London: Routledge.

Heim, E., Ajzen, I., Schmidt, P., & Seddig, D. (2017). Women's decisions to stay in or leave an abusive relationship: Results from a longitudinal study in Bolivia. *Violence Against Women.* https://doi.org/10.1177/1077801217741993

Henn, E. V. (2019). *International Human Rights Law and Structural Discrimination: The Example of Violence against Women.* Berlin: Springer.

Her Majesty's Inspectorate of Constabulary (2014). *Everybody's Business: Improving the Police Response to Domestic Abuse.* London: HMSO.

Holmer Nadesan, M. (2008). *Governmentality, Biopower, and Everyday Life.* London: Routledge.

Inghilleri, M. (2008). The ethical task of the translator in the geopolitical arena: From Iraq to Guantánamo Bay. *Translation Studies*, 1(2), 212–223. https://doi.org/10.1080/14781700802113556

Lemke, T. (2011). *Biopolitics: An Advanced Introduction.* New York: New York University Press.

Liesen, L. T., & Walsh, M. B. (2012). The competing meanings of "biopolitics" in political science: Biological and postmodern approaches to politics. *Politics and the Life Sciences : The Journal of the Association for Politics and the Life Sciences*, 31(1/2), 2–15. https://doi.org/10.2990/31_1-2_2

McCormack, D., & Salmenniemi, S. (2016). The biopolitics of precarity and the self. *European Journal of Cultural Studies*, 19(1), 3–15. https://doi.org/10.1177/1367549415585559

McNay, L. (2009). Self as enterprise: Dilemmas of control and resistance in Foucault's the birth of biopolitics. *Theory, Culture and Society*, 26(6), 55–77. https://doi.org/10.1177/0263276409347697

Parson, N., & Heckert, C. (2014). The golden cage: The production of insecurity at the nexus of intimate partner violence and unauthorized migration in the United States. *Human Organization*, 73(4), 305–314. https://doi.org/10.17730/humo.73.4.9v34586u2835411\2

Pennycook, A. (2002). Language policy and docile bodies: Hong Kong and governmentality. In: J. W. Tollefson (Ed.), *Language Policies in Education: Critical Issues* (pp. 91–110). Mahwah, NJ: Lawrence Erlbaum Associates.

Robinson, A. L. (2006). *Advice, Support, Safety & Information Services Together (ASSIST): The Benefits of Providing Assistance to Victims of Domestic Abuse in Glasgow.* Cardiff: Cardiff University.

Rubio-Marín, R., & Estrada-Tanck, D. (2013). Violence against women, human security, and the rights of women and girls: Reinforced obligations in the context of structural vulnerability. In: A. M. Tripp, M. M. Ferree, & C. Ewig (Eds.) *Gender, Violence and Human Security: Critical Feminist Perspectives* (pp. 238–259). New York: New York University Press.

SafeLives (2017). Impact report. https://safelives.org.uk/sites/default/files/resources/Impact%20Report%202017-18.pdf

Southall Black Sisters (2019, July 16). Where is the protection for BME and migrant women? https://southallblacksisters.org.uk/press-releases/protection-for-bme-and-migrant-women/

The Guardian (2020, March 3). https://www.theguardian.com/society/2020/mar/03/domestic-abuse-laws-to-be-brought-back-before-parliament

The Independent (2019, October 22). https://www.independent.co.uk/news/uk/home-news/domestic-abuse-refuges-government-funding-announcement-a9166691.html

Tipton, R. (2017a). Interpreting-as-conflict: PSIT in third sector organisations and the impact of third way politics. In: C. Valero-Garcés, & R. Tipton (Eds.), *Ideology, Ethics and Policy Development in Public Service Interpreting and Translation* (pp. 38–62). Bristol: Multilingual Matters.

Tipton, R. (2017b). 'You are foreign, you are nothing in this country': Managing risk in interpreter-mediated police interviews with victims of domestic abuse. *Revista Canaria de Estudios Ingleses*, 75, 119–138. https://riull.ull.es/xmlui/handle/915/6969

Tipton, R. (2018). Translating/ed selves and voices: Language support provisions for victims of domestic violence in a British third sector organization. *Translation and Interpreting Studies*, 13(2), 163–184. https://doi.org/10.1075/tis.00010.tip

Tipton, R. (2019a). Exploring the ESOL-PSIT relation: Interpellation, resistance and resilience. *Language and Communication*, 67, 16–28. https://doi-org.manchester.idm.oclc.org/10.1016/j.langcom.2018.12.004

Tipton, R. (2019b). 'Yes I understand': Language choice, question formation and code-switching in interpreter-mediated police interviews with victim-survivors of domestic abuse. *International Journal Police Practice and Research*. https://doi.org/10.1080/15614263.2019.1663733

Tipton, R. (2020). A guide for spoken language interpreters working with adult survivors of domestic abuse. http://mlm.humanities.manchester.ac.uk/wp-content/uploads/2020/05/Blog-post-Interpreter-Guidelines.pdf

Women's Aid (2020). *Women's Aid National Quality Standards 2020*. https://1q7dqy2unor827bqjls0c4rn-wpengine.netdna-ssl.com/wp-content/uploads/2018/01/National-Standards-2018.pdf

2 Dialogue Interpreting and Person-Centred Care in a Clinical Mental Healthcare Setting

Natalia Rodríguez Vicente, Jemina Napier, and Raquel de Pedro Ricoy

Introduction

Healthcare interpreting is a unique form of language mediation because it is ancillary to the demands of the larger speech event that frames it: cross-cultural care (Hsieh, 2016). This means that the dynamics typically associated with interpreted talk are shaped by the expectations, values, and goals of the event in which the interpreting activity unfolds. The interplay between interpreting practice and the discursive features of healthcare encounters is so significant that healthcare interpreting cannot be properly understood in isolation from its context (Angelelli, 2019). The highly situated nature of healthcare interpreting makes this practice interdisciplinary to the fullest degree, as it is located at the intersection of medicine, language, and culture (Hsieh, 2015). This intersection has implications for interpreting performance standards and what is required for an interpreter-mediated encounter (IME) to be successful. For example, a degree of cooperation between the healthcare practitioner and interpreter is usually necessary to fulfil the requirements of the medical agenda (Flores, 2005). For this cooperation to be successful, the interpreter needs to be attuned to the healthcare practitioner's interactional goals (Rodríguez-Vicente, 2020). Against this background, interpreter awareness of the guiding values of person-centred care (PCC) seems to be a prerequisite for language-discordant patients to fully benefit from the advantages of this approach to healthcare delivery and communication. The academic interest in the intersection of language mediation and person-centredness in healthcare is increasing (see Angelelli, 2020). However, the unique ways in which interpreting intersects with the values of PCC in different medical specialities remain largely unexplored. This gap in the literature is worth addressing given the implications of this issue for language-discordant patients' access to equitable healthcare services. In order to examine the intersection between language mediation and PCC, this chapter provides a discussion of the enactment of three core PCC principles in a series of interpreter-mediated episodes that took place in an outpatient mental health clinic in Scotland. The discussion is structured around the interplay between language mediation and the following PCC principles: respect for the patient's autonomy, consideration of the patient's spiritual views on treatment, and relational continuity. With the aim of theoretically grounding the discussion, we first outline some fundamental notions of the PCC paradigm and discuss their relevance from the point of view of interpreting studies.

Person-Centred Care and Its Relevance for Interpreting Studies

Person-Centred Care

Person-centred care is defined in Scottish Government publications (2019, p. 1) as "mutually beneficial partnerships between patients, their families and those delivering health and care services which respect individual needs and values, and which demonstrate compassion, continuity, clear communication and shared decision-making." Occasionally, the terms "person-centred care" and "patient-centred care" are used interchangeably in the literature as there is some overlapping meaning between the two concepts. However, the notion of "person-centredness" is gaining ground in health research as this concept seeks to portray a more integral view of the patient. Person-centred care regards patients as individuals who have needs, strengths, and preferences that may go beyond the clinical aspects of their care but can be relevant for their health journey and, thus, need to be actively considered in clinical decision-making processes (Starfield, 2011; Håkansson et al., 2018). From the PCC standpoint, patients must not be seen as passive recipients of care. Instead, they should feel encouraged to actively engage in the making of decisions that may influence their health outcomes.

Whilst PCC has an explicit legislative expression in health and social care policy in Scotland, this concept is by no means limited to the Scottish context. Instead, PCC is a theory that initially originated in the fields of medical sociology and humanistic psychotherapy (Rogers, 1951) and has evolved to the extent that it is now currently implemented in numerous countries and applied across diverse medical specialities (WHO, 2016). The evolution of PCC is tangible as a worldwide rising trend, as its philosophy has driven multiple quality improvement initiatives (Santana et al., 2017). While the practical implementation of PCC may adopt different forms across a range of medical domains, the unifying factors underlying diverse PCC-driven initiatives are their critical view of doctor-centric approaches to healthcare and their support for models of healthcare service delivery that actively attempt to cater for the patients' individuality (*ibid.*).

Communication in Person-Centred Care Approaches

As mentioned above, one of the core principles of PCC is that healthcare service users should feel encouraged to express their preferences for the

care and treatment plans available to them. However, this patient engagement–focused approach does not truly work if patients assert their preferences in a decontextualised manner. Instead, effective PCC is reliant on
the following bidirectional communication process. Firstly, in order for
patients to assert their preferences in a way that is beneficial, the healthcare practitioner must equip them with the necessary education tools and
information about their condition, their prognosis, and the care and treatment options available to them (Delaney, 2017). Without these resources,
patients may not have the agency needed to make decisions that are fully
informed. Secondly, involving the patient in clinical decision-making
processes also requires healthcare practitioners to actively consider the
cultural, spiritual, individual, family-related, and/or other sociological factors that might help contextualise the patient's preferences (Epner & Baile,
2012). Active consideration of such contextual factors is pre-required for
the integration of the patient's lifeworld into the biomedical debate. This
bidirectional process is strongly reliant on effective language use as a tool
to find common ground between the healthcare practitioner's medical
goals and the patient's preferences, which is the foundation upon which
PCC is built. Building on this idea and drawing on Mishler's[1] (1984) terminology, it may be argued that PCC relies upon a process of collective
meaning negotiation propelled by the contraposition of two voices. A
"voice" is understood in this chapter as the speech realisation of norma-
tive values. On the one hand, the Voice of Medicine (VoM), normally
enacted by the healthcare practitioner, embodies the values of the medical
establishment – mainly, the biomedical approach to healing and the scientific assumptions that underpin such an approach. One the other hand, the
Voice of the Lifeworld (VoL), typically adopted by the healthcare service
user, refers to the patient's understanding of their health journey, which
may be shaped by socioeconomic, cultural, and/or environmental conditions. From this perspective, the prioritisation of the VoM in a healthcare
encounter represents a doctor-centric approach to healthcare communication. By contrast, the active consideration of the VoL in a medical consultation places the patient's lifeworld at the centre of the biomedical debate,
thus enabling the implementation of an approach to healthcare delivery
and communication that is person-centred.

Interpreter-Mediated Person-Centred Care

Considering the vital role of language use in conciliating the VoM and VoL,
we hypothesise that language discordance between a healthcare practitioner
and a patient may pose a challenge in ensuring that linguistically and culturally diverse patients fully benefit from PCC values. Building on this statement, we propose that, in the light of language and cultural differences,
professionally trained interpreters are vital in enabling person-centred
communication.

The role of interpreters as enablers of person-centred communication may be expressed in different ways. For example, Cambridge (2012, p. 26) drew on the findings of her study on interpreter-mediated psychotherapy and concluded that interpreters are often looked upon as a "major tool for creating common ground, which clinicians often feel unable to share fully." This is relevant because common ground is key in enabling PCC, as discussed in the previous section. Additionally, the fact that interpreters naturally share a language and potentially a degree of cultural affinity with the patient places them in an influential position to either enable or hinder person-centredness. This is because interpreters have direct access to the patient's lifeworld and also have the agency to alter discursive features of the healthcare practitioner's talk. So, depending on how this power is managed, interpreters might align themselves differently in relation to person-centred communication, be that consciously or inadvertently. On the one hand, interpreters might hinder opportunities for PCC-based discussions to be initiated and/or maintained. This happens when interpreters act as agents of the health system by prioritising biomedical talk over the voice of the lifeworld (Bolden, 2000; Davidson, 2000; Leanza, 2005). On the other hand, interpreters may contribute to enabling person-centredness when rendering or even reinforcing the healthcare practitioner's displays of concern for and interest in the individual's lifeworld (Merlini & Favaron, 2005).

Acknowledging interpreters' ability to channel an exchange in the two above-mentioned directions entails the recognition of interpreters as active managers of discourse. That is, interpreters are able to actively influence the communicative processes and outcomes of a speech event. Such processes may be influenced by the interpreting process because, according to the tenets of dialogism, communication is a collective sense-making activity achieved *in* and *through* interaction (Bakhtin, 1981; Linell, 1998). In other words, *meaning* results from the interplay between the three following factors: first, the speaker's intended meaning and pragmatic force when producing an utterance; secondly, the hearer's interpretation of the speaker's utterance; and finally, the social, cognitive, and wider contextual factors surrounding the production and interpretation of the interlocutors' interventions (Thomas, 1995). This multi-layered architecture of meaning establishes that sense-making processes are dynamically co-constructed as the speech event unfolds through speakers' turns. Wadensjö (1998) applied the notion of meaning co-construction to the conceptualisation and analysis of interpreter-mediated talk. Following this line of thinking, she established that interpreters' functions go beyond strictly translating texts and coordinating speakers' turns. Instead, interpreters are actively involved in the sense-making processes that underpin the production and reception of original utterances, thus influencing the progression of talk. Additionally, Wadensjö was able to systematise how this active involvement may manifest in observable practice by providing a taxonomy of potential interpreters' renditions. Differences between types of interpreters' renditions were marked by the quantity and quality of information included within them. Among the renditions included in this taxonomy, three types will be studied in this chapter. First, a *close rendition* reflects the quantity and quality of the propositional content conveyed in the source utterance. Conversely, when a rendition offers more information than originally conveyed, the interpreter's move becomes an *expanded rendition*. By contrast, if the interpreter's intervention conveys less explicitly expressed information than the original, it is called a *reduced rendition*. As originally proposed in Wadensjö's work, the accuracy of renditions should not only consider their closeness or divergence in relation to the original, but also the context surrounding the utterances at hand. This idea was further developed by Major and Napier (2012). The authors applied Wadensjö's taxonomy to the examination of a series of interpreter-mediated healthcare interactions and concluded that achieving accuracy in the healthcare setting is a dynamic and context-dependent undertaking. This is because interpreters seek to produce utterances that reproduce the interactional goals of the original statements, and the notion of accuracy becomes linked to the fulfilment of such goals. From this point of view, producing expanded or reduced renditions is not detrimental to the fulfilment of communicative goals. Following this line of thought and considering that achieving person-centred communication is one of the main interactional goals in PCC approaches, it is worth examining the discursive enactment of PCC values in interpreter-mediated talk.

Research Questions

Building on the above ideas and considering the vital role of effective communication in enabling PCC in practice, we set out to address the following questions:

1) Do interpreters become involved in the discursive enactment of PCC values? If so, how and with what consequences?
2) To what extent can interpreting performance contribute to enabling or hampering the realisation of PCC principles?

Research Methods and Data

The three excerpts and corresponding participants' views discussed below have been extracted from two datasets gathered as part of a doctoral research project on mental health interpreting (Rodríguez-Vicente, 2020). The interpreter-mediated encounters under scrutiny took place in an outpatient mental health clinic called Psychological Medicine, located within a public hospital in Scotland. Dataset 1 consisted of transcriptions of audio-recorded consultations featuring an English-speaking consultant psychiatrist, a Spanish-speaking patient, and three different interpreters. The researcher conducting the original study, co-author of this chapter, attended these consultations as a non-participant and was granted permission to audio-record them. Data collection was conducted following strict instructions to ensure compliance with ethical requirements established by a Research Ethics Committee (REC) from the UK National Health Service (NHS). Among other issues, ethical guidelines required gathering informed consent by all participants taking part in the sessions before they took place.

Dataset 2 consisted of retrospective interviews conducted with the participants involved in the sessions featuring in dataset 1. These interviews were semi-structured, and the design of their script was guided by the results from the discourse analysis of dataset 1. More in-depth information on the data-collection processes involved in the original study can be found in Rodríguez-Vicente (2020). In this chapter, subsets of the original data are re-interpreted based on the PCC framework. Excerpts of interest from dataset 1 and dataset 2 were jointly analysed to shed light on how three PCC values are enacted in interpreter-mediated talk: respect for the patient's autonomy, consideration of her spiritual views, and relational continuity.

In order to fully understand the context surrounding the excerpts shown in excerpt 4, it is useful to know about the remit of the healthcare setting within which they take place. As mentioned above, the consultations featured in dataset 1 took place in an outpatient mental healthcare clinic called Psychological Medicine. Patients referred to this clinic typically suffer from multiple ailments, normally with one physiological condition and another of a psychological nature. This type of multimorbidity may arise because mental and physical wellbeing exert a powerful influence over one another (McFarlane, 2010). Physical and psychological comorbidities might feed one another and, therefore, need to be treated jointly (*ibid.*). The conditions facing the patient in the excerpts presented below represent a clinical picture to be addressed in Psychological Medicine. The patient is an elderly woman who suffers from three co-occurring ailments: kidney failure, depression, and mild cognitive impairment. The complexity of her health status means that she needs to be supported by a physician who has expertise both in the physical and the psychological/psychiatric side of her clinical needs. The excerpts provide examples of how the doctor in charge of this patient's case leads discussions on the treatment options available to her, as a way to manage her renal disease and comorbidities. The interpreters featured in the three excerpts are professionally trained freelancers who regularly work in healthcare settings.

Data Analysis and Discussion

"Even If That Would Save Your Life?": PCC and Patient Autonomy

Excerpt 1 took place as part of a larger discussion on the medical treatments that the patient might need in the future, given that her health status is gradually deteriorating due to her terminal illness. In accordance with section 5 of the Adults with Incapacity (Scotland) Act (2000), it is important to have anticipatory discussions on treatment options if the patient's prognosis is poor, because discussing treatments in advance enables patients to express their preferences in a competent, and therefore informed, manner as their capacity to do so has not yet been compromised. Against this background, one of the medical treatments that the clinician offers the patient is a blood transfusion, which she refuses on religious grounds, as shown below.[2]

EXCERPT 1

[S. 527] Clinician

Can I just check something you said earlier? You said that, as a Jehovah's Witness, you will not like to have a blood transfusion. Did I understand that correctly?

[S. 528] Interpreter

Para que me quede claro: como testigo de Jehová, ¿es cierto que usted no aceptaría una transfusion de sangre en caso de que fuera necesaria? ¿entendí eso correctamente? ¿no la aceptaría aunque le salvara la vida?

(Just so I am clear: as a Jehovah's Witness, is it true that you would not accept a blood transfusion in case it was necessary? Did I understand that correctly? You would not accept it even if that would save your life?)

Segment (S.) 527 shows how the clinician recaps an immediately preceding discussion in which the patient disclosed that she is a member of a religious group whose doctrine does not approve of medical procedures involving blood products. The doctor seeks the patient's confirmation that she does not want to receive blood transfusions. Thus, the clinician is seeking the patient's informed consent to *not* be treated, even in the potential case of acute need. In medical practice, discussions on informed consent are framed within the debate on the patient's right to autonomy and self-determination, two core principles of person-centred care. The notion of "autonomy" has been defined as "the right of competent adults to make informed decisions about their own medical care" (BMA, 2020). As a result, respect for the patient's autonomy entails the duty to explicitly pursue their informed consent prior to the administration of any medical treatment. Drawing on these concepts, it can be argued that Excerpt 1 shows how the patient is enacting her right to self-determination by refusing to provide her consent to be treated with a blood transfusion in the future.

In the field of biomedical ethics, there are two types of actions that health-care practitioners can engage with in relation to a patient's right to autonomy and self-determination. First, the principle of "negative obligation" entails refraining from taking coercive action or actively trying to convince a patient to make a certain decision (Coggon & Miola, 2011). Secondly, "positive obligation" refers to the actions that a medical practitioner may take to compensate for any difficulties the patient faces in making decisions in a competent, and therefore autonomous, manner (*ibid.*). Excerpt 1 shows a scenario where the patient needs the practitioner to adopt a positive obligation stance because she suffers from several conditions that may compromise her capacity to make informed decisions: an affective disorder (depression) as well as difficulty processing and remembering information due to her cognitive impairment. Consequently, the healthcare practitioner's engagement with positive obligation behaviour is vital to increase this patient's capacity for self-determination and, thus, safeguard her involvement in competent decision-making. In Excerpt 1, the clinician's positive obligation stance is displayed through his attempts to obtain the patient's explicit confirmation that she is unwilling to receive a blood transfusion, should she need one in the future.

S. 528 shows how the interpreter seems to be *aligned* with the clinician's positive obligation stance through an expanded rendition in which she adds the Spanish equivalents of "in case it were necessary" and "you would not accept it even if it saved your life?" S. 528 demonstrates how the interpreter actively retrieves information previously discussed in the encounter and incorporates it into this sequence. In doing so, she evidences her desire to remind the patient that her life might become dependent on a blood transfusion.

Having identified Excerpt 1 as worth analysing further, the researcher showed it to the clinician and interpreter who featured in this excerpt as part of two separate interviews, in an attempt to explore the participants' decision-making processes. When the clinician was asked to comment on the interpreter's enhanced rendition in Excerpt 1, he stated:

> I am okay with the interpreter's action because, even though what she says is not fully accurate, it is *consistent* with what I am trying to do.

This comment evidences the clinician's positive disposition towards divergent renditions (what he refers to as "not fully accurate"), as long as the communicative intent of the interpreter's utterance is aligned with his own communicative goals.

When the interpreter was asked to comment on Excerpt 1, she stated:

> [I]n my opinion, life is sacred. It is a God-given miracle, so I guess I felt unconsciously compelled to not let her give up so easily.[3]

The interpreter proceeded to acknowledge that Catholic values give meaning and purpose to her own life. This suggests that the interpreter's expanded rendition in Excerpt 1 is motivated by a moral drive to protect life, underpinned by her Catholic values.

We argue that the interpreter's action is aligned with the clinician's engagement in positive action behaviour, as she tries to make sure that the patient is fully informed when refusing potentially life-sustaining treatment. This action echoes Major and Napier's (2012) finding that interpreters make interpreting decisions while engaging in a balancing act between clinical, linguistic, and interpersonal goals. Excerpt 1 shows how the interpreter is trying to ensure the protection of the patient's right to autonomy and self-determination, thus enabling the implementation of person-centred communication in this encounter.

Nonetheless, Excerpt 1 raises questions regarding interpreters' principles and the institutional goals for this encounter, materialised through the healthcare provider's actions. We propose that interpreters' awareness of the communicative goals being pursued in a given interaction, such as the enactment of PCC values, may increase the chances for alignment between such goals and interpreting performance.

"God Will Decide How Long I Will Live": PCC and Spirituality

In Excerpt 2, as below, the clinician discusses with the patient the possibility of receiving a transplant, as her body is no longer adequately responding to treatment. This discussion was started in a previous consultation and resumed as shown here. To further contextualise this excerpt, we should also mention that religious beliefs are a core aspect of the patient's life, and they even shape the way that she conceives of her illness. Spirituality has a place in PCC models of healthcare delivery and communication. The philosophy of PCC promotes the identification of the patient's spiritual, including religious, beliefs. This is because spirituality might be a core part of a patient's individuality and serve as an asset when they are enduring health-related hardship (McSherry & Ross, 2010). For this reason, person-centred models of communication encourage healthcare providers to casually incorporate aspects of the patient's spiritual beliefs into clinical conversations as a way to humanise the care provided (Ruddick, 2010). Finally, using Mishler's (1984) terminology, the spiritual dimension of a patient's individuality could be seen as a cornerstone of the patient's lifeworld (VoL), a key aspect in the PCC model. Drawing on these notions, we discuss below how the patient's spirituality is interactionally negotiated in the following subsection of our dataset.

EXCERPT 2

[S. 286] Patient

Al principio yo me negaba rotundamente porque me daba miedo que me obligasen a tener un transplante pero luego un día cambió todo porque escuché a Dios. Dios me dijo que quería que yo viviera más tiempo, que me quedaban cosas por hacer en vida. Entonces ahora me siento más positiva con esa idea del transplante porque si me lo está usté ofreciendo es por algo. De todas formas, Dios dirá hasta donde vivo.

(At first I totally refused [a transplant] because I was scared I might be forced to have it but then one day everything changed because I listened to God. God told me that he wanted me to live longer, [and] that I still had things to do in life. So now I feel more positive about the idea of a transplant because there must be a reason why you are offering it to me. In any case, God will decide how long I will live.)

[S. 287] Interpreter

At the beginning I refused because I was scared that they will force me to have a transplant but one day all changed when I listened to God's voice and I think I can live longer to do more things while I live so now I am more open to the idea of the transplant. There must be a reason why you are offering it to me.

[S. 288] Clinician

First of all, you can rest assured that you cannot be forced to have a transplant. There is no medical way, no legal way to do that.

Excerpt 2 shows how the patient tells the clinician about the aspects that influenced her decision-making processes when considering receiving a transplant. The patient directly connects her motivation to accept it with God's mandate to live longer. The final sentence in S. 286 evidences the patient's belief that the clinician's offer of a transplant must be a sign of God's will. The patient's feelings of gratitude towards what she perceives to be a God-sent signal drive her decision to accept the transplant. This display of spirituality is an example of what Mishler (1984) refers to as the Voice of the Lifeworld (VoL), as it is a direct expression of the patient's contextualised perspective on her health journey. The intricate relationship between the patient's spiritual standpoint and the potential course of her health journey makes the VoL in this case a subject worth integrating into the medical discussion.

However, the spiritual dimension of the patient's utterance does not seem to come across clearly enough in the interpreter's rendition. There is no clear link in S. 287 between the patient hearing God's voice and her motivation to accept the transplant. The final sentence of S. 286 is also fully omitted in the interpreter's utterance. For these reasons, S. 287 can be classified as a *reduced* rendition, using Wadensjö's (1998) terminology.

It is well established in the interpreting community that omissions may serve as a strategy by which to prioritise a rendition of key information (Napier, 2005). Omissions may provide a way to condense the essential meaning in an original utterance by eliminating what is perceived to be redundant, thus reducing the interpreter's cognitive load (*ibid.*). Due to the immediacy involved in the dialogue interpreting modality, interpreters are constantly and rapidly making decisions concerning what is redundant and what is essential information. This means that subjective judgements are necessary to enable a speedy and therefore competent performance. The subjectivity of this process means that judgements on what information is relevant or not are made in accordance with the interpreter's cognitive frame and values. For this reason, we decided to explore the decision-making processes behind the interpreter's reduced rendition in S. 287. In a retrospective interview, the interpreter stated:

> [A]s an interpreter, sometimes you need to gear the patient's answer towards what the doctor needs to hear because sometimes patients answer in a way that is not relevant, and everybody wastes time when that happens.

This quote suggests that the interpreter perceives the spiritual component of S. 286 to be irrelevant and thus not worth including in her rendition. This position is controversial from the point of view of PCC, given that spiritual aspects in a patient's conception of their health journey are a direct expression of the VoL, a core aspect to be considered in the person-centred model. Interpreters' omissions of VoL aspects and their prioritisation of biomedical talk is a tendency that has been noted in previous literature. For example, Bolden (2000) explained how interpreters can block out patients' VoL through reduced and discursively reframed renditions in an attempt to preserve efficiency in the use of consultation time, a key aspect in healthcare settings.

In the retrospective interview with the clinician, he was invited to comment on S. 287. Upon examination of the excerpt, he admitted that it would have been useful for him to be aware of the importance that the patient attributed to religion. In fact, he added that he normally finds it useful to encourage patients' faith narratives due to the significance that they may have in times of distress. For example, he mentioned that a way of fostering this discussion would be to ask the following questions: "Do you think God has a plan for you?" or "Do you agree with God's plan for you to live longer?" This doctor's standpoint offers an illustrative example of the communicative pattern that Leanza, Boivin, and Rosenberg (2013, p. 13) call the "integration of Lifeworld and biomedicine." By integrating the VoL and VoM, two different ways of conceiving the patient's health journey co-exist and even complement each other as they refer to two different dimensions: the psychosocial and biomedical sides of patient care. This might partly explain why, during the retrospective interview with the clinician, at the end of the discussion on Excerpt 2, he referred to the episode as "a missed opportunity."

Therefore, it may be concluded that Excerpt 2 provides evidence that interpreters are actively involved in the discursive negotiation between the VoM and the VoL, thereby actively contributing to managing the tension between the two voices. Interpreter agency might safeguard or block the patient's VoL and the progression of talk might, in turn, also be influenced by it. For this reason, it is important that interpreters are attuned to the doctor's communicative goals and reflect such goals in their performance. This is relevant from a PCC standpoint given that the protection of the patient's VoL is key to enabling person-centred communication.

"The One We Talked About in Our Last Appointment": PCC and Relational Continuity

All the sessions audio-recorded as part of the original study, also the source of data for this chapter, involved the same patient and clinician. This was the case because the patient's condition was chronic. Thus, the progression of her illness needed to be monitored by a doctor familiarised with her clinical needs and psychosocial circumstances. In our data, the clinician's presence is consistent. By contrast, there is a different interpreter in each consultation.

Promoting relationship continuity throughout a patient's health journey is one of the main principles of PCC. This becomes particularly salient in cases involving patients suffering from chronic conditions, as they need to regularly access healthcare services to manage their ailments (Paddison, 2015). Ongoing contact helps clinicians better understand patients' circumstances and social history, as well as explore their health needs and priorities in the context of their lifeworld (*ibid.*). This has consequences in terms of patient experience, evidenced by the fact that higher scores in patient satisfaction are associated with care provided by a regular physician (Nutting et al., 2003).

Whilst the benefits of consistent doctor–patient contact are well-acknowledged in the medical literature, not much attention has been paid to the notion of interpreter continuity in multilingual healthcare encounters involving long-term patients. In fact, defending the importance of continuity in interpreting provision might seem like a contentious issue, particularly for those who have a conduit-model view of language mediation.

Benefits of interpreter continuity have been documented in studies set in a range of public service settings including healthcare (see Perez & Wilson, 2006; Hsieh et al., 2010; Major, 2013; Schofield & Mapson, 2014). Several benefits of continued interpreter allocation documented in these studies are worth highlighting: first, enhanced accuracy and speediness in interpreters' renditions due to terminological and conceptual familiarity; secondly, increased familiarity, which results in improved relational dynamics between participants. These aspects are illustrated in subsections of our data, such as in Excerpt 3 below.

Excerpt 3 took place in the third consultation observed and audio-recorded by the author in the data collection stage of the original study (Rodríguez-Vicente, 2020). To contextualise this excerpt, we must mention that the discussions held in the observed sessions were mostly about the patient's choice of dialysis treatment: either haemodialysis or peritoneal dialysis. In the end, the patient opts for the peritoneal version. The clinician and patient have this conversation several times in different consultations, and this topic is resumed in a follow-up session as shown in Excerpt 3.

EXCERPT 3

[S. 131] Clinician

In the last session, you said that you do not want to continue receiving dialysis. Is this still the case?

[S.132] Interpreter

¿En la última session dijo que no quería seguir con la diálisis?
(In the last session you said that you did not want to continue with dialysis?)

[S. 133] Patient

No, era...[hesitant]. Ay, ¿cómo se llamaba? Esa otra diálisis, la de volver al hospital. ¡Esa de la que hablamos en la última cita!
(No, it was... [hesitant]. Ay, what was the name? the other one, the one [that requires me] to come back to the hospital. The one we talked about in our last appointment!)

[S. 134] Interpreter

She does not want to come back to the hospital for the dialysis. She can't remember the name.

[S. 135] Clinician

I am not sure I understand that.

[S. 136] Interpreter

No entiende.
    ([He] doesn't understand.)

[S. 137] Patient

Eh, a ver, la peritoneal sí, pero la otra no. [Addressing interpreter] ¡Ay! ¿cómo se llamaba la otra?
    (Eh, yes to the peritoneal but not the other one. [Addressing interpreter] Ay! what was the name of the other one?)

[S. 138] Interpreter

[*Addressing clinician*] Yes for the peritoneal but not for the other one. What is the name of the other one?

[S. 139] Clinician

Does she mean haemodialysis?

Excerpt 3 shows the clinician seeking the patient's confirmation that she does not want haemodialysis. Perhaps assuming that the patient is well-acquainted with the names of the two types of dialysis, the clinician does not explicitly mention them when asking the patient about her preferences (S. 131). At this point, the patient seems to have a memory lapse as she is unable to remember the word "haemodialysis." As a result, the patient expresses frustration at being unable to remember the word and even asks the interpreter for help (S. 137). However, this interpreter is unable to provide an immediate response because she is unfamiliar with the terminology and, most importantly, with this patient's clinical case. The issue is finally resolved when the interpreter redirects the patient's query to the clinician (S. 138).

We argue that the tension built up between S. 133 and S. 138, shown in Excerpt 3, could have been more effectively resolved if the interpreter had been able to quickly suggest the term "haemodialysis" to the patient. Nonetheless, it must also be acknowledged that, for this seemingly small action to occur and be effective, the interpreter would have had to be acquainted with the different types of dialysis, particularly in the context of this patient's case. This would have been an example of enhanced lexical retrieval caused by continuity of interpreter provision. We propose that an interpreter's familiarity with the clinical case of a long-term patient might result in an enhanced interpreter capacity to draw on contextual assumptions and more effectively fill in meaning gaps, which would potentially result in a smoother communication flow.

Going a step beyond the discursive benefits of interpreter continuity, some authors have focused on the relational dimension of consistent contact between an interpreter and interpreting users. For example, it has been proposed that interpreter continuity enhances rapport and trust dynamics between the interpreter and service users (Perez & Wilson, 2006). In a similar vein, it has also been suggested that sustained contact between an interpreter and a service provider might lead to a more effective working relationship between them, as they familiarise themselves with one another's communication patterns (Hsieh et al., 2010). Some of these aspects were echoed in comments offered by the participants in our study. For example, one of the interpreters provided the following account:

> You can tell what seeing you in different sessions means for some peo-
> ple with complex physical or mental health issues. A lot of the content
> discussed in these sessions [psychological medicine] is very sensitive and
> can bring them [the patients] shame, so I can see why some of them
> might not feel comfortable talking about them in front of a different
> interpreter every time. Who the interpreter is *does* matter.

What this quote suggests is that interpreter continuity can have a direct impact on a patient's experience of, and satisfaction with, the care provided. This interpreter's statement has multiple implications. It challenges notions of interpreter invisibility that still predominate in the minds of some healthcare practitioners and codes of ethics (Hsieh, 2016). If interpreters are translation machines, then why would continuity of interpreter provision make a difference? The quote above raises more questions that would benefit from further research: what are the advantages and/or risks of ongoing contact between a healthcare practitioner, a long-term patient, and a specific interpreter? Might boundaries be blurred due to increased familiarity? What would be the implications in terms of confidentiality and patient choice? Considering that many interpreting services in healthcare are outsourced, what level of coordination would be required between healthcare organisations and language service providers to ensure interpreter continuity? Finally, considering that relationship continuity is a key aspect of person-centred care, does this aspect also apply to interpreting provision for patients who are language discordant?

Conclusion

Our overarching finding is that interpreters have the agency to affect participants' talk in ways that may influence the accomplishment of person-centred communication. Interpreters may consciously or unconsciously enable or hamper person-centred communication through their performance, either by conveying and even reinforcing PCC cues or by suppressing them. The way in which interpreters influence the implementation of PCC depends on the *alignment*, or lack thereof, that exists between the interactional goals in the primary speakers' original utterances and the interpreters' renditions. Interpreters make interpreting decisions based on their understanding of the clinical, linguistic, and interpersonal goals at play in the encounter (Major, 2013). Therefore, if such understanding correlates with the goals originally intended by the speaker's intervention, a primary speaker–interpreter alignment will be brought about, such as in Excerpt 1. By contrast, Excerpt 2 illustrates the notion of misalignment as it shows how an interpreter's partial omission of the spiritual component in a patient's account hampers the doctor's ability to access the patient's lifeworld. The interpreter's actions in these episodes have direct consequences for the accomplishment of person-centred communication because respect for the patient's autonomy (Excerpt 1) and spirituality (Excerpt 2) are fundamental principles of PCC. Overall, interpreter alignment with these values contributes to ensuring the implementation of PCC, and the opposite is true if misalignment happens. Finally, Excerpt 3 shows that there are circumstantial factors that may affect the provision of PCC for long-term patients who are language discordant.

These findings have practical implications. If interpreter alignment is driven by the understanding of primary speakers' communicative goals, then it may be assumed that interpreters' greater awareness of speakers' goals may increase the potential for alignment. Drawing on this, we propose that interpreter familiarity with PCC values may increase their agency in helping to enact the values of person-centred communication in multilingual healthcare encounters. Thus, when interpreters are familiar with the protocols and goals being pursued in clinical communication, they can make more informed interpreting decisions and multiply occurrences of alignment between their communicative practices and those of their clients. This supports the case for multidisciplinary training that encompasses aspects of both language mediation and healthcare communication protocols, in line with the work of Krystallidou (2018).

However, helping ensure interpreter-mediated person-centred care is not limited to interpreter performance. There are organisational factors that might play a role in ensuring that linguistically diverse patients access PCC principles, such as interpreter continuity. We suggest that the intersection between PCC and language mediation should be carefully considered by healthcare organisations and language service providers.

Acknowledgements

We would like to acknowledge Dr Robyn Dean's contribution to the discussion of Excerpt 1.

Notes

1 Mishler developed the concepts of the "Voice of Medicine" (VoM) and the "Voice of the Lifeworld" (VoL) by applying Habermas's Theory of Communicative Action (1984) to the analysis of medical interaction. For a further discussion of the VoM and the VoL in interpreter-mediated talk, see Leanza, Boivin, and Rosenberg (2013).
2 Segment (S.) numbers refer to their place in the original transcripts. Back translations are displayed using parentheses.
3 The interpreters' quotes shown in this chapter are translations of the original accounts, provided in Spanish.

References

Adults with Incapacity (Scotland) Act (2000). *Part 5 – Medical Treatment and Research*. UK Statue Law Database.

Angelelli, C. (2019). *Healthcare Interpreting Explained*. London: Routledge.

Angelelli, C. (2020). Language mediation and patient-centred communication. In: E. Postigo-Pinazo (Ed.) *Interpreting in a Changing World: New Scenarios, Technologies, Training Challenges* (pp. 13–36). Berlin: Peter Lang.

Bakhtin, M. M. (1981). *The Dialogic Imagination: Four Essays*. Austin: University of Texas Press.

Bolden, G. (2000). Toward understanding practices of medical interpreting: Interpreters' involvement in history taking. *Discourse Studies*, 2(4), 387–419.

British Medical Association (BMA) (2020). Autonomy or self-determination as a medical student. *Ethics Toolkit for Medical Students*. Available at: https://www.bma.org.uk/advice-and-support/ethics.

Cambridge, J. (2012). *Interpreter Output in Talking Therapy. Towards a Methodology or Good Practice*. Unpublished doctoral dissertation. Warwick medical school, University of Warwick.

Coggon, J. & Miola, J. (2011). Autonomy, liberty and medical decision-making. *The Cambridge Law Journal*, 70(3), 523–547.

Davidson, B. (2000). The interpreter as institutional gatekeeper: The social-linguistic role of interpreters in Spanish-English medical discourse. *Journal of Sociolinguistics*, 4(3), 379–405.

Delaney, L. J. (2017). Patient-centred care as an approach to improving health care in Australia. *Australian College of Nursing*, 25(1), 119–123.

Epner, D. E. & Baile, W. F. (2012). Patient-centered care: The key to cultural competence. *Annals of Oncology : Official Journal of the European Society for Medical Oncology*, 23(3), 33–42.

Flores, G. (2005). The impact of medical interpreter services on the quality of health care: A systematic review. *Medical Care Research and Review: MCRR*, 62(3), 255–299.

Habermas, J. (1984). *The Theory of Communicative Action* (Vol. 1). Boston: Beacon Press.

Håkansson, E. et al. (2018). Same or different? A review of reviews of person-centered and patient-centered care. *Patient Education and Counselling*, 102(1), 3–11.

Hsieh, E. (2015). Healthcare interpreting. In: F. Pöchhacker (Ed.) *Routledge Encyclopaedia of Interpreting Studies* (pp. 177–182). Oxon: Routledge.

Hsieh, E. (2016). *Bilingual Health Communication: Working with Interpreters in Cross-Cultural Care*. New York: Routledge.

Hsieh, E., Ju, H. & Kong, H. (2010). Dimensions of trust: The tensions and challenges in provider-interpreter trust. *Qualitative Health Research*, 20(2), 170–181.

Krystallidou, D. et al. (2018). Training "doctor-minded" interpreters and "interpreter-minded" doctors: The benefits of collaborative practice in interpreter training.' *Interpreting. International Journal of Research and Practice in Interpreting*, 20(1), 132–150.

Leanza, Y. (2005). Roles of community interpreters in paediatrics as seen by interpreters, physicians and researchers. *Interpreting. International Journal of Research and Practice in Interpreting*, 7(2), 167–192.

Leanza, Y., Boivin, I. & Rosenberg, E. (2013). The patient's lifeworld: Building meaningful clinical encounters between patients, physicians and interpreters. *Communication and Medicine Journal*, 10(1), 13–25.

Linell, P. (1998). *Approaching Dialogue: Talk, Interaction and Contexts in Dialogical Perspectives* (Vol. 3). Amsterdam: John Benjamins Publishing.

Major, G. (2013). *Not Just 'How the Doctor Talks': Healthcare Interpreting as Relational Practice*. Unpublished doctoral dissertation. Australia: Macquarie University.

Major, G. & Napier, J. (2012). Interpreting and knowledge mediation in the healthcare setting: What do we really mean by 'accuracy'? *Linguistica Antverpiensia*, 11, 207–225.

McFarlane, A. (2010). The long-term costs of traumatic stress: Intertwined physical and psychological consequences. *World Psychiatry: Official Journal of the World Psychiatric Association*, 9(1), 3–10.

McSherry, W. & Ross, L. (2010). *Spiritual Assessment in Healthcare Practice*. Cumbria: M&K Publishing.

Merlini, R. & Favaron, R. (2005). Examining the "voice of interpreting" in speech pathology. *Interpreting. International Journal of Research and Practice in Interpreting*, 7(2), 263–302.

Mishler, E. G. (1984). *The Discourse of Medicine: Dialectics of Medical Interviews*. Norwood, NJ: Ablex.

Napier, J. (2005). Teaching interpreters to identify omission potential. In: C. Roy (Ed.) *Advances in Teaching Sign Language Interpreters* (Vol. 2, pp. 123–137). Washington, DC: Gallaudet University Press.

Nutting, P. A. et al. (2003). Continuity of primary care: To whom does it matter and when? *Annals of Family Medicine*, 1(3), 149–155.

Paddison, C. (2015). How can we get better at providing patient centred care: Does continuity matter? *British Medical Journal – Letters*, 350, h1127.

Perez, I. & Wilson, C. (2006). *Translating, Interpreting and Communication Support: A Review of Provision in Public Services in Scotland. Scottish Executive Social Research*. Oxford: Blackwell.

Rodríguez-Vicente, N. (2020). *Dialogue Interpreting in Psychological Medicine: An Exploration of Rapport Management Practices*. Unpublished doctoral dissertation. Heriot-Watt University (UK).

Rogers, C. R. (1951). *Client-Centered Therapy: Its Current Practice, Implications and Theory*. Boston: Houghton Mifflin.

Ruddick, F. (2010). Person-centred mental health care: Myth or reality? *Mental Health Practice*, 13(9), 24–28.

Santana, M. J. et al. (2017). How to practice person-centred care: A conceptual framework. *Health Expectations: An International Journal of Public Participation in Health Care and Health Policy*, 21(2), 429–440.

Schofield, M. & Mapson, R. (2014). Dynamics in interpreted interactions: An insight into the perceptions of healthcare professionals. *Journal of Interpretation*, 23(1), 1–15.

Scottish Government (2019). Person-centred care. *Community Health and Social Care Directorate*. Available at: https://www.gov.scot/publications/person-cent red-care-non-executive-members/.

Starfield, B. (2011). Is patient-centered care the same as person-focused care? *The Permanente Journal*, 15(2), 63–69.

Thomas, J. (1995). *Meaning in Interaction: An Introduction to Pragmatics*. London: Routledge.

Wadensjö, C. (1998). *Interpreting as Interaction*. London: Longman.

World Health Organisation (WHO) (2016). *Framework on Integrated, People-Centred Health Services*. Summary record of the executive board at its 138th session, 10th meeting, section 2 (document EB138/2016/REC/2).

Part II
Process of T&I

3 Effect of Perceived Translation Difficulty on the Allocation of Cognitive Resources Between Translating and Consultation

An Eye-Tracking and Screen-Recording Study

Yixiao Cui and Binghan Zheng

Introduction

Hvelplund (2016) defined an efficient translation process as "one in which the translator exerts time and effort effectively so that cognitive resources are allocated only to those subtasks necessary to the completion of the overall translation task" (p. 2). The efficient allocation of time and effort is particularly crucial in the type of translation process that involves consulting external resources. Translation with consultation is formed of two interdependent and conflicting activities: translating[1] and consultation. During translating, which is a "knowledge based" (Enríquez Raído, 2014, p. 1) activity, consultation often serves as an aid for problem-solving (Hvelplund, 2017). However, as translators have to stop translating during consultation, they need to spare part of their time and cognitive resources for consultation, which might lead to a reduction in overall efficiency. Therefore, in order to obtain the most efficient translation process, one of the key points should be maintaining a balance between translating and consultation in the allocation of time and cognitive resources.

Few studies have been conducted to tap into the integration of consultation into the translation process from a resource-allocation perspective. Hvelplund (2017) found that the proportion of time allocated to digital resources in translating LSP (Language for Special Purposes) texts was higher than in translating literary texts. He argued that this was because LSP texts implied "more frequent dictionary lookups to solve a higher number of terminological problems" (p. 76). Since the difficulty levels of the source texts were not compared, it was not certain that LSP texts would indicate more frequent consultations, which could lead to a larger proportion of time allocated to digital resources.

Inspired by Hvelplund (2017), we investigate whether an increase in perceived translation difficulty affects the balance of resource allocation to translating and consultation, with three research hypotheses being given as follows.

Firstly, student translators would spend more time on consultation. Consultation is essentially an information behaviour, which is triggered by information need (Wilson, 2000). As perceived translation difficulty increases, it is assumed that the number and the difficulty level of translation problems would increase, leading to a higher level of need for information. Hence, in order to produce acceptable translation outputs, translators will have to seek more information through consultation and spend a longer time on their consultation.

Secondly, more types of online resources would be consulted. Previous research has found that student translators tended to rely too much on lexical resources, which was in many cases not the most appropriate type of resource (Massey & Ehrensberger-Dow, 2011; Sales et al., 2018). As more external information would be required, more diversified resources might be consulted to fulfil the increased information need in translating a more difficult text.

Thirdly, more between-task transitions would be conducted. Translation with consultation could be considered a multitasking behaviour, as translators simultaneously handle the demands of multiple tasks through task-switching (Just et al., 2001; Rubinstein et al., 2001; Spink et al., 2006). The frequency of task-switching could be revealed by the transitions between translating and consultation. As perceived translation difficulty increases, we assume that student translators would conduct more transitions between tasks.

The Measurements

Measurement of Perceived Translation Difficulty

Defining and measuring translation difficulty has always been a crucial but challenging issue in cognitive translation studies. Borrowing from reading studies, Pavlović and Jensen (2009) used readability alone as the indicator of translation difficulty for texts with similar length and genre. Jensen (2009) improved this method by using a combination of text complexity, word frequency, and non-literalness. Although text complexity and text difficulty could not be equated, researchers "can go some way towards predicting the probable degree of difficulty of a text by employing a battery of objective measures" (p. 77). Apart from text complexity, translation difficulty can be affected by "translation-specific difficulty" and "translator factors" (Sun & Shreve, 2014, p. 100). In this regard, cognitive load could be used to measure perceived translation difficulty, since difficulty "refers to the amount of cognitive effort required to solve a problem" (Sun & Shreve, 2014, p. 99). Paas et al. (2003) concluded that cognitive load could be measured by mental load, mental effort, and performance. In translation studies, Sun and Shreve (2014) asked participants first to predict the translation difficulty level with a Likert scale before translating, and then applied the NASA Task Load Index (TLX) as a multidimensional scale for measuring participants' workload so as to assess translation difficulty. They confirmed the validity of using mental effort in measuring perceived translation difficulty. Liu et al. (2019) used fixation and saccade duration (FSD) and pupil size as two physiological measurements of cognitive load and found that the perceived translation difficulty had a strong correlation with FSD but had no correlation with pupil size. They also confirmed the usability of measuring perceived translation difficulty with psychophysiological techniques.

In this study, we conducted a two-phase rating in order to compare the translation difficulties of the two source texts. In the pre-translation phase, the complexity of source texts was tested by using a combination of readability indices, percentage of complex words, and non-literalness (Jensen, 2009). Besides this, 12 freelance translators were recruited to rate the perceived translation difficulty using a rating scale. Their expert evaluation was collected to estimate the mental load for conducting the translation. The pre-translation phase was conducted as part of the experimental design for source text selection. In the post-translation phase, the participants' cognitive load in translation would be measured using two methods, which served as further support of the pre-translation assessment. Firstly, the participants' post-translation rating was conducted using NASA-TLX to estimate the mental effort. Secondly, their fixation duration was collected as the physiological measurement of the cognitive load. Although pupil size is "often taken as an indicator of the working load placed on the cognitive system" (Hvelplund, 2014, p. 214), it was not used to assess the cognitive load in the present study. As Liu et al. (2019) argue, pupil size during translating might be influenced by various factors including ambient illumination, task complexity, and gaze angle, and it was difficult to control all the factors in an eye-tracking experiment while maintaining the real translation scenario. In addition, pupil size was found to be largely affected by emotional arousal (Bradley et al., 2008). During consultation for translation, participants' emotions might be affected by the information they have found, which thus has an impact on their pupil size. Based on the above discussion, we used only fixation duration as the indicator of cognitive load in our study.

Transitions Between Tasks

In the translation process with consultation, participants have to frequently make transitions between the two tasks, translating and consultation, which would lead to a *switch cost* in time and cognitive resources. The basis for switch costs is still a controversial topic (Arrington & Logan, 2004). Some researchers interpret the costs as reflecting active processes, which involves updating working memory, retrieving information from long-term memory, or activating the production rules associated with a particular task (Logan & Gordon, 2001; Mayr & Kliegl, 2000; Rubinstein et al., 2001), while others suggest that these costs reflect passive interference from memories of past task sets or interference from associations between the current stimulus and its interpretation under the last task set (Allport & Wylie, 2000; Wylie & Allport, 2000). Nevertheless, both types of interpretation confirm that task-switching would lead to a cost in cognitive resources.

In this study, we do not calculate the accurate amount of time and cognitive resources cost in each task-switch. Instead, we use the number of transitions between tasks as an indicator of the cost. Hvelplund (2019) divided three attention-demanding areas, comprising source text (ST), target text (TT), and digital resources (DR), observed the transitions among these areas, and categorised them into four types: ST-DR-ST, ST-DR-TT, TT-DR-ST, and TT-DR-TT. The present study compared the number of occurrences of the four patterns and found that ST-DR-TT was the most frequent one. Following this study, we defined the translation and consultation interfaces as two attention-demanding areas and calculated the number of transitions between them.

Research Design

Participants

Thirty-eight MA translation students (32 females and six males) from a UK university with an average age of 24 (range = 21–35, SD = 2.67) were voluntarily recruited as student participants. They all had Mandarin Chinese as their first language and English as their second language and had not been brought up in a bilingual context. As one of their admission requirements for the MA programme, all participants had obtained an IELTS score of at least 7 (mean = 7.38, range = 7–8, SD = 0.36). Participants were asked not to drink coffee or alcoholic beverages before the experiment and not to wear heavy mascara during the experiment. Anonymity and confidentiality were ensured and a consent form was signed. Each participant received a £10 Tesco voucher as a reward for their work. Our experiment complies with the June 1964 Declaration of Helsinki and has been approved by the research ethics committee of Durham University.

Experiment Setting

The experiment was prepared and run in an eye-tracking lab. A Tobii TX300 eye-tracker was used to record participants' eye movement during translation and consultation. The eye-tracker was connected to a 23-inch LCD monitor that functioned as the presentation screen. The screen resolution was set at 1280×1024 pixels and the fixation radius was the default setting of the Tobii system, 35 pixels per inch.

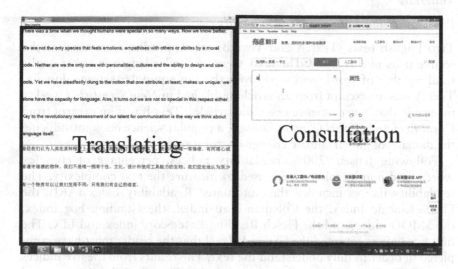

Figure 3.1 Interface Design for the Experiment.

We divided the screen into two areas of equal size (shown in Figure 3.1), with the Translog II user interface on the left for translating and the web browser (Internet Explorer 11) on the right for consultation. The English source texts were displayed in the upper window of the Translog interface,[2] with a Microsoft sans serif typeface set at 18 points, and triple line spacing. The Chinese target texts were produced in the lower window, with a SimSun typeface set at 18 points, also with triple line spacing. The web browser was set on a blank page before the translation task began. After each task, the search history was erased in order to avoid any potential influence on the next participant.

Experiment Procedure

All participants were tested individually. After an acceptable five-point calibration had been saved, each participant started to translate the warm-up text and then the two experimental texts with no time constraints in a randomised order. They were allowed to use any online resources apart from machine translation and CAT tools. In order to minimise the negative effect of fatigue, the participants could take a break between tasks when necessary. After translating the texts, they were asked to take part in a retrospective interview providing us with more information about each individual consultation behaviour.[3] Finally, they were asked to complete a questionnaire about their familiarity with background knowledge for the two source texts and their internet-usage experience. The total session for each participant lasted roughly 90 minutes.

Materials

Pre-Translation Rating: Text Complexity

Two English texts (Text A and Text B, see Appendix) were used as the source texts in this study. The texts were of similar length in terms of the total number of words and were from the same popular science domain. Text A was an excerpt from an article published in *New Scientist*, a weekly magazine that covers science news and articles. Text B was an excerpt from *Coral Reef and Global Climate Change*, a popular science book introducing the damage of global climate change on coral reefs.

Following Jensen (2009), readability indices, percentage of complex words, and non-literalness were used to measure the text complexity. The readability indices included the Automated Readability Index (ARI), the Flesch-Kincaid index, the Coleman-Liau index, the Gunning Fog index, the SMOG index, and the Flesch Reading Ease Score index and LIX. The first five indices returned the US grade level that the reader must have completed in order to fully understand the text. The results from the five indices showed that Text A is lower in complexity than Text B, with 8.68 years and 18.02 years of schooling, respectively, for successful comprehension (see Figure 3.2).

The Flesch Reading Ease Score index and LIX returned numerical scores. In the former, higher scores (up to 100) indicated that the text was easier to read, while lower scores (as low as 0) indicated that the text was more difficult to read. LIX-scale was divided into five categories of difficulty: very easy texts (< 25), easy texts (25–35), average texts (35–45), difficult texts (45–55), and very difficult texts (> 55). According to these two standards, Text A was evaluated as an easy text and Text B as a very difficult text (see Figure 3.3).

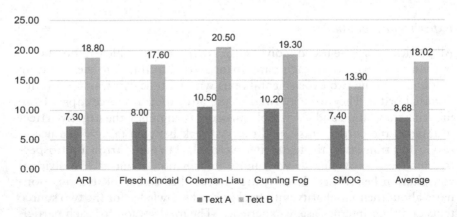

Figure 3.2 US Grade Level Indices Scores of Texts A and B.[4]

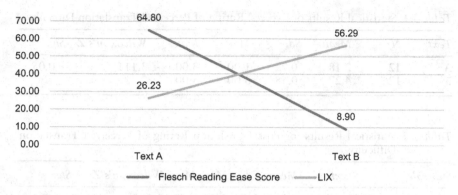

Figure 3.3 Flesch Reading Ease Scores and LIX Scores of Texts A and B.[5]

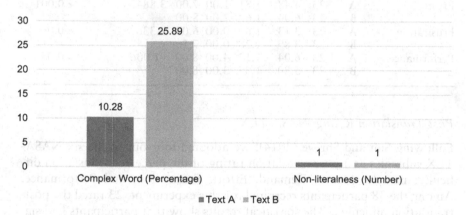

Figure 3.4 Complex Word Percentage of Non-Literalness Number of Texts A and B.[6]

Percentage of complex words and number of non-literalness were also used to indicate the text complexity. Figure 3.4 shows that Text B had a larger proportion of complex words than Text A; and both texts contained the same amount of non-literalness.

To sum up, the three indicators of text complexity showed that Text B was more complex in nature than Text A.

Pre-Translation Rating: Evaluation from Experts

Twelve freelance translators were recruited to rate the perceived translation difficulty of the two texts on a five-point Likert scale, with 1 being "very easy" and 5 being "very difficult." Table 3.1 shows that Text B is perceived to be significantly more difficult to translate than Text A.

Table 3.1 Statistical Results of Experts' Rating of Perceived Translation Difficulty

Text	N	Mean	Sd.	Min	Max	Wilcoxon's Z	Sig.
A	12	2.18	0.72	1.00	3.00	3.111	< 0.05
B	12	4.27	0.58	3.00	5.00		

Table 3.2 Statistical Results for Post-Translation Rating of Perceived Translation Difficulty

Subscale	Text	N	Mean	Sd.	Min	Max	Wilcoxon's Z	Sig.
Mental Demand	A	23	4.09	1.31	2.00	6.00	3.865	< 0.001
	B	23	5.96	1.43	4.00	8.00		
Effort	A	23	4.48	1.81	1.00	7.00	3.884	< 0.001
	B	23	6.04	1.69	2.00	8.00		
Frustration	A	23	3.13	1.60	0.00	6.00	2.336	< 0.05
	B	23	3.89	2.28	0.00	7.50		
Performance	A	23	6.04	1.15	4.00	8.00	–1.006	> 0.05
	B	23	5.80	1.37	3.00	8.00		

Post-Translation Rating: NASA-TLX

Following Sun and Shreve (2014), we adopted four out of the six NASA-TLX subscales as a post-translation rating of the perceived translation difficulty, namely: Mental Demand, Effort, Frustration, and Performance. Among the 38 participants recruited for this experiment, 23 rated the post-translation difficulty.[7] The statistical results show that participants had significantly higher mental effort and slightly worse performance in translating Text B than Text A (see Table 3.2).

Post-Translation Rating: Physiological Measurement

Two separate AOIs in Tobii Studio were drawn to divide the areas of translating and consultation. Overall, 147,692 fixations with valid fixation duration data on the translation area were collected, and the mean values of fixation duration in translating Texts A and B are presented in Table 3.3.

Since the data of the two groups have unequal variances (Levene's test, $F = 99.033$, $p < 0.001$) and are not normally distributed (the Kolmogorov-Smirnov normal distribution test, $Z = 0.168$ for Text A, $Z = 0.171$ for Text B, $p < 0.001$), the Welch's t-test on the rank transformation of the raw data was conducted (Mellinger & Hanson, 2017; Ruxton, 2006; Zimmerman & Zumbo, 1993). The result shows that the difference is statistically significant, indicating that participants devoted more cognitive load in translating Text B than Text A.

Table 3.3 Mean Values of Fixation Duration (Milliseconds) on the Translation Area

Text	N	Mean	Sd.	Min	Max
A	59325	241.97	181.86	60.00	5943.00
B	88367	251.89	191.94	60.00	5073.00

Table 3.4 Result of the Welch's *t*-Test

Measurement	Df	t-Value	Sig.	Cohen's d
Fixation Duration	147690	−130.897	< 0.001	1.50

In conclusion, indicated by all the above assessments on text complexity and the cognitive load of translation, Text B was perceived as more difficult for translation than Text A.

Results

Quality Assessment of Eye-Tracking Data

The quality of the collected eye-tracking data was assessed prior to the data analysis. With reference to Hvelplund (2014), the following three criteria were adopted in this study for assessment: Mean Fixation Duration (MFD), which was calculated as [total fixation duration/the number of fixations]; Gaze Time on Screen (GTS), which was calculated as [(total fixation duration/total task time) × 100%]; and Gaze sample to Fixation Percentage (GFP), which was calculated as [(number of gaze samples/number of fixation gaze samples) × 100%]. In this study, the bars of MFD, GTS, and GFP were set to be 206.85 ms, 46.60%, and 74.67%, respectively (one SD below the mean). Data that satisfied at least two out of the three criteria were considered as valid data. Data obtained from eight participants (P_5, P_{10}, P_{12}, P_{16}, P_{21}, P_{25}, P_{30}, and P_{38}) were deemed invalid, with the percentage of invalid data being 21.05% (see Table 3.5).

Time Spent on Consultation

Sun and Shreve (2014) observed that, with the increase in translation difficulty level, student translators tended to spend more time on translation. In their experiment, participants were allowed to consult their own dictionaries during translation. Since the time spent on consulting dictionaries was considered an internal part of the entire translation process, it was difficult to tell whether the increase in the holistic time length was caused by the increase in

Table 3.5 Summary of Eye-Tracking Quality Assessment with Invalid Data (Marked as ×)

Participant (P_n)	Text A			Text B		
	MFD	*GTS*	*GFP*	*MFD*	*GTS*	*GFP*
P_5	×	×	×	×	×	×
P_10	×		×	×		×
P_12		×	×			×
P_16	×	×		×		
P_21	×	×	×	×	×	×
P_25	×	×	×	×	×	×
P_30	×			×	×	
P_38				×	×	

Table 3.6 Mean Values of the Holistic Translation Time (Seconds) for Texts A and B

Text	N	Mean	Sd.	Min	Max
A	30	889.32	358.09	432.67	1968.98
B	30	1436.57	531.52	766.33	2985.31

the time spent on translating or on consultation. In the present study, we specifically calculated: 1) the total time spent on finishing the whole task; 2) the time spent on translating; and 3) the time spent on consultation.

As can be seen from Table 3.6, participants spent a longer time finishing Text B than Text A. A Welch's *t*-test is performed to confirm the difference, showing that the difference is significant ($t(50.828) = -4.677$, $p < 0.001$, $d = 1.21$). These results indicate that an increase in perceived translation difficulty leads to an increase in the total time length of translation, which is in line with Sun and Shreve (2014).

In our attempt to further calculate the time spent on translating and consultation, respectively, we noticed that the participants' attention flitted frequently between the translation interface and the web browser, which made it difficult to precisely assess the time length of translating and consultation. As a consequence, we used TFD and FC instead as indicators of attention allocated to translating and consultation. Table 3.7 shows the mean values of TFD and FC in processing Texts A and B. The results indicate that an increase in perceived translation difficulty leads to an increase in the time spent on both translating and consultation.

Wilcoxon matched-pairs signed-ranks tests were performed to confirm the differences in TFD and FC as allocated to translating and consultation, respectively, for the two texts, and the differences are all statistically significant (see Table 3.8).

Table 3.7 Mean Values of TFD (Seconds) and FC Allocated to Translating and Consultation for Texts A and B

Behaviour	Measurement	Text	N	Mean	Sd.	Min	Max
Translating	TFD	A	30	475.94	148.43	222.56	782.79
		B	30	699.07	226.89	319.94	1223.20
	FC	A	30	1975.57	527.92	1059	3342
		B	30	2765.43	834.90	1436	4595
Consultation	TFD	A	30	94.39	83.95	1.93	418.37
		B	30	278.96	186.40	96.12	929.23
	FC	A	30	360.40	361.50	12	1929
		B	30	1079.63	723.38	374	3366

Table 3.8 Results of Wilcoxon Tests (TFD and FC Allocated to Translating and Consultation, Respectively)

Behaviour	Measurement	Z	Sig.	Cohen's d
Translating	TFD	4.535	< 0.001	1.16
	FC	4.288	< 0.001	1.13
Consultation	TFD	4.700	< 0.001	1.28
	FC	4.576	< 0.001	1.26

Table 3.9 Mean Value of Percentages of TFD and FC on Consultation

Measurement	Text	N	Mean	Sd.	Min	Max
TFD (Percentage)	A	30	15.12%	8.92%	0.52%	35.83%
	B	30	26.92%	9.15%	0.70%	36.60%
FC (Percentage)	A	30	13.85%	8.38%	15.18%	56.87%
	B	30	26.18%	9.01%	14.65%	53.34%

Since no time constraint was given in our experiment, the length of time spent on translating and consultation could vary depending on the participants' personal processing behaviours. We thus moved a step further to calculate the proportion of visual attention distributed to consultation, indicated by the percentages of TFD and FC on consultation over the entire task. Table 3.9 shows the mean value of the proportion of the two indicators allocated to consultation in processing Texts A and B. The differences in the percentages of TFD and FC between the translations of the two texts are both statistically significant (paired t-test, $t(29) = -6.844$, $p < 0.001$, $d = 1.31$; $t(29) = -6.989$, $p < 0.001$, $d = 1.42$, respectively). The results show that, compared with the proportion of attention allocated to consultation in processing Text A, the proportion in processing Text B is significantly larger. In conclusion, while translating texts with a similar length but different levels of perceived difficulty, participants spend a longer time on consultation for tasks with higher perceived difficulty, and a significantly larger proportion of attention is spent on consultation.

Types of Online Resources

The number of types of online resources used in translation was calculated based on PACTE's categorisation of online resources (Kuznik & Olalla-Soler, 2018, pp. 31–32). The list contained eight items: 1) search engines, such as Google or Baidu;[8] 2) bilingual dictionaries, such as Youdao Dictionary or Bing Dictionary; 3) monolingual dictionaries, such as the *Oxford English Dictionary*; 4) dictionaries of synonyms, such as WordReference; 5) encyclopaedias, such as Wikipedia; 6) databases, such as UNTERM; 7) online corpora, such as Collins; and 8) online or field-specific portals, such as information related to the subject of the source texts. In the present research, six types of online resources (except databases and corpora) were used by the participants.

Table 3.10 shows the mean number of resource types used in processing Texts A and B, with the difference between the two sets of figures being statistically significant (paired t-test, $t(29) = -3.885$, $p < 0.05$, $d = 0.81$). This result indicates that more types of online resources are used in processing Text B than Text A.

Figure 3.5 shows the number of participants that used each type of online resource in translating Texts A and B. Except for dictionaries of synonyms, which was only consulted by one participant in translating Text A, all the other five types of online resources were consulted by more participants in translating Text B than Text A. The largest difference is shown in the use of encyclopaedias. Only one participant consulted encyclopaedias in translating Text A, but half of them did so in translating Text B. Compared with the differences in consulting the three types of dictionary, the differences between translating Texts A and B in consulting the rest of the three types of online resources are larger. These results indicate that, in translating a difficult text, lexical-related resources on their own cannot fulfil participants' information needs, which should be supported by resources containing extra-linguistic information.

Table 3.10 Mean Number of Resource Types in Translating Texts A and B

Text	N	Mean	Sd.	Min	Max
A	30	1.47	1.01	0	4
B	30	2.37	1.22	1	5

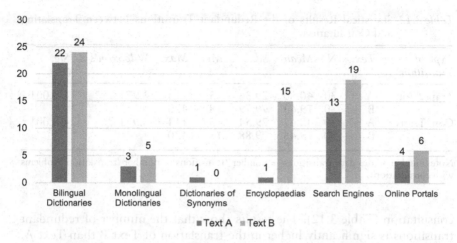

Figure 3.5 Number of Participants Using Different Online Resources.

Table 3.11 Statistical Results for the Transitions Between Translating and Consultation

Type of Transition	Text	N	Mean	Sd.	Min	Max	Wilcoxon's Z	Sig.
Trans2Con	A	30	46.27	31.13	6	119	4.115	< 0.001
	B	30	92.67	81.05	24	433		
Con2Trans	A	30	46.13	31.30	5	120	4.104	< 0.001
	B	30	92.47	81.15	23	433		

Transitions Between Tasks

As mentioned above, we calculated the number of transitions between translating and consultation. Table 3.11 shows the statistical results for this number in processing Texts A and B, indicating a significantly higher number of between-task transitions in processing Text B than Text A.

The number of transitions might be affected by the frequency of consultations, as they were triggered by the need for external information. For each translation segment that required consultation, at least two transitions would be involved: one from translating to consultation, and one from consultation back to translating. Since Text B was perceived to be more difficult to translate, the number of translation problems that required external information was naturally higher, which inevitably led to more between-task transitions. Therefore, in order to eliminate this effect, we then calculated the number of redundant transitions, which equals the total number of transitions deducted by the number of translation problems with

Table 3.12 Statistical Results of the Redundant Transitions Between Translating and Consultation

Type of Transition	Text	N	Mean	Sd.	Min	Max	Wilcoxon's Z	Sig.
Trans2Con	A	30	40.80	29.36	5	113	3.971	< 0.001
	B	30	79.63	79.79	18	420		
Con2Trans	A	30	40.67	29.54	5	114	3.971	< 0.001
	B	30	79.43	79.88	18	420		

Note: number (redundant transitions) = number (transitions) − number (translation problems with consultation).

consultation (Table 3.12). The results show that the number of redundant transitions is significantly higher in the translation of Text B than Text A, indicating a higher switch cost in translating Text B.

Discussion

Time Length of Consultation

We compared the length of time spent on translating and consultation in processing Texts A and B. Our study aligns with Sun and Shreve (2014), verifying that an increase in perceived translation difficulty would lead to an increase in the time spent on translating. We went one step further by comparing the length of consultation time between Texts A and B and observed that an increase in perceived translation difficulty also led to longer time spent on consultation.

In order to elaborate the reasons for this effect, we first need to understand the relationship between task complexity and information behaviour. According to Vakkari's (1999) model on task complexity and information actions (see Figure 3.6), the complexity of a task determines "its performance and consequent information needs" (p. 825). For the present research, as perceived translation difficulty increased, the consequent information needed was higher in the translation of Text B than Text A, which results in a widened gap between participants' prior knowledge and the required knowledge. In order to successfully complete the task, participants had to conduct information actions, which refers to consulting online resources, to fill the knowledge gap.

This result suggests a new method of measuring perceived translation difficulty: measuring the length of time spent on consultation and using this as an indicator to assess the gap between participants' prior knowledge and the required knowledge when translating.

Furthermore, the proportion of attention allocated to consultation over the entire translation process shows an increase as perceived translation

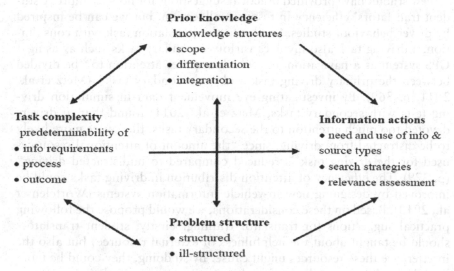

Figure 3.6 Vakkari's Model of Task Complexity and Information Behaviours (1999, p. 830).

difficulty increases. Hvelplund (2017, 2019) compared the proportions of digital resource consultation in translating literary and LSP (Language for Special Purposes) texts and found that text type had a significant impact on the attention distribution in consultation. The results obtained in the present study indicate that translation difficulty is another influential factor that affects attention distribution in the translation process. This also sheds some light on translator training. Our results suggest that consultation consumes a significant proportion of cognitive resources in translation (about 15–26%). Since the consultation and translating activities cannot be conducted simultaneously, a larger proportion of attention allocated to consultation would inevitably lead to a smaller proportion allocated to translating. However, Shih (2019) found that if student translators ignored the importance of consultation and only conducted superficial searches, they might spend a shorter time on a translation task but obtain an undesirable quality, which was called "a false economy in efficiency" (p. 920). Shih argues that "it was not necessarily the amount of time spent overall, but how and where it was spent that seemed to offer optimum return in web search" (p. 920). Therefore, in order to follow the "minimax principle" in translation proposed by Levý (1967/2000), that is, producing maximised translation products with minimised effort, student translators should be trained to be skilful in balancing the cost of resources for translating and consultation. Otherwise, consultation could not fully play its role as the support but might be an interference in the translation process. In the translation competence model proposed by PACTE (2003), the ability to reach the highest efficiency of translation was also included as a "strategic sub-competence" (p. 16).

Few studies have provided practical suggestions for how to improve student translators' efficiency in resource allocation, but we can be inspired by driver behaviour studies. Similar to the translation task with consultation, a driving task also involves various secondary tasks such as using a GPS system as a navigation aid, which requires attention to "be divided between the primary driving task and the secondary task" (Metz et al., 2011, p. 369). By investigating eye movement data in simulation driving tests with secondary tasks, Metz et al. (2011) found that, if drivers devoted too much attention to the secondary tasks, they were more likely to be distracted from driving, since "the amount of attentional resources used for the driving task is reduced compared to undistracted driving" (p. 379). The efficiency of attention distribution in driving tasks could be improved by designing new in-vehicle information systems (Wortelen et al., 2013). Based on these considerations, we would propose the following practical suggestions for translator training. Firstly, student translators should be taught about the helpfulness of external resources but also the interference these resources might cause. By so doing, they could be more conscious of potential distraction during consultation in their translation process. Secondly, the use of external resources should receive more consideration in translation pedagogy. If we consider the entire internet to be an information system for translators, we could either improve the development of external resources specialised for translators or improve the proficiency in their use, with both aims requiring more attention and further empirical investigation.

Preferences of Resource Types

Our study reveals that student translators used significantly more types of resources for consultation in translating Text B than Text A, and that more of the resources were general-purpose resources.

Byströml and Järvelin (1995) defined different types of information required in a general problem-solving process: problem information (PI), which describes the structure, properties, and requirements of the problem; domain information (DI), which consists of known facts, concepts, laws, and theories in the domain of the problem; and problem-solving information (PSI), which covers the methods of problem treatment. According to their research, an increase in task complexity brings more requirements for DI and PSI, which leads to an increase in the number of sources used and the share of general-purpose sources, but a decrease in the share of problem- and fact-oriented sources. Angelone (2010) defined the translation task as "a chain of decision-making behavior relying on multiple, interconnected sequences of problem solving behavior for successful task completion" (p. 17). In our experiment, when participants were conducting a more difficult translation task, their need for DI and PSI increased, as their information need could not be fulfilled by fact-oriented sources only; in fact, they extended their consultation scope to some more general-purpose sources such as information from relevant websites or Wikipedia.

Participants' behaviour in using more types of online resources also indicates that an appropriate level of challenge could motivate students in taking more problem-solving approaches. Several previous studies have indicated that student translators rely heavily on dictionaries and try to solve extra-linguistic problems with multilingual online dictionaries. Massey and Ehrensberger-Dow (2011) observed that undergraduate students tended to consult online dictionaries for extra-linguistic problems, while the instructors preferred to use parallel texts and search engines. Similarly, Sales et al. (2018) reported that first-year translation students often did not select the most appropriate information sources in relation to their information need (such as contextualising the text they should translate and searching for specific information). However, in our study, student translators have shown a capability of using multiple online resources for their consultation, especially when translating a more difficult text. We propose two possible explanations for this result. First, compared to the participants in the above-mentioned studies who were all undergraduate students, our participants have all finished a postgraduate programme, which means that they have undergone a higher level of training and accumulated more translation experience. Based on the questionnaire data, the participants had an average of 12.35 years of using the internet for information searching (range = 7–19, SD = 3.04), which indicates that they have built up sufficient experience in using various online resources for information consultation. Secondly, a challenge might motivate students to conduct more complicated consultation behaviour. Betts (1946) first proposed the idea of an *instruction level*, or the *appropriate level of challenge*, in the field of reading studies. Based on this concept, a great variety of studies have demonstrated that providing students with an optimal level of challenge can improve their learning outcomes, since they are more actively and productively engaged in the learning task (Burns, 2002; Gettinger & Seibert, 2002; Gickling & Thompson, 1985). In our study, students conducted significantly more complicated consultation behaviours in translating the more difficult text, which shows that an increase in translation difficulty might be a motivation for student translators.

Transitions Between Tasks

As perceived translation difficulty increased, participants conducted significantly more redundant between-task transitions, which indicates a higher switch cost. This can be attributed to the following two reasons. Firstly, as the participants were allowed to access external resources, the process of translation was naturally divided into smaller segments by individual consultations. In our study, Text B triggered more translation problems than Text A, which automatically brought about more information consultations, and consequently resulted in more between-task transitions. Besides this, working memory capacity should have an impact on the transition number in this circumstance. According to Baddeley (2007, p. 1), "working memory is a temporary storage system under attentional control that underpins our capacity for complex thought." When participants conduct consultation in translation, the obtained information from external resources is stored in their working memory ready for solving translation problems. If the stored information is too complex, participants will have to look back into the consultation area and repeat the previous consultation procedure, leading to more between-task transitions and costing more cognitive resources. As discussed earlier, the increase in perceived translation difficulty could lead to an increase in the information need. Hence, participants have to search for a larger amount of information (including complex information) in the Text B translation, which requires a heavier demand on their working memory capacity and brings about more transitions between translating and consultation.

Our finding in this regard can provide some pedagogical suggestions for training students' instrumental sub-competence. In order to reduce the amount of cognitive-resource cost by task-switching, student translators should be given designated training in improving their working memory capacity. By comparing different searching behaviours given by eight dyslexic and eight non-dyslexic university students, MacFarlane et al. (2012) report that working memory capacity had a substantial effect on their individual information-searching behaviours. This argument corroborates our results, which suggests that training on working memory capacity would be effective in improving student translators' instrumental sub-competence.

Conclusion

This study investigated how student translators changed their allocation of time and cognitive resources to the sub-tasks (translating and consultation) during the translation process when the perceived translation difficulty increased. Indicators used in this study included the time length of consultation, the proportion of TFD and FC on consultation, the number of online resource types, and the number of transitions between translating and consultation. Our findings can be summarised as follows. Firstly, as perceived translation difficulty increases, participants spend a longer time on consultation, and consultation accounts for a larger proportion of visual attention over the entire translation process. This result proves that as translation difficulty increases, the need for consulting external information increases accordingly so that participants will allocate a larger proportion of time and cognitive resources to consultation. Secondly, as perceived translation difficulty increases, participants prefer to consult more types of online resources, with more general-purpose resources. These results indicate that student translators at the MA level are able to consult a variety of online resources in translation. Thirdly, in the translation of a more difficult text, more transitions between translating and consultation are conducted.

The findings of this study contribute to translation pedagogy, especially in the training of instrumental sub-competence. However, we are aware that some limitations exist in this study. We only investigated student translators' resource allocation. Professional translators' behaviour towards an increase in perceived translation difficulty might be different. Besides this, time pressure might be an influential factor in resource allocation, which was not investigated in this study. Future studies on this topic could be conducted considering these issues.

Appendix

Warm-Up Text

Source: *ScienceDaily*

Plant pollens vary in quality as food sources for bees, and pollen from the sunflower family is known to have some unpleasant qualities. Bees fed exclusively sunflower pollen often develop poorly, slowly, or not at all. Yet many bee species collect pollen exclusively from this family; in fact, specialization on sunflower pollen has evolved multiple times in bees.

(Number of words: 58)

Text A

Source: *New Scientists*

There was a time when we thought humans were special in so many ways. Now we know better. We are not the only species that feels emotions, empathises with others or abides by a moral code. Neither are we the only ones with personalities, cultures and the ability to design and use tools. Yet we have steadfastly clung to the notion that one attribute, at least, makes us unique: we alone have the capacity for language. Alas, it turns out we are not so special in this respect either. Key to the revolutionary reassessment of our talent for communication is the way we think about language itself.

(Number of words: 107)

Text B

Source: *Coral Reef and Global Climate Change*

Coral reefs have the highest biodiversity of any marine ecosystem, and they provide important ecosystem services and direct economic benefits to large and growing human populations in coastal zones. Although the natural habitat of coral reefs can be a stressful environment, recent global increases in reef ecosystem degradation and mortality suggest that the rate and nature of recent environmental changes often exceed the adaptive capacity of coral reefs. This crisis is almost certainly the result of interactions between multiple stresses. These include increased nutrient and sediment loading, direct destruction, contamination, overharvesting, disease and predation. Rising ocean temperatures have been implicated in chronic stress, disease epidemics, mass coral bleaching episodes and reduced calcification.

(Number of words: 112)

Notes

1 In this chapter, "translating" is specifically used to indicate the pure translation activity without involving any consultation, and to differentiate from the broad concept of translation.
2 The key-logging data from Translog II were not analysed in this study. Translog II was only used as the interface to display source text and produce target text.
3 The data from retrospective interviews are mostly about consultation for individual translation problems, which are not discussed in this study.
4 These indices were retrieved from https://www.webfx.com/tools/read-able/.
5 The Flesch Kincaid Ease score was retrieved from https://www.webfx.com/tools/read-able/. LIX was calculated based on its formula [words/sentences + 100 × (words ≥ 6 characters)/words].
6 The Complex Word percentage was retrieved from https://www.webfx.com/tools/read-able/.
7 The experiment was conducted in two phases. Based on the results of the first-phase experiments, we added post-translation rating with NASA-TLX in the second phase.
8 If the search engine was only used to find a specific website (such as searching for "Youdao dictionary"), this would not be considered as consulting the search engines.

References

Allport, A., & Wylie, G. (2000). Task switching, stimulus-response bindings, and negative priming. In: S. Monsell & J. Driver (Eds.), *Control of Cognitive Processes: Attention and Performance XVIII* (pp. 35–70). Cambridge, MA: MIT Press.
Angelone, E. (2010). Uncertainty, uncertainty management and metacognitive problem solving in the translation task. In: G. M. Shreve & E. Angelone (Eds.), *Translation and Cognition* (pp. 17–40). Amsterdam: John Benjamins.
Arrington, C. M., & Logan, G. D. (2004). The cost of a voluntary task switch. *Psychological Science*, *15*(9), 610–615. https://doi.org/10.1111/j.0956-7976.2004.00728.x.
Baddeley, A. (2007). *Working Memory. Thought and Action*. Oxford: Oxford University Press.
Betts, E. A. (1946). *Foundations of Reading Instructions*. New York: American Book.
Bradley, M. M., Miccoli, L., Escrig, M. A., & Lang, P. J. (2008). The pupil as a measure of emotional arousal and autonomic activation. *Psychophysiology*, *45*(4), 602–607. https://doi.org/10.1111/j.1469-8986.2008.00654.x.

Burns, M. K. (2002). Comprehensive system of assessment to intervention using curriculum-based assessments. *Intervention in School and Clinic, 38*(1), 8–13. https://doi.org/10.1177/10534512020380010201.

Byströml, K., & Järvelin, K. (1995). Task complexity affects information seeking and use. *Information Processing and Management, 31*(2), 191–213. https://tu tcris.tut.fi/portal/en/publications/task-complexity-affects-information-use(e926 6504-71b0-4439-a772-89677cb4e5cf).html.

Enríquez Raído, V. (2014). *Translation and Web Searching.* New York: Routledge. https://doi.org/10.4324/9780203798034.

Gettinger, M., & Seibert, J. K. (2002). Best practices in increasing academic learning time. In: A. Thomas & J. Grimes (Eds.), *Best Practices in School Psychology* (4th ed., pp. 773–787). Bethesda, MD: National Association of School Psychologists.

Gickling, E. E., & Thompson, V. P. (1985). A personal view of curriculum-based assessment. *Exceptional Children, 52*(3), 205–218. https://doi.org/https://doi-org .ezphost.dur.ac.uk/10.1177/001440298505200302.

Hvelplund, K. T. (2014). Eye tracking and the translation process: Reflections on the analysis and interpretation of eye-tracking data. *MonthTI Speciale Issue 1: Minding Translation,* 201–223. https://doi.org/10.6035/monti.2014.ne1.6.

Hvelplund, K. T. (2016). Cognitive efficiency in translation. In: R. M. Martin (Ed.), *Reembedding Translation Process Research* (pp. 149–170). Amsterdam: John Benjamins. https://doi.org/10.1075/btl.128.08hve.

Hvelplund, K. T. (2017). Translators' use of digital resources during translation. *HERMES - Journal of Language and Communication in Business, 56*(56), 71–87. https://doi.org/10.7146/hjlcb.v0i56.97205.

Hvelplund, K. T. (2019). Digital resources in the translation process–attention, cognitive effort and processing flow. *Perspectives, 27*(4), 510–524. https://doi .org/10.1080/0907676X.2019.1575883.

Jensen, K. T. H. (2009). Indicators of text complexity. In: S. Göpferich, A. L. Jakobsen, & I. M. Mees (Eds.), *Behind the Mind: Methods, Models and Results in Translation Process Research* (pp. 61–80). Copenhagen: Samfundslitteratur.

Just, M. A., Carpenter, P. A., Keller, T. A., Emery, L., Zajac, H., & Thulborn, K. R. (2001). Interdependence of nonoverlapping cortical systems in dual cognitive tasks. *NeuroImage, 14*(2), 417–426. https://doi.org/10.1006/nimg .2001.0826.

Kuznik, A., & Olalla-Soler, C. (2018). Results of PACTE group's experimental research on translation competence acquisition. The acquisition of the instrumental sub-competence. *Across Languages and Cultures, 19*(1), 19–51. https://doi.org/10.1556/084.2018.19.1.2.

Levý, J. (1967/2000). Translation as a decision process. In L. Venuti (Ed.), *The Translation Studies Reader* (pp. 148–159). London: Routledge.

Liu, Y., Zheng, B., & Zhou, H. (2019). Measuring the difficulty of text translation. *Target, 31*(1), 125–149. https://doi.org/10.1075/target.18036.zhe.

Logan, G. D., & Gordon, R. D. (2001). Executive control of visual attention in dual-task situations. *Psychological Review, 108*(2), 393–434. https://doi.org/10.1037 /0033-295X.108.2.393.

MacFarlane, A., Albrair, A., Marshall, C. R., & Buchanan, G. (2012). Phonological working memory impacts on information searching. In: *Proceedings of the IIIX 2012 Therapeutic 4th Information Interaction in Context Symposium* (pp. 27–34). https://doi.org/10.1145/2362724.2362734.

Massey, G., & Ehrensberger-Dow, M. (2011). Investigating information literacy: A growing priority in translation studies. *Across Languages and Cultures, 12*(2), 193–211. https://doi.org/10.1556/acr.12.2011.2.4.

Mayr, U., & Kliegl, R. (2000). Task-set switching and long-term memory retrieval. *Journal of Experimental Psychology: Learning Memory and Cognition, 26*(5), 1124–1140. https://doi.org/10.1037/0278-7393.26.5.1124.

Mellinger, C. D., & Hanson, T. A. (2017). *Quantitative Research Methods in Translation and Interpreting Studies*. Abingdon: Routledge.

Metz, B., Schömig, N., & Krüger, H. P. (2011). Attention during visual secondary tasks in driving: Adaptation to the demands of the driving task. *Transportation Research Part F: Traffic Psychology and Behaviour, 14*(5), 369–380. https://doi.org/10.1016/j.trf.2011.04.004.

Paas, F., Tuovinen, J. E., Tabbers, H., & Van Gerven, P. W. M. M. (2003). Cognitive load measurement as a means to advance cognitive load theory. *Educational Psychologist, 38*(1), 63–71. https://doi.org/10.1207/S15326985EP3801_8.

PACTE (2003). Building a translation competence model. In: F. Alves (Ed.), *Triangulating Translation: Perspectives in Process Oriented Research* (pp. 43–66). Amsterdam: John Benjamins. https://doi.org/10.1075/btl.45.

Pavlović, N., & Jensen, K. T. H. (2009). Eye tracking translation directionality. In: A. Pym & A. Perekrestenko (Eds.), *Translation Research Projects 2* (pp. 93–109). Tarragona: Intercultural Studies Group.

Rubinstein, J. S., Meyer, D. E., & Evans, J. E. (2001). Executive control of cognitive processes in task switching. *Journal of Experimental Psychology: Human Perception and Performance, 27*(4), 763–797. https://doi.org/10.1037/0096-1523.27.4.763.

Ruxton, G. D. (2006). The unequal variance t-test is an underused alternative to Student's t-test and the Mann-Whitney U test. *Behavioral Ecology, 17*(4), 688–690. https://doi.org/10.1093/beheco/ark016.

Sales, D., Pinto, M., & Fernández-Ramos, A. (2018). Undressing information behaviour in the field of translation: A case study with translation trainees. *Journal of Librarianship and Information Science, 50*(2), 186–198. https://doi.org/10.1177/0961000616666131.

Shih, C. Y. (2019). A quest for web search optimisation: An evidence-based approach to trainee translators' behaviour. *Perspectives, 27*(6), 908–923. https://doi.org/10.1080/0907676X.2019.1579847.

Spink, A., Park, M., Jansen, B. J., & Pedersen, J. (2006). Multitasking during web search sessions. *Information Processing and Management, 42*(1), 264–275. https://doi.org/10.1016/j.ipm.2004.10.004.

Sun, S., & Shreve, G. M. (2014). Measuring translation difficulty: An empirical study. *Target. International Journal of Translation Studies, 26*(1), 98–127. https://doi.org/10.1075/target.26.1.04sun.

Vakkari, P. (1999). Task complexity, problem structure and information actions: Integrating studies on information seeking and retrieval. *Information Processing and Management, 35*(6), 819–837. https://doi.org/10.1016/s0306-4573(99)00028-x.

Wilson, T. D. (2000). Human information behavior. *Informing Science, 3*(2), 49–55. https://doi.org/10.28945/576.

Wortelen, B., Lüdtke, A., & Baumann, M. (2013). Integrated simulation of attention distribution and driving behavior. In: *Proceedings of the 22nd Annual Conference on Behavior Representation in Modeling and Simulation* (pp. 69–76).

Wylie, G., & Allport, A. (2000). Task switching and the measurement of "switch costs." *Psychological Research*, *63*(3–4), 212–233. https://doi.org/10.1007/s004269900003.

Zimmerman, D. W., & Zumbo, B. D. (1993). Rank transformations and the power of the Student t test and Welch t' test for non-normal populations with unequal variances. *Canadian Journal of Experimental Psychology/Revue Canadienne de Psychologie Expérimentale*, *47*(3), 523–539. https://doi.org/10.1037/h0078850.

4 Navigating the Web

A Study on Professional Translators' Behaviour

Claire Y. Shih

Introduction

When the World Wide Web was first invented, it was hard to imagine its prevalence in most people's lives today. The nature of the WWW means that masses of data are interconnected via hyperlinks and become easily accessible to anyone. Yet, with an explosive volume of data available, to locate relevant information requires skilled navigation. Search engines are supposed to facilitate this process. But, for translators, navigating and locating relevant information can still seem like searching for a needle in a haystack. The importance of navigating the web successfully cannot be underestimated, since it serves as a key (input) in shaping translators' inference in comprehending the source text (ST) and/or rendering the target text (TT) (Chang, 2018, p. 198).

Despite being acknowledged as an important translator competence (e.g. EMT Competence Framework, 2017) and professional translators spending a substantial amount of time on web search (e.g. Hvelplund, 2017, 2019), there are still relatively few studies focusing on these phenomena. This study, therefore, aims to shed further light on professional translators' web search behaviours, particularly with respect to their "primary action" and "secondary action" (White, 2016, pp. 21–37), why and in what circumstances such behaviours occur, and what the interplay is between primary action and secondary action. The dichotomy of primary action and secondary action was first adopted from information retrieval (IR) studies by Shih (2019, pp. 912–913) to largely illustrate translators' interaction with search engines and online resources. Primary action indicates query-related behaviours, such as entering queries in search boxes, whereas secondary action indicates browsing and clicking behaviours that are associated with search engine result pages (SERPs). Table 4.1 provides a schematic overview of the aims and their corresponding research questions.

Previous Studies

A number of previous studies on translators' web search behaviours focused on student translators. For example, Enriquez Raido's (2014) study focuses

Table 4.1 Schematic Overview of Research Questions

Types of Web Search Behaviours	Corresponding Research Questions
Primary action: query-related action	• What types of queries do professional translators tend to use? • What are their query intents? • How and in what circumstances do queries relate to query intent?
Secondary action: browsing and clicking behaviours	• What are the potential patterns of professional translators' browsing and clicking behaviours? • When and in what circumstances is a hyperlink clicked at a search engine result page (SERP)?
Interplay between primary and secondary action	• What is the interplay between primary and secondary actions in professional translators' behaviour?

on four student translators translating two separate texts from Spanish into English. Similarly, Shih (2017, 2019) first investigated the web search process of six student translators translating a scientific text and then 18 student translators translating three medical texts on three separate occasions from English into Chinese. In contrast, Gough (2015) focused more specifically on professional translators working from English into various languages. All these studies adopted a mixed-method approach, primarily using screen recording as their main data collection method supplemented by surveys, questionnaires, search reports, or concurrent verbal reports, etc. Most recently, Hvelplund (2017, 2019) conducted an eye-tracking study with 18 professional translators exploring their overall visual attention, cognitive efforts, and "processing flow," defined as the eye movement transition between the ST, TT, and web resources. His results showed that translators' visual attention (hence cognitive efforts) is more substantial in the drafting rather than the revision stage, highlighting the importance of web searching during the early/drafting stages of the translation process (for a broader overview of studies on web search in translation, see Shih, 2019, pp. 908–911). In the following section, I will focus specifically on primary action and secondary action in these existing studies.

About Primary Action in Translation

Query was probably one of the most overt aspects of investigation in existing studies, probably due to the widespread use of screen recording (since what is typed in the search box is clearly visible on the computer screen). However, related concepts and definitions about the use of the term "query," such as "query type," "query (re-)formulation," and "query intent" are worth clarifying, as they are not only prominent features of primary actions in translators' search behaviour but also the focus of the present study.

Shih (2017, pp. 50–66) examined query types (i.e. categorisations of different types of queries) in her study of Chinese student translators. She reported that ST terms, or occasionally, tentative TT terms, were the primary queries undertaken by her subjects working on a semi-specialist text. However, four other variations of query types were also noted, including 1) ST term and its (partially) corresponding TT equivalent (e.g. LNG + 燃料船), 2) ST term and [natural language] questions (e.g. gt + 是什么单位), 3) ST term and the name of the TL (e.g. owner operator + 中文), and 4) provisionally translated sentence/title of the ST (Shih, 2017, pp. 57–59). Partly due to the limitation of the subject population and the focus on a single language combination (English–Chinese), as noted by Shih, the list of query types was non-exhaustive. Shih's (2019, pp. 912–913) subsequent study also partially focused on "query re-formulation," a term she adopted from the field of IR studies to indicate how queries were constructed and (re)formulated over time in a web search episode. Findings confirmed that student translators' queries were largely homogeneous and the author concluded that query (re) formulation did not appear to contribute to the success or optimisation of a search episode. What contributed to student translators' success or optimisation of web search lay in their secondary actions, implying that student translators should probably shift their focus to utilising their SERPs rather than queries.

Nevertheless, somewhat in contrast to Shih's study, one of the conclusions of Enriquez Raido's (2014, p. 183) study still centres around queries, indicating that successful query construction seemed to depend on clear analysis of web search purposes. This brings us the concept of "query intent." In fact, it is imperative to elucidate the concept of "query intent," not least because this is one of the research questions of the present study, but also because there is some level of terminological confusion in the field. In previous literature, a number of related terms were used, such as "information need," "information goal," and "information-seeking trigger." In Enriquez Raido's study (2011, p. 152), "information need" was described as "the desire to solve a translation problem" and found to be primarily "lexical," whereby problematic ST terms or lexis often prompt a search on the web, or "thematic," thus requiring a search for background information (Enriquez Raido, 2014, pp. 112–171). The scholar further clarified that there were two possible 'information goals', either for ST comprehension purposes or for both comprehension and production purposes (*ibid.*, 118). Enriquez Raido therefore appeared to consider "information need" as a more overt drive for different types of information, while "information goal" was deemed to be a more generic purpose for translation. In addition to "information goal" and "information need," Wang (2018, pp. 49–52) also used the term "information-seeking trigger," which was defined as a particular point in the ST triggering an information need. This appeared to be comparable to the notion of "Rich Point" as delineated in Shih's study (2019, p. 914; cf. PACTE, 2009, p. 41). Notwithstanding the potential overlap and confusion of the terms mentioned above, previous scholars' efforts seem to focus on studying translators' general information needs or their purposes for web search. However, translators' web search intent more specifically at the query level has largely been ignored in the existing literature. Query intent in the present study indicates the reasons why certain query types were used or constructed by professional translators and how or in what circumstances query types relate to their query intent. Worth pointing out here is that, similar to "query intent," the concept of "search intent" (Broder, 2002) is commonly referred to in IR studies as either "navigational" (i.e. locating a particular site), "informational" (i.e. acquiring information), or "transactional" (i.e. performing an activity). However, this taxonomy holds limited value for translation, as presumably web search for translation is largely "informational." Therefore, one of the contributions of the present study is to offer further insights into query and query intent for a specific group of web searchers, i.e. professional translators.

About Secondary Action in Translation

Unlike primary actions, secondary actions did not appear to attract too much attention in previous studies. Although not specifically focusing on secondary actions, Gough's (2015) study tapped into a broader overview of how professional translators interact with online resources, partially involving browsing and clicking behaviours. Gough collected her data initially from a large-scale survey (N = 540) and subsequently with a screen-recorded translation task in conjunction with post-task questionnaires (N = 16). The scholar analysed the number of search episodes, their length, and the types of online resources used. Professional translators' web search behaviours were deemed to be a reflection of translators' idiosyncrasies (2015, p. 31), characterised by five user styles: "explorer," "prolific translator," "methodical translator," "economical translator," and "understated translator," with the "explorer" spending the most amount of time and efforts on web search and, at the opposite end of the scale, the "understated translator" spending the least amount of time and efforts.[1]

Similar to Gough, secondary actions did not appear to be Enriquez Raido's (2011, 2014) prime focus in her study, although the scholar reported that two of her subjects had a style of "interactionistic browse searching" (2014, p. 140), whereby certain websites were investigated further and internal hyperlinks were clicked. Such style of behaviours seemed to contribute to search success.

Following on from previous scholars' work, Shih focused on her student translators' (N = 18) secondary actions more specifically and found that the success or optimisation of a web search episode could be pinned down to a more "explorer" approach, especially when attempting to locate a harder-to-find TL terminology (2019, pp. 919–920). This finding suggested that in certain circumstances, a more persistent and profound engagement in secondary actions, i.e. browsing and clicking, rather than the primary actions, may pay off.

The present study can be seen as a further attempt to gauge translators' secondary actions, particularly in terms of the patterns of browsing and clicking behaviours, in what circumstances a hyperlink is clicked, and perhaps more importantly, the interplay between primary actions and secondary actions.

Research Methodology: A Qualitative Approach to Eye-Tracking

Methods

As mentioned previously, so far, existing web search studies in translation have mostly adopted screen-recording as a main method, in conjunction with other data sources, such as interviews, questionnaires, think-aloud protocols, etc. To the best of my knowledge, apart from Hvelplund's (2017, 2019) study, the present study does not just represent one of the earliest attempts to use eye-tracking to investigate web search behaviour but is also one of the first studies that adopts a qualitative approach to eye-tracking data in translation studies.

Eye-tracking as a research method in translation studies is nothing new. In fact, it has become a customary data collection method in many sub-fields of translation process research (TPR) (O'Brien, 2010, pp. 251–266). Yet, currently, eye-tracking research in TPR almost exclusively focuses on analysing statistical aggregated data on fixations, saccades, and occasionally, pupil dilation. This results in a very granulated view of various aspects of translator behaviour, which does not align with the aims of the present study. In order to provide a more holistic and contextualised overview of translators' web search behaviour, an alternative eye-tracking methodology was adapted in the present study. Essentially, this methodology exploited the screen-recording component of the eye-tracking data where translators' eye movements (i.e. gazes) were superimposed in real time onto the screen recording. This eye-tracked screen recording was then used as a video cue to prompt translators to verbally report on their web search immediately after completing the translation task. Part of the reasons for adopting this methodology was the decision to maintain a slightly more naturalistic design[2] for the present study, which entailed that translators were able to translate and use any online resources that they wanted with minimal restrictions on their screen setup. This constraint made it virtually impossible to plot aggregated eye-tracking data (using AOI for example), as no two translators were using online resources exactly the same way. Nevertheless, the advantage of this methodology was twofold. First, it provided a far richer and less fragmented illustration of translators' behaviours compared to the numerical analysis of eye-tracking data (see Van Gog et al., 2010). Secondly, it also offered more precise and accurate screen-based data (due to the gaze being superimposed on the screen) than the traditional screen recording that has previously been used in the study of web search in translation.

Despite its novelty in translation studies, this qualitative methodology has been widely used in web-based research commercially and academically in the field of human–computer interaction (HCI). Particularly, in a sub-field of HCI, known as user experience (UX) research, this methodology is commonly referred to as "eye-tracking stimulated or cue-based retrospective think-aloud" (RTA) (see Guan et al., 2006). By adopting a combination of real-time eye-tracking gaze and RTA in this study, it is hoped that data such as translators' inferences and strategies can be elicited, which in turn will enhance our understanding of not just specific aspects of translators' web search behaviours but, more importantly, the interplay and potential reasons why such interplay occurs.

Participants

A group of professional translators (n = 10) were recruited (using open call and snowball sampling technique) to translate a short piece of medical text from English into their respective mother tongues, including (in alphabetical order) Arabic (n = 1), Chinese (n = 5), German (n = 1), Japanese (n = 1), Russian (n = 1), and Spanish (n = 1). These professional translators are all freelance translators based in the UK, with their experiences ranging from 2 to 30+ years, working in different fields (see Table 4.2). While due to the sampling technique, the language combinations, years of experience, and specialisms are not deliberate, the participants do represent a good selection of various experiences of freelance translators in the UK. Consent was sought and ethical approval was obtained at the researcher's academic institution. Upon completion of the study, each participant received a voucher as a thank-you token for participating.

Data Collection Procedures

Participants were asked to translate their source text in Microsoft Word (font size 18) and use the browser Google Chrome (zoomed at 150%) for their web search. Shortly after their translation, the eye-tracked screen recording was replayed, and participants' retrospective think-aloud was recorded (using the RTA function in SMI's BeGaze software). The replay of the recording was paused intermittently if necessary during the RTA. After the RTA, participants completed a questionnaire containing questions related to their demographic information and translation web search experiences. The whole process from start to finish took approximately two hours.

Table 4.2 Translators' Background and Experiences

Subject Code	Gender	Years of Experience	Specialised Domains	Language Combinations
P01	F	35 years	Legal Business translation/ interpreting	English–Japanese
P02	F	9 years	Audio-visual translation Localisation	English–Chinese Chinese–English
P05	F	24 years	Media/news reports Medical translation Advertisement/marketing	English–Chinese Chinese–English
P06	F	3 years	Literary translation Business translation/ interpreting	English–Russian Russian–English
P07	F	25 years	Technical/scientific translation Localisation	English–German
P08	F	2–3 years	Audio-visual translation Economics and finance	English–Chinese
P09	F	26 years	Legal translation Technical/scientific translation	English–Chinese Chinese–English
P14	M	7 years	Legal translation Official documents Conference interpreting	English–Chinese Chinese–English French–Chinese
P16	M	4 years	Audio-visual translation Legal translation Tourism	English–Spanish Spanish–English
P23	F	15 years	Technical/scientific translation Business interpreting/ translation	English–French French–English English–Arabic Arabic–English

The source text was a medical case report (word count: 136 words) extracted from the website of the Medical Protection Society (https://www.medicalprotection.org/hongkong/casebook-resources/case-reports/case-reports/paraplegia-follows-epidural). The source text consists of a good selection of medical terminologies and concepts which was tested in a pilot study and considered to be suitable to elicit relevant data in the present study.

The eye tracker, SMI RED250 Mobile (sample rate of 250 Hz), and a laptop with a 15-inch screen were set up at the researcher's office and used to record participants' web search and translation processes. Participants' sitting position was roughly 60 centimetres from the laptop screen. Calibrations via SMI's iView software (with six-point calibration) were conducted prior to the data collection and repeated if necessary. Subjects were all able to touch-type and either had normal vision or were vision-corrected, wearing their own glasses. The experiments took place under natural daylight with blinds pulled down wherever possible.

Results and Discussion

Query Types

Prior to reporting the findings in the present study, it is important to clarify "query" for the purpose of analysis, i.e. what constitutes a query in the analysis of the typologies as illustrated below. Query types in the present study indicate words or symbols typed in a search field, which may include any search fields outside search engines. This slightly wider definition is crucial because professional translators may choose to use a variety of different online tools other than search engines, such as dictionaries, glossaries, corpora, or even MT tools, etc. Overall, it was found that the use of a (sole) ST or TL term (i.e. keyword-based query) appeared to be a prominent feature of many queries, although the degree of its prominence very much depended on each individual translator, as the types of online resources preferred can also dictate the types of queries being used. For example, it was pointless for translators to construct complex queries in online dictionaries since most online dictionaries did not support complex queries. Query types illustrated below show common queries being used by translators, apart from the keyword-based queries as mentioned earlier in this section. These query types were largely categorised based on their linguistic features. Table 4.3 shows the typologies of such queries and their corresponding online resources.

Query Type 1: The Use of (Non-Keyword) Natural Language in Search Engines

This study found that many professional translators regularly used natural language sentences or clauses in their queries in search engines, as opposed

Table 4.3 Typologies of Non-Keyword Queries and Their Corresponding Online Resources

Query Type Code	Query Types	Types of Online Resources
Type 1	The use of natural language	Search engines
Type 2	The use of a "casting-a-net" approach	Search engines Online encyclopaedia
Type 3	The use of literal translation or potential "false-friend"	Search engines Online corpora/concordancer Online dictionaries
Type 4	The use of collocation in search engines and/or other specialised online resources	Search engines Online dictionaries Online corpora/concordancer
Type 5	The use of an ST term, an ST sentence, or even a whole ST paragraph	Online machine translation tools (e.g. Google Translate)

to using a keyword-based query. Such natural language can be found either in the form of a statement or a question. For example, while researching the term, "triple coronary artery bypass graft," Subject P14 posed the following query in Google: "心脏搭桥可以几个?" (literal translation: How many heart bypass[es] are there?). Subject P14 reported that he was trying to find which measure word to use for the translation of "triple." A measure word is a common grammatical feature in many oriental languages, where each noun has a corresponding measure word. In this case, even though Subject P14 had already located the TL equivalent for "coronary artery bypass graft," he was not familiar with how to translate "triple" or whether "triple" was directly linked to bypass, artery, or even graft, as association with different nouns might require different measure words. By typing the question in the TL, he was hoping to locate a correct measure word in this context. Another example can be found with Subject P05 where she posed the following query: "心脏手术词汇" (literal translation: heart surgery glossary). Subject P05 described this query as her strategy to pull together relevant glossaries or terminologies related to the ST and partly as a way to familiarise herself with the field.

Interestingly, the use of natural language was also found in Shih's (2017, pp. 57–59) study. However, in contrast to the present study, the natural language used in Shih's study was largely used in conjunction with a specific ST term and appeared as an answer to questions such as "What is this?" or "What does this mean?" This was linked to Shih's (*ibid.*) finding that student translators tended to use ST keyword-based queries in search engines as if they were using a paper-based dictionary. In a wider context, search engines are increasingly developing their capability to understand natural language queries, as opposed to the traditional keyword-based queries. In fact, it was reported that Google has recently rolled out a new AI algorithm specifically designed for enhanced understanding of sophisticated natural language.[3] This means that for translators, the use of natural language in queries is likely to become a more efficient and probably more prevalent query type in the future.

Query Type 2: The Use of the "Casting-a-Net" Approach in Search Engines or in Online Resources (e.g. Wikipedia)

Professional translators in the present study used a wide array of query techniques to narrow down their search. In fact, Subject P05 labelled this as the "casting-a-net approach," as if she were trawling the internet to "fish" for specific information in the open water. However, she was not just casting a net blindly but meant to use different nets to catch different types of fish. For instance, Subject P16 posed the query, "revision surgery site:es" in Google, as it was reported that he was consciously aware of regional variations of Spanish being used in different countries and it was imperative to narrow down the search for this purpose. This type of query serves a similar purpose to Boolean operators (e.g. AND, OR) or advanced search functions in search engines. However, the "casting-a-net" approach does not necessarily have to include Boolean operators. For example, Subject P09 posed the query, "weaning, 中文, 医学" (literal translation: weaning, Chinese, medicine). According to Subject P09, she was trying to narrow down the search for the ST term, weaning, in the field of medicine and in Chinese. In other words, simply entering the name of the language and the name of the field (or possibly other terms) alongside an ST term is also a possible "casting-a-net" approach.

Query Type 3: The Use of Literal Translation or Potential "False-Friends" (as Keywords) in Both Search Engines and/or in Other Online Resources (e.g. Linguee.com, Cosnautas.com)

At first glance, this finding may appear to resemble the provisional TL equivalent (i.e. a rough translation of an ST sentence or title) in Shih's study (2017, pp. 57–59) (see the section on primary action in translation for more details). However, unlike Shih's study, this query type was often not attached to an ST sentence or title but more specifically appeared to be habitually used by translators working between European languages, probably due to the fact that "false friends" exist among such languages and translators were very aware of them. For example, Subject P07 (working in the language combination of English to German) indicated that she often typed a literal German translation based on an ST terminology as the query. According to her, this was a strategy to check whether a literal equivalent existed in German, or whether such literal translation was merely a "false-friend." This strategy was used both in search engines and in online concordance tools, such as Linguee.com or Cosnautas.com/es.

Query Type 4: The Use of Collocation in Search Engines and/or Other Specialised Online Resources

This was probably one of the most interesting query types found in the present study, as often professional translators did not just pose the terminology by itself but also its collocated verb as their query. In fact, some professional translators reported that locating a TL equivalent for an ST term was often the easier part of their web search process, as frequently, the thorny issue they encountered was to locate the collocated verb in the TL or to determine whether a collocation existed at all in the TL. A typical example of this could be found in the query behaviour relating to translating the following ST passage: "the graft had gradually become blocked." Many translators painstakingly searched a combination of "graft" and "block" in an attempt to find a collocation in the TL. Similarly, the collocation of "evacuation" and "haematoma" in the ST passage, as in "evacuation of the haematoma [was] performed," was also frequently posed together in a query. This probably demonstrated professional translators' acute aware-ness of possible polysemy and mismatch of collocation in translating spe-cialised texts.

Query Type 5: The Use of an ST Term, an ST Sentence,
or Even a Whole ST Paragraph in Online Machine
Translation (MT) Tools (e.g. Google Translate)

Shih (2017, p. 59) has previously reported the phenomena of MT tools being used by student translators. Gough (2015, p. 163) also had similar findings amongst the professional translators in her study. In the present study, Subject P01 was found to copy and paste the whole paragraph of the ST into an MT tool and effectively conducted post-editing in the present study. Other translators used it as a terminology tool to verify a possible TL equivalent for an ST term. The present study therefore further confirmed this finding that posing an ST term or a longer ST passage (as queries) could be found in professional translators' behaviour, even when CAT tools were not used. It also illustrated that, increasingly, translation, MT post-editing, and possibly web searching should not be seen as separate entities but as an integral part of the whole translation process.

Query Intent and Its Relationship with Query Types

Largely based on the RTA data, seven different types of query intent were reported by professional translators in the present study. They were:

1) Locating a TL term.
2) Locating further background information (about a specific term or about a field in general).
3) Validating a TL term or expression.
4) Seeking inspiration for alternative terms or expressions.
5) Locating TL collocation.
6) Post-editing intent.
7) Language-specific intent.

The first two query intents (i.e. locating a TL term and locating further background information) were probably the most common intents. In fact, as previously mentioned, Enriquez Raido (2014, pp. 112–140) described them as "information needs" being either "lexical" or "thematic." Query intent 3 (i.e. validating terminology) and query intent 4 (i.e. seeking alter-native terminology) were often found to be linked to query intent 1 (i.e. locating terminology), as they often centred around terminology. The dif-ference was that query intent 1 was often found to precede query intent 3 and query intent 4, since often a TL term needed to be located before it could be verified or before alternative terms could be sought. Query intent 3 and query intent 4 may also exist independently, however, as sometimes translators already had a good idea about a particular terminology without locating it first online.

As demonstrated earlier, many query intents were shown to be closely linked to the query type and the resources being used. In other words, different query types could be tailored to suit each query intent and, in turn, query intent could also dictate which query types were used by professional translators. On the one hand, certain query types were closely associated with certain query intents. For example, query type 4 (i.e. the use of collocation) was clearly linked to query intent 5 (i.e. collocation purposes). An illustrative example can be found in the section on query type 4. The same applied to query type 5 (i.e. the use of ST terms and sentences in online MT) and query intent 6 (i.e. the intent of post-editing). On the other hand, certain query types appeared to be more generic (or even open-ended), as they could be adapted for many different purposes. Both query type 1 and query type 2 belong to this category. In addition, query intent could also be language-specific (e.g. query intent 7), as shown in the example mentioned above whereby Subject P14 intended to locate a measure word for a specific ST term. Finally, it is important to stress that query intents are not mutually exclusive. In fact, it is a dynamic process where query intents could co-exist or even evolve over time, probably as a result of the contents presented in the search engine result pages (SERPs).

Browsing and Clicking Behaviours

To explain and elaborate on the model of translators' browsing and clicking behaviours in search engines (see Figure 4.1), it is important to clarify two concepts first. These are: "scanning action" and "reading action." In eye-tracking IR research (see Cole et al., 2011; Holmqvist et al., 2011), specialised algorithms tended to be used to analyse fixation and saccade data in order to establish the starting point and ending point of "reading fixation" and "scanning fixation." "Scanning fixation" was defined as web users' eyes being fixated at the foveal (i.e. smaller) visual field, whereas "reading fixation" referred to the larger parafoveal region (see Rayner & Fischer, 1996; Rayner et al., 2003). This means that merely isolated words or phrases can be processed visually and cognitively at one time during "scanning fixation" but longer stretches of texts (such as clauses or sentences) can be processed during "reading fixation." These concepts were adapted for the purpose of the present study. However, instead of directly relating to the aggregated fixations and visual fields, in the present study, such concepts were used to refer to the observable orientations of eye movement (i.e. gaze). "Scanning action" indicated rapid eye movements that largely travel vertically. "Reading action" indicated slower eye movements that largely travel horizontally. "Scanning action" and "reading action" must be understood as a more holistic overview of translators' behaviour in the present study rather than at the granulation level. Related to the concept of "scanning," in a wider context of IR research, it was generally recognised that web-based information behaviour often featured quick scanning and browsing, a potentially very different behaviour to the traditional paper-based information behaviour (Walsh, 2016, pp. 160–173). In fact, Rowlands et al. (2008) dubbed this as information behaviour of the "Google generation."

As seen in Figure 4.1, professional translators' secondary actions (or browsing and clicking behaviours) commenced after a query was posed. After posing queries, professional translators were found to process the SERPs with "scanning action," largely scanning of the title of the SERPs and their corresponding snippets (i.e. a short descriptor of the webpages in SERPs). Essentially, their eyes were found to move quickly up and down along the SERPs. These rapid eye movements only slowed down (at which point the translator's eyes appeared to "fixate" on a specific search result) if the translator decided that something relevant might have been found. During the "scanning action," the translator appeared to be constantly making judgements on SERPs and their relevance in relation to query intent so that they could slow down the rapid eye movements. If none of the SERPs was deemed to be relevant, the translator might decide to go back to the drawing board (i.e. primary action) to pose a new query. But, once relevance was identified, the browsing behaviours would turn from "scanning action" to "reading action." "Reading action" was characterised by horizontal eye movements that were much slower than the "scanning action." Crucially, at this stage "reading action" was restricted to snippets. In other words, the translator only read snippets and did not necessarily click on any of the SERP hyperlinks. For instance, Subject P09 reported that often reading snippets themselves had already satisfied her query intent; therefore, there was no need to click on them. This represented an interesting phenomenon, which will be elaborated upon later on in this section. However, if the translator judged from the snippets that a hyperlink might provide further relevant information, she would then click on the SERP hyperlink to investigate further. After clicking on the hyperlink, the translator tended to commence the "skimming action," typically characterised by rapid eye movements that could be vertical, horizontal, or even diagonal, presumably depending on how information was displayed on the website. According to the RTA, this serves to have an overview of the site. This initial "skimming action" may be accompanied by a cycle of further clicks of hyperlinks and/or further "reading action" within the site; alternatively, the translator may decide to abandon the whole site altogether and pose a new query instead.

As mentioned earlier, hyperlinks resulting from the SERPs were often browsed (via "scanning action" and "reading action") but not clicked. Translators in the present study claimed that this was often the norm (rather than the exception) because there was no point in clicking hyperlinks when

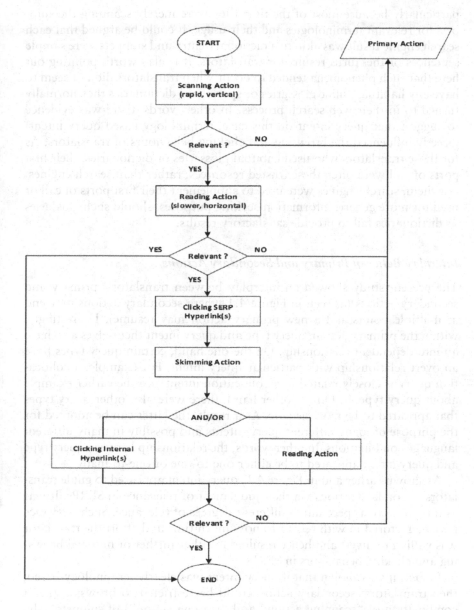

Figure 4.1 Professional Translators' Browsing and Clicking Behaviours (in Search Engines).

snippets alone were considered to be sufficient enough to answer their query. Upon a closer examination, it was found that such phenomena tended to be associated with queries (intent) that were predominately terminology-based, such as query intents 1, 3, and 4. For instance, Subject P01, Subject P07, and Subject P09 all reported (via RTA) that they rarely clicked on hyperlinks, particularly because most of the time they were merely scanning the snippets for relevant terminologies and their usage. It could be argued that each search engine result was akin to a dictionary entry and snippets were sample sentences or thesaurus results for translators. It is also worth pointing out here that such phenomena tended to occur when translators did not seem to have any habitual online glossaries or specialised dictionaries they normally turned to in their web search process. In other words, there was evidence to suggest that query intent (in this case, terminology-based query intent) directly influenced the browsing and clicking behaviours of translators. As for those translators who used habitual glossaries or dictionaries, their first ports of call were often these trusted resources, rather than search engines. For them, search engines were used to supplement their first ports of call or used for more generic information-seeking purposes, should such glossaries or dictionaries fail to provide satisfactory results.

Interplay Between Primary and Secondary Actions

The present study showed an interplay between translators' primary and secondary actions (as seen in Figure 4.1 where secondary actions may end at multiple points and a new primary action may resume). Interestingly, within the primary action, query type and query intent themselves also have an interdependent relationship. On the one hand, certain query types have an overt relationship with particular query intent. For example, a collocation query is closely related to a collocation intent (see the earlier example about query type 4). On the other hand, there were also other query types that appeared to be more generic. As a result, the latter can be adopted for the purpose of many different query intents and possibly in many different language combinations. In other words, the relationship between query type and query intent appeared to be either one-to-one or one-to-many.

As shown earlier and in Figure 4.1, query intent appeared to guide translators' secondary actions via their judgement of relevance in SERPs. It was as if there were a spectrum of different degrees of relevance. Such relevance may be factored in with regard to how much time and effort the translator was willing to invest and hence resulted in either further or minimal browsing and clicking behaviours in SERPs.

In fact, it was shown that if query intent was clearly terminology-based, then translators' secondary action could be restricted to browsing (i.e. a combination of "scanning action" and "reading action") of snippets only. However, if the query intent was for general background information, translators were probably more likely to explore further afield by clicking the SERPs. Interestingly, in Shih's (2019, pp. 908–923) study, it was shown that students' over-reliance on snippets alone could be problematic, as without clicking on hyperlinks or having further engagement in secondary action, the chances of locating harder-to-find terminology could be hindered. This finding appears to be in contradiction to that of the present study. However, it is worth reiterating that whilst Shih's study focused on student translators' (more) optimised web search behaviours, particularly for harder-to-find terminology, and it essentially contrasted students' successful and unsuccessful web search behaviour, the present study focused on professional translators' web search behaviour exclusively. Although the two studies differed in their focus, it may be mooted that relying on snippets is something that professional translators can do due to their increased experience in identifying reliable sources, a skill that students may not yet have.

Conclusion

This study set out to find out professional translators' primary and secondary actions and the interplay between them. It was found that there were at least five different types of queries. Among these five query types, one of them was potentially more language-specific, i.e. query type 3, as "literal translation" or "false-friend" is used frequently between European languages. Nevertheless, other query types appeared to be more universal among all languages. Seven types of query intent were also found. Among the query intent, many of them appeared to be terminology-based specifically. In terms of how and in what circumstance query type related to query intent, it was found that certain query types distinctly matched with certain query intents but there were also clear indications that other query types could be adapted to suit many different query intents. This finding may have potential pedagogical implications, as it advocates that students could be taught which query types are more generic, i.e. can be adapted or customised, which ones are more specific, and how different query types and query intents could be utilised so as to optimise their web search. Likewise, language-specific queries could also be taught to students working in specific language combinations.

With regard to professional translators' secondary actions, a pattern of browsing and clicking behaviours was observed. In sum, their browsing behaviours started with "scanning action" and "reading action," subsequently followed by "skimming action" and possible "reading action." These browsing actions were partly punctuated with clicking actions, which were monitored and guided by the judgement of relevance to query intent. Interestingly, the sequence of professional translators' secondary actions could be limited to browsing action exclusively. In fact, for some professional translators, particularly when the query intent was for terminology purposes, it was deemed unnecessary to click on any of the hyperlinks, as clicking on hyperlinks could be potentially time-consuming. They did, however, take full advantage of snippets in search engines. The action of reading snippets therefore became a vantage point in translators' secondary actions, as it was a decision point as to whether there was enough information in the snippets to justify clicking, whether further clicking was required, or even whether it was worth abandoning the whole sequence of secondary actions and returning to the primary actions. The strategy of "no clicking" could be seen as a minimax strategy (Levy, 1967/2000, pp. 148–159) that professional translators apply in the sense that they would usually aim for maximum effect with minimum cognitive effort. This strategy also revealed a key feature of professional translators' web search, that is, the fact that search engines themselves were often used as if they were vast online dictionaries.

These findings about professional translators' web search behaviours have their limitations, as they may not apply to professional translators working in different genres and in different language directions. Indeed, the list of query types and query intents was never intended to be exhaustive. Therefore, similar studies should be duplicated in the future on a larger scale with different genres, different search engines, and potentially with a focus on the link between translation quality and web search. In particular, implications of using different search engines along with their associated neural machine translation (NMT), such as Google Translate, with respect to the different availability of data and how information is displayed should be considered by future researchers.

One of the main contributions of the present study, however, lies in its methodology, as it challenges the quantitative approach to eye-tracking in TPR and in translation studies. It demonstrated that the use of qualitative methodology for eye-tracking research is not only feasible but also an effective way of eliciting inference and reflective data in the translation process. It also shows that there is a potential to triangulate qualitative RTA data with quantitative eye-tracking data in future TPR studies, as this way the granulated and holistic aspects of translators' behaviour are both accounted for.

Notes

1 In Gough's study (2015), efforts largely indicate the number and variety of online resources used, and the number of queries made.
2 It has to be pointed out here that the more naturalistic design refers to the screen setup (i.e. the use of Mircosoft Word and the web browser, Google Chrome) rather than the location of the data collection.
3 See https://searchengineland.com/welcome-bert-google-artificial-intelligence-for-understanding-search-queries-323976

References

Broder, A. (2002). A taxonomy of web search. *SIGIR Forum*, 36(2), 3–10.
Chang, L. Y. (2018). *A Longitudinal Study on the Formation of Chinese Students' Translation Competence: With a Particular Focus on Metacognitive Reflection and Web Searching* (Unpublished PhD thesis). London: University College London.
Cole, M. J., Gwizdka, J., Liu, C., Bierig, R., Belkin, N. J. & Zhang, X. (2011). Task and user effects on reading patterns in information search. *Interacting with Computers*, 23(4), 346–362.

Enríquez-Raido, V. (2011). Developing web searching skills in translator training. *Revista Electrónica de Didáctica de la Traducción e Interpretación*, 6, 60–80.

Enríquez-Raido, V. (2014). *Translation and Web Searching*. New York: Routledge.

European master's in translation (EMT) (2017). *Competence Framework*. Retrieved from https://ec.europa.eu/info/sites/info/files/emt_competence _fwk_2017_en _web.pdf.

Gough, J. (2015). *The Patterns of Interaction between Professional Translators and Online Resources* (Unpublished doctoral dissertation). Guildford: University of Surrey.

Guan, Z., Lee, S., Cuddihy, E. & Ramey, J. (2006). *The Validity of Stimulated Retrospective Think-Aloud Method as Measured by Eye Tracking*. Montreal, Canada: CHI.

Holmqvist, K., Nyström, M., Andersson, R., Dewhurst, R., Jarodzka, H. & van de Weijer, Joost (2011). *Eye Tracking: A Comprehensive Guide to Methods and Measures*. Oxford: Oxford University Press.

Hvelplund, K. T. (2017). Translators' use of digital resources during translation. *Journal of Language and Communication in Business*, 56, 71–87.

Hvelplund, K. T. (2019). Digital resources in the translation process–attention, cognitive effort and processing flow. *Perspectives*, 27(4), 510–524, doi:10.1080/ 0907676X.2019.1575883.

Levy, Jiri (1967/2000). Translation as a decision process. In: Venuti, L. (Ed.) *The Translation Studies Reader*. London: Routledge, 148–159.

O'Brien, S. (2010). Eye tracking in translation process research: Methodological challenges and solutions. In: Mees, I. M., Fabio, A. & Gopferich, S. (Eds.) *Methodology, Technology and Innovation in Translation Process Research: A Tribute to Arnt Lykke Jakobsen*. Copenhagen: Samfundslitteratur, 251–266.

PACTE (2009). Results of the validation of the PACTE translation competence model: Acceptability and decision making. *Across Languages and Cultures*, 10(2), 207–230.

Rayner, K. & Fischer, M. (1996). Mindless reading revisited: Eye movements during reading and scanning are different. *Perception and Psychophysics*, 58(5), 734–747.

Rayner, K., White, S. J., Kambe, G., Miller, B. & Liversedge, S. P. (2003). On the processing of meaning from parafoveal vision during eye fixations in reading. In: Hyönä, J., Radach, R. & Deubel, H. (Eds.) *The Mind's Eye: Cognitive and Applied Aspects of Oculomotor Research*. Amsterdam: Elsevier, 213–234.

Rowlands, I., Nicholas, D., Williams, P., Huntington, P., Fieldhouse, M., Gunter, B., Withey, R., Jamali, H. R., Dobrowolski, T. & Tenopir, C. (2008). The Google generation: The information behaviour of the researcher of the future. *Aslib Proceedings: New Information Perspectives*, 60(4), 290–310, doi:10.1108/00012530810887953.

Shih, C. Y. (2017). Web search for translation: An exploratory study on six Chinese trainee translators' behaviour. *Asia Pacific Translation and Intercultural Studies*, 4(1), 50–66, doi:10.1080/23306343.2017.1284641.

Shih, C. Y. (2019). A quest for web search optimisation: An evidence-based approach to trainee translators' behaviour. *Perspectives*, 27(6), 908–923, doi:10.1080/090 7676X.2019.1579847.

Van Gog, T. & Scheiter, K. (2010). Eye tracking as a tool to enhance multimedia learning. *Learning and Instruction*, 20(2), 95–99.

Walsh, G. (2016). Screen and paper reading research –A literature review. *Australian Academic and Research Libraries*, 47(3), 160–173, doi:10.1080/00048623.201 6.1227661.

Wang, J. (2018). *Information Seeking Behaviour in Two-Way Translation: An Empirical Study* (Unpublished MPhil thesis). Guildford: University of Surrey.

White, R. W. (2016). *Interactions with Search Systems*. Cambridge: Cambridge University Press.

Part III
Product of T&I

5 Conference Interpreting in Diplomatic Settings

An Integrated Corpus and Critical Discourse Analysis

Fei Gao and Binhua Wang

Introduction

This study investigates how political speeches delivered by Chinese government officials are rendered by Chinese conference interpreters in diplomatic settings. Diplomacy is essentially concerned with tactfully conducting practices of dialogue, negotiation, and nonviolent means between nations with the aim of influencing the conducts of foreign governments (Jönsson & Langhorne, 2004); in a broad sense, it primarily pertains to inter-state discursive practices at a government level. The twentieth and twenty-first centuries have become an epoch of diplomatic discursive practices due to world-scale wars, post-war reconstruction, and globalisation. The formation of a global village means that dialogue and decision-making are often done internationally. Such inter-state discursive practices would not have been possible without a cohort of interpreters, who lend their cross-linguistic and cultural expertise to government officials, as diplomats, on the international scene. In *Interpreters as Diplomats*, Ruth Roland (1999) argues for the vital, but often under-acknowledged importance of interpreters throughout the history of inter-state relations, positing that they are "more than interpreters" in many ways. Indeed, the range of real-life accounts in her surveys – a long history of diplomatic interpreting from its origins in recorded history (2600 BC in Mesopotamia and 165 BC in China) up to 1980 – underpins her emphasis on the importance of diplomatic interpreting. Despite the critical importance of interpreters in diplomatic settings, little empirical research is done regarding how interpreters reconstruct political discourse in diplomatic settings.

With a focus on the discursive reconstruction of political discourse by interpreters, we are interested in an integrated methodological approach in which critical discourse analysis (CDA) and corpus linguistics (CL) methods are jointly deployed. The CDA-and-CL combined approach has been only incipiently used in a few conference interpreting studies (e.g. Wang, 2012; Wang & Feng, 2017; Gu, 2018, 2019; Gao, 2021) though we believe its utility, particularly with growing interpreting corpus data, could effectively unravel otherwise-hidden linguistic and discursive patterns that address research questions at a discourse level. With the integrated approach, we intend to answer two research questions:

1) What type(s) of systemic-functional meaning has/have close renditions and what is/are subject to interpreting shifts through conference interpreting in diplomatic settings?
2) What are the salient patterns in the interpreters' mediation of renditions that contribute to the discursive reconstruction of political discourse?

Integrating Corpus Methods with CDA: Viewpoints from the Literature

CDA has been used to systematically deconstruct otherwise opaque power structures embedded in political discourse (e.g. Fairclough, 1989, 1995b; Fairclough & Wodak, 1997; van Dijk, 1997; Chilton, 2004). Emerging from critical linguistics, CDA perceives language as embedded in sociolinguistic contexts, examining how grammatical or lexical choices are used to express social processes and social phenomena (Fairclough et al., 2011). Therefore, the primary concern for CDA is not to analyse language as a static linguistic phenomenon, but to examine how texts reflect social, cultural, and political realities.

Nonetheless, CDA studies are often criticized as "cherry-picking" (e.g. Partington, 2004, 2006) or being anecdotal due to the limited amount of text fragments selected for analyses (Chilton, 2005). For example, working with Fairclough's (1989, 1995a) model alone inevitably involves researcher subjectivity in "cherry-picking" the textual data in favour of his/her own positions. Criticisms of CDA could be penetratingly summarised by Widdowson's (1998, p. 148) remark: "your analysis will be the record of whatever partial interpretation suits your own agenda" and "what is distinctive about Critical Discourse Analysis is that it is resolutely uncritical of its own discursive practices" (*ibid*., p. 151). For large corpus data sets, in particular, the qualitative methods used in CDA "proved ill-suited to handling the sizeable corpus that formed the basis of the study" (Hardt-Mautner, 1995, p. 1). However, these demerits can be offset by the use of corpus techniques.

While corpus linguistics affords various methods dealing with increasingly sizable corpus data, a main criticism of CL is that it neglects the social, cultural, or political context of discourse. The main cause resides in the invariably decontextualised corpus examples of language use (Baker, 2006, p. 25). A corpus analysis alone is often criticised as lacking interpretive and explanatory power on the grounds that in-depth exploration of context seems infeasible with large corpora.

CDA that emphasises sociopolitical context compensates for the context-vagueness of CL so that the strength of CL can be effectively harnessed.

Corpus linguists Baker et al. (2008) argue effectively for the strength of combing CDA and CL in analysing political discourse. Such strength is predominantly attributed to three intrinsic properties of corpus approach, 1) data authenticity of the naturally occurring discourse, 2) the large scope otherwise not feasible, and 3) (semi-)automatic tools for analysis. Multiple CL techniques, such as frequency, concordance, collocation, and keyness, are often operationalised to give "a much more detailed insight into the working language in use" (Baker & McEnery, 2015, p. 10) to assist the CDA analysis. In a nutshell, the integration of CDA with CL not only off-sets each other's weaknesses but also maximises their strengths in analysing language use in a real social, cultural, or political context.

Integrating corpus methods with CDA-oriented approaches is not new in monolingual investigations of social, cultural, and political issues. Nevertheless, its integrated deployment is only incipient in translation and interpreting studies, in particular, in conference interpreting research. The next section introduces the corpus and details for integrating CDA and CL methods for analytical purposes with a bilingual interpreting corpus.

The Corpus and Methods

A Bilingual Interpreting Corpus of Diplomatic Speeches

The parallel interpreting corpus includes 17 speeches delivered by Chinese government officials and their interpretation in diplomatic settings from 2006 to 2013. These speeches are carefully crafted to cater to diplomatic purposes, possibly jointly, by high-level government officials and their secretaries/advisers within the Chinese government, and delivered with the speech scripts (as seen from video footage) by then-President Hu Jintao, then-Premier Wen Jiabao, then-Foreign Minister Yang Jiechi, and current President Xi Jinping. These speeches are interpreted on the site by Chinese institutional conference interpreters, who are probably delivering English renditions with the script or translated texts. The interpreting is done in the consecutive mode and with script since the video footage captures images of the Chinese interpreters looking at text documents while delivering consecutively. The public-facing events in which these speeches are delivered range from bilateral meetings between heads of states of China and the United States to multilateral meetings involving a group of countries, such as BRICS and APEC country-alliances. A common discourse feature of these speeches is that they are intended for diplomatic purposes, among others, rapport-building or maintaining, articulating China's and Beijing's positions in relation to other countries on matters of common concern, and calling for concerted efforts to achieve common goals.

The compilation of this corpus is based on publicly available videos from Chinese government websites, YouTube, and Baidu Videos. The audio data are orthographically transcribed as the written texts, and punctuations are assigned according to meaning units and pauses in speeches. The bilingual corpus is composed of a Chinese ST sub-corpus (23,359 words) and an English ST sub-corpus (28,772 words).

Integrating Fairclough's Three-Level CDA Model with Corpus Methods

CDA is a dynamic and interdisciplinary tradition, comprising many different approaches (cf. Wodak & Meyer, 2009; Fairclough et al., 2011). Despite the profusion in analytical approaches, Fairclough's (1989, 1995a) model for CDA is a widely used and well-established one, consisting of three interrelated processes of analysis involving 1) the text (description), 2) the discourse process (interpretation), and 3) social, historical, or political conditions that govern the former two (explanation). This three-level model allows for systematic analysis through linking text, discourse process, and the context in which the former two are produced. In addition, the analysis involves a spirally interrelated process that description, interpretation, and explanation are centripetally united for an analytical purpose.

More complicated than the studies with monolingual English data (as a dominant line) could be the studies using bilingual translation/interpreting data because it involves at least two systems of languages, cultures, and values, and thus it requires different treatments of the source text (ST) and the target text (TT) sub-corpora. In particular, corpus-driven methods, such as keyness, wordlist, and collocation networks need to be utilised, given the STs and TTs constitute different "wholes" (cf. Gao, 2020).

For this study with the interpreting corpus of diplomatic speeches, we primarily utilise data-driven methods – that do not use *a priori* theories and respect the total accountability of a given data set (cf. Baker, 2010) – to identify the locus of semantic closeness to and shifts from the source texts that inform subsequent analyses. We apply corpus methods to the retrieval of relevant lexicogrammatical items that include both lexical items and grammatical items on the expression plain (cf. Halliday, 1994). The following three steps are implemented to identify, describe, interpret, and explain how interpreting shifts at the textual level affect the discursive construction of China in diplomatic settings.

Step One

Use the wordlist function to identify key contents, topics, and countries/ regions in both the ST and TT sub-corpus. Compare them in view of ideational (or factual) and interpersonal dimensions of texts and relevant discourses with an aim at revealing locus of similarities and differences between the STs and TTs. High-frequency linguistic items that contribute to ST–TT differences are to be identified; results are fed into subsequent steps.

Step Two

Deploy, in the TT sub-corpus, the collocation network analysis (an extended "multiple" form of collocation analysis, see later sections on first-person plurals and modal verbs to investigate how linguistic items are collocated with relevant semantic clusters. Identify dominant formations/constructions that change the ST discursive structure.

Step Three

Closely examine these formations/constructions in the running co-texts and explain their discursive effects in the light of contextual aspects, not least to diplomatic intentions and intended country audiences. This is done with an ST–TT contrastive lens through which interpreting shifts are explained accordingly.

Analysis and Findings

Global Pattern: Closely-Rendered Ideational Meaning Vis-à-Vis Shifted Interpersonal Meaning

As demonstrated by the list of top 20 high-frequency words[1] in both STs (Chinese) and TTs (English) in Table 5.1, the ideational information that construes world realities (Halliday, 1994) has close renditions in these diplomatic settings through interpreting. There emerge relative correspondences in terms of discourse actors (*China, countries, we, people, world,* and *Asia*) and surrounding contents (*development, cooperation, international,* and *economic*). Such close semantic approximation is expected given the nature of speeches and accompanying interpreting in diplomatic settings, where Chinese political leaders speak with pre-crafted speeches and interpreters are likely to deliver with a copy of the speech or with pre-translated scripts in the consecutive mode in public-facing meetings.

Despite approximate correspondences of ideational meaning between STs and TTs, divergence is noticeable in terms of Halliday's (1994) "interpersonal meaning" in two clusters. First, the aggregate of the first-person plural and its possessive form (*we, our*) in TTs far exceeds the occurrences of the Chinese word 我们 (*we/our/us*), which suggests the addition of first-person plurals in renditions. This pattern resonates with findings in conference interpreting for Chinese Premiers' press conferences (e.g. Gu, 2019; Gu & Tipton, 2020). Another semantic shift concentrates on the use of modality, where the contrastive obligatory modal verb (*should*) in the TTs is not in this ST wordlist. Interpreting shifts in first-person plurals and modality index changed interpersonal positioning in the TTs. In what follows, we explain the ways in which interpersonal positioning is changed by the two specific patterns.

Table 5.1 Top 20 High-Frequency Words in the STs and TTs

No.	STs (Chinese)	Absolute Freq.	Normalised Freq. (per Million)	TTs (English)	Absolute Freq.	Normalised Freq. (per Million)
1	发展 (develop(ment))	472	17,074	*we*	514	15,947
2	中国 (China)	371	13,420	development	338	10,487
3	我们 (we/our/us)	292	10,562	countries	283	8,780
4	合作 (cooperation)	256	9,260	China	265	8,222
5	经济 (economy/ic)	251	9,079	cooperation	227	7,043
6	国家 (country/ies)	237	8,573	*our*	224	6,950
7	国 (country/ies)	194	7,717	will	222	6,887
8	世界 (world)	159	7,017	economic	163	5,057
9	人民 (people)	156	5,751	people	153	4,747
10	我 (I)	151	5,643	I	151	4,685
11	国际 (international)	141	5,462	world	149	4,623
12	东盟 (ASEAN)	131	5,100	*should*	142	4,405
13	共同 (together/all)	128	4,738	international	125	3,878
14	亚洲 (Asia)	126	4,630	all	122	3,785
15	将 (will)	124	4,557	Asia	93	2,885
16	关系 (relation)	103	3,725	developing	87	2,699
17	两 (two)	102	3,689	Chinese	86	2,668
18	年 (year(s))	96	3,472	two	84	2,606
19	促进 (promote)	95	3,436	growth	77	2,389
20	问题 (problem/issue/matter)	88	3,183	years	76	2,358

Specific Patterns: Increased First-Person Plurals and Modal Verbs of High-Intensity Obligation

Following the results from the global analysis, Table 5.2 presents details of the ST–TT divergence in relation to first-person plurals and high-intensity modality. It is obvious that the use of first-person plural pronouns in different forms (*we*, *our*, and *us*) in the TTs is more than double that in the STs (*freq*: 773 > 292). While additions of *we* as subjects in the TT English might be attributed to the ST Chinese, which is known as a "pro-drop" or "null-subject" language, the prominent addition of these first-person plurals discursively shifts the interpersonal positioning towards a more solidary position. As such, China is projected as a solidary country that is committed to rapport-building and solidifying "us" (China) and "them" (other counties) in various diplomatic settings. The second category of interpreting shifts concentrates on the increase of obligation modals in the TTs, which notably outnumber those in STs (*freq*: 212 > 142). The increase in these high-intensity modals (*must*, *should*, and *need*) render the overall discourse of the TTs more obligation-bound; that is, China is represented as an obligation-bound country internationally, with a strong sense of responsibility and obligation for the general good of a diplomat partnership or alliance. In a nutshell, the interpreted speeches discursively create a more solidary and obligation-bound discourse about China and the Chinese government.

A Stronger Sense of Solidarity Reconstructed through Increased Use of First-Person Plurals of We and Our

Most fundamental to the interpersonal positioning of political speeches is the selection of pronouns, which discloses the speaker's mental representation of the audience and grouping of them, for instance, with or against the speaker (Van Dijk, 2008, p. 226). For example, the European

Table 5.2 Frequencies of First-Person Plurals and High-Intensity Modals of Obligation in the STs and TTs

STs (Chinese)	Freq.	TTs (English)	Freq.
First-Person Plurals			
我们（的）（we, our, us）	292	we	514
		our	224
		us	35
Total	292		773
High-Intensity Modals of Obligation[2]			
必须 (must)	17	must	23
(需)要 (should/need)	107	should	142
应 (should)	18	need	57
Total	142		212

Parliament interpreters demonstrate in-group mentality through the use of pronouns (Beaton-Thome, 2013). Essentially, the use of pronouns serves to negotiate the overall relationship of solidarity and distance between interlocutors (Halliday, 1994; Halliday & Matthiessen, 2014). In particular, the use of first-person plurals reveals the way speakers view others in a possible unity. There are two types of first-person plurals – an inclusive *we* (speaker + addressee) and an exclusive *we* (speaker + third party) (Wales, 1996, p. 58), the two of which are often used with combined effects because the political speaker "often uses *we* with the double reference and presumption that he or she is not only speaking on behalf of the party or government (exclusive), but also on behalf to the audience (inclusive)" (*ibid.*, p. 62). In diplomatic settings, the inclusive use is preeminent because the diplomatic discourse tends to serve a rapport-building and solidifying function. While the first-person pronouns in the STs are rendered verbatim in the TTs in our data, the most salient interpreting shift of pronouns is the increase of first-person plurals in terms of their inclusive usage, which discursively renders the relevant TT discourse more solidary. The graphs shown in Figures 5.1–5.4 illustrate how *we* and *our* are used in their co-texts in the TTs.

The analyses of the two words (*we* and *our*) are carried out in their collocation network, which is an extended "multiple" form of collocation analysis. The mutual information (MI) score is used to measure the strength of association because it stresses semantic exclusivity and de-emphasises grammatical frequency. As shown in Figures 5.1–5.4, GraphColl 1.0 is utilised to generate visual representations of the word in question as nodes and its collocates, with regular settings (statistic 03 – MI span: 3–3; collocation freq. threshold: 5.0; statistic value threshold: 3.0). We do not set cut-off points for MI scores for illustrating the cases under investigation

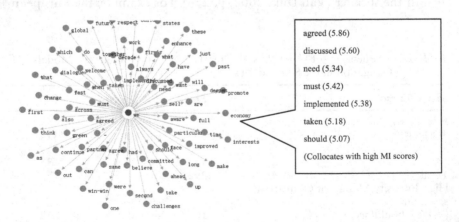

Figure 5.1 Collocation Network of *We* (Association Strengths Measured by MI).

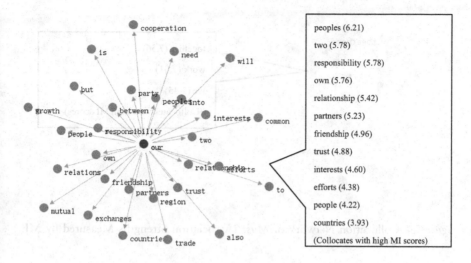

Figure 5.2 Collocation Network of *Our* (Association Strengths Measured by MI).

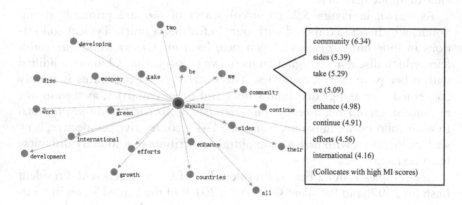

Figure 5.3 Collocation Network of *Should* (Association Strengths Measured by MI Scores).

(see Figures 5.1–5.4) because they are node-word specific. Rather, we list relevant, top-ranking collocates with high MI scores.

For the node word, *we* (in Figure 5.1), its collocates (collocated words) with high MI scores fall into two categories – actions verbs in past/perfect tense and modal verbs. The former, such as in collocations of *we agreed*, *discussed*, *implemented*, and *taken*, indicates things that have been done. The latter, such as *we need*, *must*, and *should*, suggests a sense of obligation

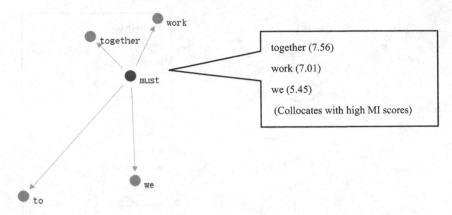

Figure 5.4 Collocation Network of *Must* (Association Strengths Measured by MI Scores).

and responsibility on the part of China and possibly other countries with a view of an inclusive *we*.

As shown in Figure 5.2, close collocates of *our* are primarily group nouns, which are juxtaposed with *our*, indicating a unity. Typical collocations include *our peoples*, *our two peoples*, *our partners*, and *our countries*, which discursively signal an inclusive message that China is solidified with other peoples and countries. The other type of collocates is mainly concerned with things that bind China and other countries, as seen in *our responsibility*, *our relationship*, *our friendship*, *our trust*, and *our interests*. In what follows, we illustrate, from an ST–TT contrastive perspective, how such collocations with first-person plurals contribute to a solidary discourse in co-texts.

In Examples 1 and 2 below, President Hu of China meets with President Bush (in 2007) and President Obama (in 2010) of the United States in bilateral meetings. In a friendly atmosphere, President Hu speaks about the development of China–US relations with one first-person plural *we* to start off a sentence. The additions of two *we* in Example 1 and one *we* in the renditions could be attributed to the grammatical reason that Chinese is known as a "pro-drop" or "null-subject" language; discursively, however, the TT repetition of *we* serves to reinforce a solidifying message that China regards the US as an in-group. More interestingly, in both examples, the interpreters add the first-person possessive plurals (*our*) which do not exist in the STs in the collocation *our two countries*. The inclusive use of *our* in the TTs signals a stronger, clearer message to the US that China views the US in a solidary unity.

Example 1

(President Hu Jintao meets with President Bush; bilateral meeting during APEC; Sydney, Australia; 6 September 2007)

President Hu: 刚才我和布什总统在坦诚友好的气氛下进行了会谈，我们回顾了近几个月来中美关系取得的新进展，讨论了双边关系当中的一些问题。都表示要通过对话、协商，进一步促进中美经贸关系的发展。

Gloss: *Just now I and President Bush had a meeting in a candid and friendly atmosphere. We reviewed the new progress made in China–US relations in the past few months, discussed a number of issues in our bilateral relations, [and] expressed a need to promote further the growth of China–US business and commerce through dialogue and consultations.*

Chinese Interpreter: President Bush and I had a meeting in a candid and friendly atmosphere. We reviewed the new progress made in China–US relations in the past few months. We discussed a number of issues in our bilateral relations. We both expressed a desire to work for further development and growth of the business and commercial sides between *our two countries* through dialogue and consultations.

Example 2

(President Hu Jintao meets with President Obama; bilateral meeting during G20 Summit; Seoul, Republic of Korea; 11 November 2010)

President Hu: 中方愿意与美方一道加强对话、交流与合作，推动中美关系沿着积极、合作、全面的轨道向前发展。感谢奥巴马总统邀请我明年初访问美国，现在两个的有关部门正在为此做着积极准备，希望这次访问，也相信这次访问是成功的。

Gloss: *The Chinese side stands ready to work with the US side to increase dialogue, exchanges, and cooperation, to move [the] China–US relationship forward on a positive, cooperative, and comprehensive track. Thanks to President Obama for inviting me to visit the United States early next year, now the two relevant departments are making preparations for the visit, with the hope and the belief that the visit will be successful.*

Chinese Interpreter: The Chinese side stands ready to work with the US side to increase dialogue, exchanges, and cooperation so that *we* can move forward the China–US relationship on a positive, cooperative and comprehensive track. I'd like to thank President Obama for inviting me to visit the United States early next year. The competent departments in *our two countries* are making preparations for the visit. I hope and do believe that the visit will be successful.

The TT discursive propensity for solidarity is more prominent in Example 3, when President Hu speaks at the Fourth China–US Strategic and Economic Dialogue. While President Hu delivers his speech with an overtly welcoming and friendly tone, the interpreter amplifies such discourse through adding three first-person possessive plurals (*our*) in the collocations of *our American friends*, *our two countries*, and *our government departments*. The inclusive message covers different levels – people as friends, countries, and governments; diplomatically, the solidary discourse combines states and people, which may have a more cogent implication for a unifying sense between China and the US.

Example 3

(President Hu Jintao speaks at the Opening Ceremony of the Fourth China–US Strategic and Economic Dialogue; 5 March 2012)

President Hu: 首先，我谨对第四轮中美战略与经济对话开幕，表示祝贺！对远道而来的美国朋友们，表示欢迎。2009年，我同奥巴马总统在伦敦会晤时共同商定，建立中美战略与经济对话机制。3年多来，中美战略与经济对话作为两国级别最高、参与部门最多、讨论议题最广的机制。

Gloss: *First, I wish to extend congratulations on the opening of the fourth round of the S&ED and welcome to American friends coming from afar. President Obama and I agreed to establish the S&ED when meeting in London in 2009. This is the highest-level China–US mechanism that involves the most extensive participation by government departments of two countries and has a most wide-ranging agenda.*

Chinese Interpreter: I wish to extend congratulations on the opening of the fourth round of the S&ED and welcome to *our American friends* coming from afar. President Obama and I agreed to establish the S&ED when *we* met in London in 2009. This is the highest-level mechanism between *our two countries* that involves the most extensive participation by *our government departments* and has a most wide-ranging agenda.

On top of the bilateral diplomatic settings, the pattern of increased first-person plurals is also found in multilateral settings. In Example 4, President Xi addresses an audience from BRICS countries, calling for concerted efforts for common good. The interpreter then inserts a *we* before *the BRICS countries* and an *our* before *own development*. The inclusive use of the first-person plurals discursively intensifies the bond between China and other BRICS countries.

Example 4

(President Xi Jinping speaks at the 5th BRICS Leaders Meeting; Durban; 27 March 2013)

President Xi: 我们要大力推动建设全球发展伙伴关系，促进各国共同繁荣。独木不成林。在经济全球化深入发展的时代条件下，金砖国家发展不能独善其身，必须在谋求本国发展的同时促进各国共同发展。

Gloss: *We should strongly promote the building of a global development partnership and promote the common prosperity of all countries. One tree does not make a forest. In an era of deepening economic globalization, BRICS countries cannot only seek benefits for themselves, [but] should seek for development of [their] own countries, and meanwhile work for the common development of all countries.*

Chinese Interpreter: We should vigorously promote the building of a global development partnership and strive for the common prosperity of all countries. One tree does not make a forest. In an era of deepening economic globalization, *we the BRICS countries* should not just seek *our own development*, but also work for the common development of all countries.

A Stronger Sense of Our Obligation Reconstructed through Increased High-Intensity Obligation Modal Verbs: Should and Must

From a functional systemic linguistics (SFL) perspective, linguistic forms are linked with their functions (Halliday, 1994), so the modal verbs of obligation are linked with their functions in use. The modal verbs of obligation fall into the category modulation of SFL's modality system; Halliday and Matthiessen (2014) avoid the philosophical terms epistemic and deontic modality to distinguish between different modal domains but introduce the categories "modalization" (roughly epistemic modality) and "modulation" (roughly obligation and inclination). The modal verbs of obligation, like other modal expressions, are scaled along a high-median-low intensity cline (*ibid.*). In other words, the use of high-intensity obligation modals signals stronger senses of obligation and urgency to fulfil such obligations. Considering the prominent increase of high-intensity modal verbs (see Tables 5.1 and 5.2), the following collocation analyses use *should* and *must* as a case in point.

As shown in Figure 5.3, the node word *should* in the TTs is closely associated with nouns or adjectives used in subject positions: *community*, *sides*, *we*, and *international*, as well as action verbs in predicate positions: *take*, *enhance*, and *continue*. The construction (subject + *should* + action verb), used in high frequency (*n* = 142), creates a strong sense for the discourse actors to take actions for fulfilling obligations. In other words, Chinese interpreters render the ST speech in such a way that the Chinese government is obligation-bound to the international community.

The collocation network for *must* (shown in Figure 5.4) is relatively straightforward since its close collocates are only a few (*together*, *work*, and *we*). However, the noticeably high MI scores indicate the stable formation of *we* + *must* + *work together* + to (action verb), which sends a strong call for a collective action taken to fulfil certain obligations.

Interestingly, both *should* and *must* are closely associated with the first-person plural *we* (discussed earlier) in the construction *we should/must* + action verb, which discursively passes on a message pertaining to China's playing a solidifying and obligation-bound role in diplomatic settings. In what follows we illustrate these constructions in co-texts through an ST–TT comparative lens.

In Example 5, Premier Wen enumerates concrete measures for the structural reform of international economic and banking sectors at the 8th ASEM Summit. In his original speech, the Premier does not use the first-person plural 我们 (we) and only uses 应 (should), 要 (should/need) to start off two sentences. However, the TT is replete with the construction *we* + *must/should/need to* + action verbs/phrases. Despite the fact *we* could be added on a syntactic ground, such a high-frequency formation with high-intensity obligation modals constructs a different discourse from that of the ST in ways that the Chinese government official is emphatically calling for solidary actions from ASEM member states for a joint cause, which seems an important obligation on the part of all member states.

Example 5

(Premier Wen Jiabao speaks at the Opening Ceremony of the 8th ASEM Summit; Brussels; 4 October 2010)

Premier   Wen: 共同推动国际经济金融体系改革。推动国际经济治理改革，是正本清源的根本举措。应探索建立更为有效的世界经济治理机制，完善国际金融机构决策程序和机制，增加发展中国家的代表性和发言权，促进各方更加广泛参与，充分照顾各方的利益和关切。要加强国际金融监管合作。坚决倡导和支持自由贸易，旗帜鲜明地反对保护主义，推动多哈回合谈判以现有案文为基础，早日达成合理、平衡的结果。

Gloss: *Jointly promote the reform of the international economic and financial systems. Global economic governance reform is a fundamental measure in overcoming the financial crisis. Should explore ways to establish a more effective global economic governance system, to improve the decision-making process and mechanism of the interna-*

tional financial institutions, to increase the representation and voice of developing countries, encourage wider participation, and fully accommodate each other's interests and concerns. Should strengthen cooperation on international financial supervision and regulation. Steadfastly advocate and support free trade, resolutely oppose protectionism, and push for early, equitable and balanced outcomes of the Doha Round negotiations on the basis of the existing text.

Chinese Interpreter: Second, *we must* work together to reform the international economic and financial systems. Global economic governance reform is of fundamental importance in overcoming the financial crisis, and *we must* explore ways to establish a more effective global economic governance system. *We need* to improve the decision-making process and mechanism of the international financial institutions, increase the representation and voice of developing countries, encourage wider participation, and fully accommodate each other's interests and concerns. *We should* step up cooperation on international financial supervision and regulation. *We must* be steadfast in advocating and supporting free trade, resolutely oppose protectionism, and work for early, equitable and balanced outcomes of the Doha Round negotiations on the basis of the existing text.

The similar pattern is also evident in Example 6, when President Xi addresses business and political leaders from numerous Asian counties at the 2013 Boao Forum. President Xi does not employ any reference nouns in subject positions until the last sentence, in which, he uses use 亚洲 (Asia) that includes China and other Asian countries. In terms of obligation modal verbs, President Xi uses 要 (should/need) to start off two sentences and another one after a clause with the subject *Asia*. The first-person plural *we* only uses 应 (should) and 要 (should/need) to start off two sentences. In the TT, most sentences start with the formation *we should* + action verbs/phrases, the repetitive use of which again reinforces the discursive construction of China as a solidary and responsible country.

Example 6

(President Xi Jinping speaks at the Boao Forum for Asia Annual Conference; Boao, Hainan; 7 April 2013)

President Xi: 第一，勇于变革创新，为促进共同发展提供不竭动力。长期以来，各国各地区在保持稳定、促进发展方面形成了很多好经验好做法。对这些好经验好做法，继续发扬光大。同时，世间万物，变动不居。"明者因时而变，知者随事而制。"要摒弃不合时宜的旧观念，冲破制约发展的旧框框，让各种发展活力充分迸发出来。要加大转变经济发展方式、调整经济结构力度，更加注重发展质量，更加注重改善民生。稳步推进国际经济金融体系改革，完善全球治理机制，为世界经济健康稳定增长提供保障。亚洲历来具有自我变革活力，要勇做时代的弄潮儿，使亚洲变革和世界发展相互促进、相得益彰。

Gloss: *First, boldly reform and innovate in order to promote an inexhaustible source of power for joint development. Over a long time, many countries and regions have developed a lot of good practices in maintaining stability and promoting growth. These good experiences and methods are to continue. Meanwhile, nothing in the world remains constant, "a wise man changes as time and event[s] change". Should abandon the outdated values, break away from the old confines that fetter development and unleash all the vitality for development. Should increase efforts to shift the growth model and adjust the economic structure, raise the quality of development and make life better for the people, steadily advance the reform of the international economic and financial systems, improve global governance mechanisms and provide support to sound and stable global economic growth. Asia with its long-standing vigour for self-reforming, should ride on the waves of the times, and make changes in Asia and global development [to] reinforce and benefit each other.*

Chinese Interpreter: First, *we should* boldly break new ground so as to create an inexhaustible source of power for boosting common development. Over the years, many countries and regions have developed a lot of good practices in maintaining stability and promoting growth. *We should* continue such practices. However, nothing in the world remains constant, and as a Chinese saying goes, a wise man changes as time and event[s] change. *We should* abandon the outdated mindset, break away from the old confines that fetter development and unleash all the potential for development. *We should* redouble efforts to shift the growth model and adjust the economic structure, raise the quality of development and make life better for the people. *We should* steadily advance the reform of the international economic and financial systems, improve global governance mechanisms and provide support to sound and stable global economic growth. Asia, with its long-standing capacity for adjusting to change, *should* ride on the waves of the times and make changes in Asia and global development [to] reinforce and benefit each other.

Conclusion

With a CDA-and-CL integrated analysis of a bilingual interpreting corpus, we investigated how political speeches delivered by Chinese government officials are rendered by conference interpreters in diplomatic settings. The overall pattern is that while the ideational information has renditions that are close to the original, the interpersonal information is susceptible to interpreting shifts. The most salient shifts concentrate on the use of first-person plurals and obligation modal verbs, both of which increase noticeably in the TTs. Despite the fact that interpreters tend to add a subject *we* for syntactic completeness in Chinese–English interpreting, the increase in first-person plurals, in particular in terms of first-person plural possessives in the construction *our two countries/peoples/governments*, discursively creates a stronger sense of solidarity in relation to a foreign government/country being addressed in diplomatic settings. Furthermore, the added obligation modal verbs in the TTs, especially in the salient formation *we should/must* + action verb, suggest a stronger sense of obligation on the part of the Chinese government to unite other countries with China and the Chinese government, possibly, for matters of common concern and shared interests. In summary, Chinese conference interpreters reconstruct the political discourse in interpreting with a stronger sense than that in the STs of solidarity and obligation in relation to other governments/countries in diplomatic settings.

The main limitation of this study is the limited corpus size, which might reduce otherwise more multifaceted patterns of interpreting data. While the corpus data is small, the patterns uncovered in this study corroborate those in other corpus-based studies with a larger corpus in the Chinese context (e.g. Gu, 2019). Despite that, the operationalisation of the CDA-and-CL approach to the analysis of bilingual interpreting data demonstrates its usefulness for interpreting research with relatively large data sets; the CL-oriented data-driven methods enable the identification of overall shift patterns contrastively (between the STs and TTs) on one hand, and, on the other, the CDA-oriented analysis reveals deeper social, cultural, institutional, and political relations with respect to the ST producers (speakers) and the TT producers (interpreters). With the affordances of corpus techniques, the methods used in this study could unleash more potential for CDA in translation and interpreting studies to uncover meaningful patterns with ever-growing translation and interpreting corpora.

Notes

1 These words include content words and some function words that affect meaning in language use, such as pronouns, modal verbs, and modal auxiliaries. Function words that mainly perform grammatical functions, such as articles and prepositions, are removed from the list. The top 20 is considered as a reasonable cut-off point because the frequencies of the words after the top 20 are relatively low.
2 It is useful to note that the Chinese language has "auxiliary verbs," which are similar to the English language's "modal verbs." Therefore, we use "modals" to refer to both the auxiliary verbs and modal verbs in our discussion.

References

Baker, P. (2006). *Using Corpora in Discourse Analysis*. London: Bloomsbury.
Baker, P. (2010). *Sociolinguistics and Corpus Linguistics*. Edinburgh: Edinburgh University Press.

Baker, P., Gabrielatos, C., Khosravinik, M., Krzyżanowski, M., McEnery, T., & Wodak, R. (2008). A useful methodological synergy? Combining critical discourse analysis and corpus linguistics to examine discourses of refugees and asylum seekers in the UK press. *Discourse and Society,* 19(3), 273–306.

Baker, P. & McEnery, T. (2015). Introduction. In P. Baker & T. McEnery (Eds.), *Corpora and Discourse Studies: Integrating Discourse and Corpora* (pp.1–19). Springer.

Beaton-Thome, M. (2013). What's in a word? Your enemy combatant is my refugee: The role of simultaneous interpreters in negotiating the lexis of Guantánamo in the European Parliament. *Journal of Language and Politics,* 12(3), 378–399.

Chilton, P. (2004). *Analysing Political Discourse: Theory and Practice.* London: Routledge.

Chilton, P. (2005). Missing links in mainstream CDA. In: R. Wodak & P. Chilton (Eds.), *A New Agenda in (Critical) Discourse Analysis* (pp. 19–51). Amsterdam: John Benjamins.

Fairclough, N. (1989). *Language and Power.* London/New York: Longman.

Fairclough, N. (1995a). *Critical Discourse Analysis: The Critical Study of Language.* Essex: Longman.

Fairclough, N. (1995b). *Media Discourse.* London: E. Arnold.

Fairclough, N., & Wodak, R. (1997). Critical discourse analysis. In: T. A. Van Dijk (Ed.), *Discourse as Social Interaction* (pp. 258–284). London: Sage.

Firclough, N., Mulderrig, J., & Wodak, R. (2011). Critical discourse analysis. In: T. A. Van Dijk (Ed.), *Discourse Studies. A Multidisciplinary Introduction* (pp. 357–378). London: Sage.

Gao, F. (2020). *Interpreters' Ideological Positioning through the Evaluative Language in Conference Interpreting* (PhD thesis). Leeds: University of Leeds.

Gao, F. (2021). From linguistic manipulation to discourse re-construction: A case study of conference interpreting at the World Economic Forum in China. In: B. Wang & J. Munday (Eds.), *Advances in discourse analysis of translation and interpreting* (pp. 24–39). London: Routledge.

Gu, C. (2018). Forging a glorious past via the 'present perfect': A corpus-based CDA analysis of China's past accomplishments discourse mediatised at China's interpreted political press conferences. *Discourse, Context and Media,* 24, 137–149.

Gu, C. (2019). *Interpreters' Institutional Alignment and (Re) Construction of China's Political Discourse and Image: A Corpus-Based CDA of the Premier-Meets-the-Press Conferences* (PhD thesis). Manchester: University of Manchester.

Gu, C., & Tipton, R. (2020). (Re-)voicing Beijing's discourse through self-referentiality: A corpus-based CDA analysis of government interpreters' discursive mediation at China's political press conferences (1998–2017). *Perspectives,* 28(3), 406–423.

Halliday, M. A. K. (1994). *An Introduction to Functional Grammar.* London: Edward Arnold.

Halliday, M. A. K., & Matthiessen, C. (2014). *An Introduction to Functional Grammar.* New York: Routledge.

Hardt-Mautner, G. (1995). *"Only Connect": Critical Discourse Analysis and Corpus Linguistics.* Retrieved from Lancaster UK: http://ucrel.lancs.ac.uk/paper s/techpaper/vol6.pdf.

Jönsson, C., & Langhorne, R. (2004). *Diplomacy.* London: Sage Publications.

Partington, A. (2004). Corpora and discourse, a most congruous beast. In: A. Partington, J. Morley, & L. Haarman (Eds.), *Corpora and Discourse* (pp. 11–20). Bern: Peter Lang.

Partington, A. (2006). Metaphors, motifs and similes across discourse types: Corpus-assisted discourse studies (CADS) at work. In: A. Stefanowitsch & S. Gries (Eds.), *Corpus-Based Approaches to Metaphor and Metonymy* (pp. 267–304). Berlin: Mouton de Gruyter.

Roland, R. A. (1999). *Interpreters as Diplomats: A Diplomatic History of the Role of Interpreters in World Politics*. Ottawa: University of Ottawa Press.

van Dijk, T. A. (1997). What is political discourse analysis. *Belgian Journal of Linguistics*, 11(1), 11–52.

van Dijk, T. A. (2008). *Discourse and Power*. New York: Palgrave Macmillan.

Wales, K. (1996). *Personal Pronouns in Present-Day English*. Cambridge: Cambridge University Press.

Wang, B. (2012). A descriptive study of norms in interpreting – Based on the Chinese-English consecutive interpreting corpus of Chinese Premier press conferences. *Meta*, 57(1), 198–212.

Wang, B., & Feng, D. (2017). A corpus-based study of stance-taking as seen from critical points in interpreted political discourse. *Perspectives*, 26(2), 246–260.

Widdowson, H. G. (1998). Review Article: The theory and practice of critical discourse analysis. *Applied Linguistics*, 19(1), 136–151.

Wodak, R., & Meyer, M. (2009). Critical discourse analysis: History, agenda, theory and methodology. *Methods of Critical Discourse Analysis*, 2, 1–33.

6 A Creative Approach for Subtitling Humour

A Case Study of the Political Comedy *Veep*

María del Mar Ogea Pozo

Introduction

Over the last decades, some authors have worked in favour of the communicative aspects of translation, such as Zabalbeascoa (1997) and Díaz-Cintas (2001). According to both authors, most of such studies concentrate on linguistic items and neglect other communicative elements such as "suprasegmental features, language variation and the combination of verbal and nonverbal elements" (Zabalbeascoa, 1997, p. 238). A focus on communication as a key to translation may be justified by the rising awareness that translation is a social process which takes place within specific cultural, spatial, and temporal settings, so translators must take an active and visible role to mediate the message (Ulrych, 2013). This trend becomes effective when dealing with audiovisual translation, as the audiovisual text is inextricably bound to other codes that constitute a complex intersemiotic structure designed to prompt an effect on the audience. For this reason, translators must pay attention to non-linguistic signs in order to portray the speaker's intended message (Zabalbeascoa, 1997).

However, this task may be hampered by factors related to the audiovisual product itself, such as synchronisation, technical features, or the presumed characteristics of the audience. Concerning subtitling, translators face challenges derived from space and time limitations, image constraints, and the form of presentation of the text, consisting of a written on-screen form reproduced simultaneously with the speaker's speech (Chaume, 2004). Furthermore, the presence of the source text makes this form of translation "vulnerable" (Díaz-Cintas & Remael, 2007, p. 55) and different from others, as subtitles are accompanied by the source text, generating the so-called "feedback effect" (*ibid.*). That is to say, users perceive source and target languages at once, so they feel able to assess the subtitles and some might feel cheated if the translator does not translate "such-and-such a word which they have clearly heard" (Díaz-Cintas & Remael, 2007, p. 56). For this reason, subtitles rendering phrases literally have become a common but not advisable practice that is usually demanded by clients with little experience with translation (*ibid.*) and perhaps by viewers not accustomed to subtitles either. This theory leads us to think that, if viewers are more familiar with subtitling and aware that the text might differ from the original script, they might be able to understand why certain vocabulary needs to be adapted or substituted, or why wordiness must be synthetised.

Regarding the familiarisation of the Spanish audience with subtitling, recent years have seen an increase in the consumption of media providing subtitles for their users. Audiovisual consumption patterns have experienced extraordinary changes since the boom of video-on-demand (VOD) platforms in 2015, as revealed by the annual report published by the Spanish General Society of Authors and Editors (SGAE), which shows a rapid increase of Spanish households subscribing to at least one VOD service, whereas traditional TV has been ditched slightly (see Figure 6.1).

In Spain, telecommunications companies and video-on-demand platforms provide a wide range of foreign films, series, and documentaries available in their original version with Spanish subtitles. Consequently, subtitles have gained popularity among viewers, as shown in the study performed by Hernández and Martínez (2016), where 57% of the 545 participants acknowledged watching audiovisual contents in their original version with subtitles.

The current case study analyses a selection of episodes of *Veep*, a series that entails a variety of challenges derived from humour based on national identities, stereotyped characters, puns, slang, and swearwords, and investigates Spanish viewers' reception of the creative translation method via a questionnaire among a group of Spanish viewers to evaluate the humorous load found in two translation choices. Finally, through a comparative

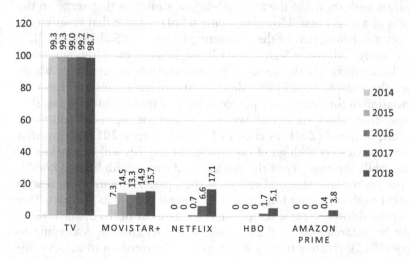

Figure 6.1 TV and Subscriptions to VOD Services in Spanish Households. Source: http://www.anuariossgae.com/anuario2019.

analysis of both source and target texts, the research will determine whether a creative approach may cause any loss of meaning or effector, quite contrarily, compensate any inevitable loss, maintaining the comical function despite some variations in the types of jokes used.

The notion of *humour* may refer to any verbal or nonverbal element used as a form of communication with the purpose of producing laughter or amusement in the receiver or, in the case of audiovisual translation, in the audience. According to Zabalbeascoa (2001), there is a cause and effect connection between humour and fun, and not only jokes can be found funny.

Creative Translation

The concept of *creative translation* refers to an approach purposefully taken by translators to set it apart from translation proper (O'Sullivan, 2013, p. 42). Barrena (2014) describes this creative process during which an idea is elucidated as "a glimpse of comprehension" that facilitates the flow of ideas for conveying meaning in an ingenious way. Hence, creative translation implies decisions that may be risky but successful when the effect on the audience is prioritised. According to Ulrych (2013), translators make the necessary adjustments during a creative process consisting of three steps (interpretation, transmission, and relocation) to compensate and account for cross-cultural gaps, even when the purpose of the source text and the target text is the same. Then, the question is whether audiovisual translation always remains as a creative task.

There seems to be little literature delving into the notion of creativity as a stage of inception prior to the production of translation solutions in the face of the many challenges posed by the audiovisual text, and opinions are disparate with regard to the acceptability of strategies that verge on the adaptation of a target text. However, some scholars argue that creativity is an important, intrinsic part of the translating process (O'Sullivan, 2013).

In his study, Martínez-Sierra (2017) explains that, although some authors like Sorroche (2010) stand up for imagination and creativity above all, some others like Kahane (1990) describe audiovisual translation as a literal translation of the original script that is later adapted. That suggests that audiovisual translators are not always free to opt for ingenious solutions. Despite this, Mayoral (2001, as cited in Martínez-Sierra, 2017) claims that translation for viewers with good knowledge of English will be marked by literalism, while the majority of the Spanish audience – with limited knowledge of the source language and culture – shall prefer a more natural style with respect to their mother tongue and its general laws of expression. This theory is plausible for the translation of *Veep*, as most of the Spanish viewers might be unfamiliar with the sociocultural background. According to McClarty (2012), creative translation provides the freedom to achieve difference and to create from the ingenious mind of a translator performing as a filmmaker or a cineliterate film viewer, rather than from a linguistic mind.

The current study sees creative translation as a translation method in which the humorous function prevails over the original linguistic form, with the objective of providing a verbal element that differs from the original text but gains in effectiveness and fun among the target audience. Therefore, this creative approach focuses on the translator's effort to produce a compelling target text in an inventive way, and to give life to the speech through a linguistic twist. A translation is creative when the target text reflects tangible variations from the source text, caused by the necessity to compensate for the viewers' lack of knowledge of the source culture, to address cultural barriers, and to solve any problem of untranslatability due to the presence of certain linguistic elements or allusions to culture-specific themes.

Humour in *Veep*

Veep and Comedy

The selected series *Veep* belongs to the comedy genre. Comedy was originally created with the main objective of offering a mocking vision of reality and, as a result, provoking a laughter reaction in the audience. Zabalbeascoa (2001) explains that, as a specific genre to be distinguished from others, comedy must meet some formal and structural requirements, such as a certain density of humour and a happy ending.

The production subject to this study is presented in TV series format, which is defined by Agnetta (2015) as a multidimensional complex constituted by different signals from semiotic systems like oral speech, written text, moving images, and soundtracks. Therefore, translators must pay attention to the presence of humorous components in any semiotic signal and comprehend the comicalness that emerges from their interaction in order to make it feasible when transferred to the target text (*ibid.*). Furthermore, translators must execute linguistic operations to preserve the specific units involved and ensure that the target text is consistent with nonverbal comical elements.

Veep is an acid-tongued political satire starring Julia Louis-Dreyfus, who plays Selina Meyer, vice president of the United States. The topics addressed are political incompetence, corruption, fraud, backstabbing, physical and verbal violence, and social forms of intolerance, all of them triggering absurd situations in a formal and professional environment.

The key to humour in *Veep* – considered as a sitcom by some media[1] – lies in its close bond with the sociocultural background of the country in which the plot takes place, as well as in the interaction of different semiotic elements operating on multiple levels. From a translatological perspective, its main defining feature is manifested at the verbal level. The characters' use of language diverges from the standard linguistic norms generally adopted in the oral speech within a specific environment, and is therefore perceived as comical (Agnetta, 2015). Humour also resides in references to fields of expertise (politics, international conflicts, law, etc.) through different codes, and that is where the complexity of its translation lies.

Types of Humour

Pursuant to the theory published by Juckel et al. (2016), in which the authors delve into sitcoms as the widest-reaching comedy form, there are some compelling reasons to study this genre. According to Juckel et al., sitcoms may reveal psychological and sociological aspects of individuals as well as national and cultural groups, and the outcomes can be fruitful for writers and producers who may benefit from investigating the types of humour that appeal to certain audiences. Besides, Buijzen and Valkenburg (2004) acknowledge that any research on humour and its perception by audiences must begin with a recognition of separate categories. Moreover, they suggest that audience groups are attracted to different forms of humour, so that leads to "different types of effects in different types of audiences" (p. 164).

As far as translation is concerned, a study of the types of humour within the audiovisual text would help translators pinpoint the prevalence of certain forms of humour, as well as the difficulties inherent to every category, so that they can effectively prepare their work and provide solutions founded on solid theoretical studies.

To undertake this research, I took Juckel et al.'s typology as the main foundation, which allows humour to be coded in US sitcoms through four categories of sitcom-specific techniques (see Table 6.1). I believe this proposal meets the forms of humour found in *Veep* and therefore is suitable for the present study.

Notwithstanding the reliability of the model above, I found some nuances that were not covered, such as cultural and social aspects. Moreover, some techniques from the model of four macro groups could be dispensable, as they referred to non-tangible psychological aspects, social behaviours, and exclusively nonverbal elements that could not be included in our written corpus. However, visual information is essential, from costume design[2] to facial expressions and body language. Thus, even when the current case

Table 6.1 Humour Typology for Sitcoms Established by Juckel et al.

Language	Logic	Identity	Action
Allusion	Absurdity	Parody	Peculiar face
Irony	Coincidence	Rigidity	Peculiar music
Puns	Conceptual surprise	Malicious pleasure	Clumsiness
Repartee	Outwitting	Deceitful behaviour	Repulsive behaviour
Ridicule	Caught out	Condescension	
Wit	Misunderstanding	Self-deprecation	

study is focused on verbally expressed humour, it includes jokes bound to nonverbal aspects. But since my main purpose is to analyse the audiovisual text from a translation approach, nonverbal elements were considered only when they accompanied lexical units.

A New Proposal for Analysing Audiovisual Comedies

To code humour in a comedy about sociocultural aspects with an underlying intention to express social and political criticism, I proceeded to the following stages:

1) Viewing of eight episodes of the sixth season.

  I may justify this choice with two reasons. First, I had the chance to contact one of the two translators involved and have access to the original scripts. Moreover, season six is worth taking into consideration for several reasons. It is the first season to take the show out of the White House, *Veep*'s executive producer David Mandel admitted that the season was still underway when Donald Trump said he was running for president, so the Trump administration boosted the level of absurdity of some characters. Therefore, it seems interesting to observe this satire when it reached its most grotesque height.[3]

2) Identification of comical situations.
3) Identification of any type of humour coded in verbal units.
4) Denomination of the types of humour distinctive of this audiovisual product.

After the completion of the four stages, I noted some biases in the forms of humour produced. Therefore, I devised a new typology (see Table 6.2) which should be tested throughout the course of this study. Some new categories and techniques are added and marked with an asterisk, and they will be explained below.

Table 6.2 Original Typology for Types of Humour Found in Veep

Language	Logic	Identity	Culture*	Taboo*
Allusion	Absurdity	Parody	Cultural	Racism*
Irony	Outwitting	Nickname*	reference*	Sex*
Puns	Misunderstanding		Fixed	Profanity*
Ridicule			expression*	Homophobia*
Sarcasm			National	Swearwords*
Misuse*			episode*	
Specialised				
language*				

In the first place, two techniques were added to the "Language" category to represent a significant amount of jokes based on special features of natural language.

- Specialised terminology. The terminology found is mostly related to politics and war and used to produce comicalness within a certain context. For example, in episode three, a funny scene occurs when Richard and Jonah are dancing at a concert and unaware that they happen to be in a Nazi pub. After reading the name of the band "Panzer," they exchange the dialogue below and then remain silent for a second, while the music intensifies and the frame displays the image of some Nazi flags, for the surprise of the characters and the audience, therefore producing a comical effect through multiple semiotic codes (see Figure 6.2).

  Richard: You know, the band's name translates to Panzer Division.
  Jonah: What?
  (Silence.)
  Jonah: Maybe we should leave?
  (Richard nods.)

- Misuse. This refers to an allegedly innocent language mistake – but intended by the scriptwriters – to denote innuendoes and absurdities. For instance, a comical situation occurs when Minna, a Finnish politician not very fluent in English, addresses Selina's stay in the "insane

Figure 6.2 Specialised Term Used in Multisemiotic Humour. Source: HBO. *Veep*. S. 06 Ep. 03.

asylum," but Selina does not want to admit she suffered a mental breakdown. The term "insane asylum" is no longer used, as this care gradually transformed into modern psychiatric hospitals, so this unintended confusion seems to be malicious (see example below):

Minna: Your stay in the insane asylum really agreed with you.
Selina: It was a spa.

In regard to the "Identity" category, I implemented the technique "Nicknames," as these have become characteristic in *Veep*. This satire is praised to have turned "the act of insulting into an art form"[4] and many of those twisted, heinous insults are blurted out in the form of nicknames assigned to some characters. Nicknames in *Veep* are a complex form of humour related to other techniques, such as puns, cultural references, or intertextuality, and they are worth being studied further. A representative example is the nickname used by Selena for Laura Montez, her opponent, who is an attractive woman with a Mexican heritage. The nickname is created by fusing the name of the *Looney Tunes* character, Speedy Gonzales, with the colloquialism "titty" referring to her breasts:

Selina: I'm gonna say what Titty Gonzales was too chicken-shit to say!

Due to the close relation between humour and culture in this political satire, I created the type of humour labelled as "Culture," comprising three techniques that are as follows:

- What I called "National episode," which implies scandals, funny anecdotes, or dark incidents usually involving politicians or celebrities who may be well-known in the United States but not heard of overseas. For example, Will alludes to Joey Chestnut, an American competitive eater who holds the world hot dog eating record, although this fact may not be understood by the Spanish audience:

  Will: I'd be swallowing dicks whole just like Joey Chestnut.

- "Fixed expressions" influenced by the source language and culture.
- "Cultural references" found in jokes inextricably linked to the source culture.

In addition to this, I detected a prominent presence of humour based on the use of taboo words, and this fact seems to be particularly distinctive of *Veep*. Through relentless insults and swearwords, dialogues caricature power-hungry politicians. I believe this offensive language is a mocking form of humour which is not the type of language expected in a professional diplomatic context and "it is the violation of an expected pattern that provokes humour in the mind of the receiver" (Buijzen & Valkenburg, 2004). The "Taboo" category includes swearwords and terms related to racism, sex, sexism, profanity, and homophobia.

The Translation of Humour and Its Reception Among Viewers

The translation of audiovisual humour is extremely complex, since it may be based on a special use of language and bound to a particular cultural context. Furthermore, this task poses the added difficulty of specific restrictions such as synchronisation, space limitations, image constraints, and technical issues. Besides, humour is a form of communication associated with certain social groups and, consequently, its translation implies a comprehensive knowledge of language and culture, as well as a creative effort when it comes to rendering the message. There is no doubt that transferring the linguistic code is not enough when the cultural heritage is not shared and understood by the target audience, because the humorous discourse turns out to be incomprehensible or unfunny (Chiaro, 2008). Therefore, the process of translating humour becomes a linguistic and cultural exchange that transforms the original text into a new one in the target language (Chiaro, 2010).

Translating humour entails a sound command of both languages and cultures, but also the acquisition of specific skills that Zabalbeascoa (2001) groups in three main types:

• Ability to interpret the meaning of the original version and to express it appropriately in the target language.
• Ability to adjust the translated version to space limitations and to synchronise the text with the auditory and visual elements.
• Ability to produce a target text that works as a funny script.

Viewers' Reception of Humour

Zabalbeascoa's (*ibid.*) theory as above leads us to think that, during the process of translating humour, it is essential to pursue a "reality effect" (Chaume, 2005, p. 12) so that the target audience can recognise the humorous elements and experience the same feelings as the original audience did. Linguistic, sociocultural, and semiotic aspects may be a barrier for the satisfactory reception of translated audiovisual humour, so the text should be adjusted by means of compensation and adaptation methods. In this regard, Botella (2017) maintains that translators must overcome the gap between the original and the target audience, since the original audience's knowledge, culture, and ways of seeing the world will not necessarily be common to the target audience. To accomplish a correct transfer of audiovisual humour, Botella (*ibid.*) states that translators must be able to recognize the audiovisual signals and their purposes, and to find the mechanisms that allow the same effect to be reached by the target audience.

The ultimate objective of audiovisual translation is to meet the viewers' expectations (Fuentes, 2003), which, in the case of comedy consumers, is to have fun (Chiaro, 2010). For this reason, Fuentes (2003) states that translators must focus on the different semiotic codes with connotative, comical, and cultural load that influence the transfer of humour to be able to convey their explicit purposefulness. Besides, he argues that viewers from different language or cultural backgrounds may experience the same or a completely different humorous effect for a variety of reasons, as their interpretation of the comedy may vary.

Humour Translation Strategies

As mentioned before, I centred this analysis on "verbally expressed humour" (Chiaro, 2010) to gather lexical units in the corpus, even though semiotic elements were considered when they performed an essential function. However, the exclusively nonverbal humour had to be excluded, as no translation strategy was involved.

In order to classify the translation strategies used throughout the process of translating this comedy, I resorted to the typologies for translation strategies developed by Hurtado (2001) and Franco-Aixelá (1996), as they were applicable to cultural and humorous textual components. Only the translation strategies detected in the texts subject to study were included, for the purpose of measuring their recurrence for the translation of humorous elements in *Veep*. Regarding Hurtado's proposal, I observed that the following strategies had been applied: adaptation, equivalence, loan, elision, compensation, substitution, and discursive creation, in addition to linguistic translation and universalisation from Franco-Aixelá's model.

In the current study, I subdivided the substitution strategy into three different strategies, in order to overcome the great variety of cases in which a substitution was applied: humorous substitution (the type of humour is replaced by another), linguistic substitution (a totally different linguistic unit is used in harmony with the context), and cultural substitution (a humorous component belonging to the source culture is replaced by another from the target culture) (see Table 6.3).

In addition, a distinction between conservative and creative strategies has been made in the current research. Creative strategies are those strategies that involve the mechanisms described in the next section and entail a great difference with respect to the original text, to counteract any possible loss

Table 6.3 Typology for Humour Translation Strategies

Conservative Translation Strategies	Creative Translation Strategies
Equivalence	Adaptation
Linguistic translation	Compensation
Loan	Cultural substitution
Elision	Humorous substitution
Universalisation	Linguistic substitution
	Discursive creation

of the humorous function in the target text. By contrast, conservative translation strategies are those that maintain the allusions specific to the source culture or are inclined towards a "literal method" (Martínez Sierra, 2017).

Hence, the final typology put into practice included the following 11 categories.

Data and Data Analysis Results

Data of Humour and Translation Strategies

During the compilation of the corpus, I gathered 97 excerpts from different scenes across the eight episodes selected, during which at least one type of verbal humour was involved.

Humorous dialogues and jokes found in the original subtitles of both English and Spanish versions were recorded (see Table 6.4 for an example). Subsequently, I identified the types of humour spotted in both audiovisual texts according to the typology designed in Table 6.2, as well as the translation strategies employed.

The results obtained would help me find out whether the translation strategies applied were in line with a creative process, using the framework described above, and whether this approach had minimised the loss of humour. Finally, the questionnaire carried out would let me verify if a good reception among the audience was accomplished.

Humour techniques found in both the original and the target text were categorised in tables designed for each category. In case a type of humour was detected on multiple occasions, the number of occurrences is bracketed, and excerpts manifesting a combination of types of humour include an enumeration of them.

The comparison revealed what translation strategies were the most recurrent, as well as the types of humour rendered after the translation process. The analysis of the lexical units was performed as shown in the example in Table 6.4.

In the tables used for the comparative analysis (Tables 6.5–Tables 6.8), translation strategies are indicated by the following abbreviations: adaptation (A), cultural substitution (CS), compensation (C), discursive creation (DC), equivalent transformation (EQ), humorous substitution (HS), linguistic substitution (LS), literal translation (LIT), loan translation (LOA), omission (O), and universalisation (UN).

Table 6.4 Comparative Analysis of Jokes in *Veep*

English	Type of Humour in ST
- *Do you want me to 69 him?* - *Oh, you mean 86.*	Fixed expression
Translation strategy: Discursive creation	
Spanish	**Type of Humour in TT**
- *¿Quieres que me lo cepille?* - *Ah, deshacerte de él.*	Pun

Table 6.5 Humour Based on a Special Use of the Language

LANGUAGE

Type of Humour in Source Text	Strategy	Type of Humour in Target Text
Allusion	LIT	Reference to SC
	DC	(2) Allusion
Misuse + Outwitting	DC	Misuse + Outwitting (different to ST)
Pun	A	Pun
	C	Pun
	DC	(3) Pun (different to ST)
		Pun + Sex swearing
	EQ	Pun
	LIT	Absurdity
	LS	(3) Pun
		Pun + Allusion
	O	Absurdity
Pun + Gesture	LOA	Reference to SC
Pun + Image	EQ	Pun
Ridicule	CS	(3) Ridicule (different to ST)
	DC	Ridicule + Allusion
	HS	Ridicule
	O	Misunderstanding
Sarcasm	DC	Sarcasm (different to ST)
	LS	(2) Sarcasm
Specialised term	LIT	(2) Specialised term
Wit	HS	Fixed expression

Table 6.6 Humour Based on Social Identities

IDENTITY

Type of Humour in Source Text	Strategy	Type of Humour in Target Text
Parody	C	Allusion
	EQ	Absurdity
		Parody
	UN	Ridicule
Nickname + Profanity	DC	Nickname + Allusion
Nickname + Parody	EQ	Nickname + Parody
Nickname + Parody	LOA	Nickname + Parody
		Swearword + Sexist
Nickname + Pun	LS	(2) Allusion
		Nickname
Nickname + Racism	LS	Nickname + Cultural ref. + Racism
Nickname	UN	Ridicule

Table 6.7 Humour Based on Cultural References

CULTURE		
Type of Humour in Source Text	*Strategy*	*Type of Humour in Target Text*
Fixed expression[5]	CS	(8) Fixed expression
Cultural reference	DC	Fixed expression (different to ST)
		Pun
	CS	(5) Cultural reference
	DC	Absurdity
		Reference to SC
		Cultural reference (different to ST)
	LS	Swearword
	UN	(2) Absurdity
		(2) Ridicule
National episode	C	Reference to SC
	HS	Fixed expression
	LOA	Reference to SC
	UN	Allusion
		Sex swearing
	DC	Allusion
		Ridicule
		Universalisation

Table 6.8 Humour Based on Taboo Words

TABOO		
Type of Humour in Source Text	*Strategy*	*Type of Humour in Target Text*
Homophobia	CS	Fixed expression (sex euphemism)
		Homophobia
Profanity	A	Profanity
	EQ	Profanity
Racist reference	DC	Racist reference
	HS	Racist + Fixed expression
	O	Absurdity
	UN	Racist reference
Sex swearing	CS	(2) Sex swearing
		Swearword
Swearword	CS	Swearword
	C	Sarcasm
	O	Outwitting

Data of Viewers' Reception

An experiment on the viewers' reception was carried out with the participation of 41 users of at least one VOD service. Participants were 21 undergraduate students of the Film and Cultural Studies degree at the University of Córdoba as experts on filmography (but not familiar with translation studies) and 20 adults with different university degrees. The age ranged from 18 to 65.

The questionnaire was made up of 11 sections containing a total of 20 examples considered to be the representative of the types of humour with greater prominence in *Veep*: allusion, national episode, cultural reference, fixed expression, nickname, parody, pun, racism, ridicule, swearwords, and specialised terms. Among them, nine had been translated by means of conservative strategies, while 11 were rendered through a creative approach. The structure of each section was as follows:

1) Phrase containing the selected joke and video of the scene in which humour occurs.
2) Evaluative measure for the viewers' understanding of the humour within the source culture and language, being 1 = Total understanding, 2 = Partial understanding, and 3 = No understanding (see Figure 6.3).
3) Two translation choices. The original translation found in the Spanish audiovisual text was included, and a second option was created for this questionnaire, which would be translated using the opposite method to the one applied by the translators (creative or conservative, respectively; see Figure 6.4).

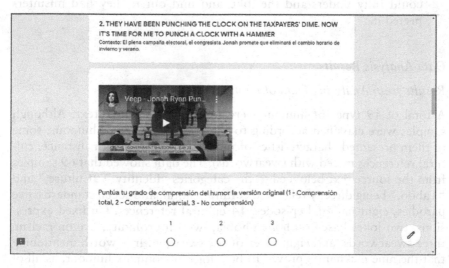

Figure 6.3 Questionnaire: Understanding the Original Humour.

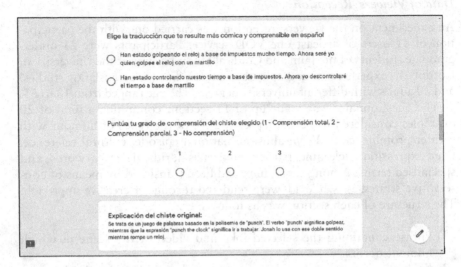

Elige la traducción que te resulte más cómica y comprensible en español

○ Han estado golpeando el reloj a base de impuestos mucho tiempo. Ahora seré yo quien golpee el reloj con un martillo

○ Han estado controlando nuestro tiempo a base de impuestos. Ahora yo descontrolaré el tiempo a base de martillo

Puntúa tu grado de comprensión del chiste elegido (1 - Comprensión total, 2 - Comprensión parcial, 3 - No comprensión)

  1   2   3
  ○   ○   ○

Explicación del chiste original:
Se trata de un juego de palabras basado en la polisemia de "punch". El verbo "punch" significa golpear, mientras que la expresión "punch the clock" significa ir a trabajar. Jonah lo usa con ese doble sentido mientras rompe un reloj.

Figure 6.4 Creative vs. Conservative Translation and Understanding of Translated Humour.

4) Evaluative measure for the viewers' understanding of the humour in the target language (being 1 = Total understanding, 2 = Partial understanding, and 3 = No understanding). The objective was to determine if any substantial loss of sense or comicalness occurred.
5) An explanation of the original joke was provided, so the participants could fully understand the joke and find out if they had misinterpreted it.

Data Analysis Results

Results from Analysing Data of Humour in the Source Text

A total of 19 types of humour were found in the source text. Although samples were classified according to the prevailing type of humour, some of them presented characteristics of more than one type (for instance, cultural references mixed with swearwords). The data showed that 69 samples from the source text belonged to the categories "Identity," "Culture," and "Taboo," being directly related to cultural, moral, and social standards: five parodies, eight national episodes, 14 cultural references, ten fixed expressions, two jokes based on homophobia, two on profanity, five on racism, three swearwords, and eight cases of sex swearing. It is worth mentioning that the nine nicknames proved to be a form of complex humour, as all of them were mixed with another type, resulting in three nickname + pun, one nickname + absurdity, three nickname + parody, one nickname + profanity, and one nickname + racism. Furthermore, three allusions – despite corresponding to the "Language" category – were connected to references to the source culture. On the other hand, 31 samples were mainly based on the use of language, although many of them were partially bound to the source culture and associated to the above categories: one language misuse, 16 puns (one mixed with visual gesture), five ridicules, one wit, three sarcastic comments, and two specialised terms used for comical purposes (one mixed with visual information).

These results demonstrate the prevalence of humour specific to a social and cultural background that may be unfamiliar to the target audience. This cultural gap calls attention to the importance of pragmatics and requires a target text that fulfils a similar communicative function as the source text in order to achieve qualitative adequacy (Nord, 1991, as cited in Chiaro, 2008). Thus, the quality of the translation may be pondered in terms of its orientation to the needs and requirements of the consumer (Chiaro, 2008).

Results from Analysing Data of Humour in the Translated Subtitles

Figure 6.5 and Figure 6.6 below represent the translation strategies used for translating each humour technique, grouped in two separate diagrams corresponding to a conservative or a creative approach, as termed in the present study.

From the data shown in both figures, it can be concluded that there is a clear predominance of creative strategies, especially when translating

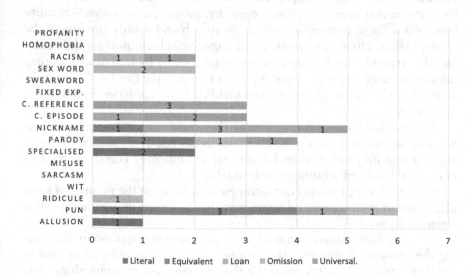

Figure 6.5 Conservative Translation Strategies.

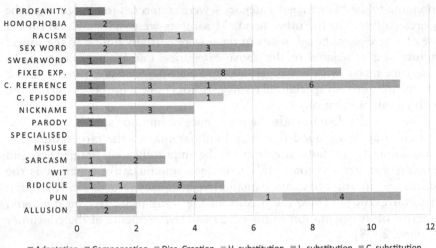

■ Adaptation ■ Compensation ▨ Disc. Creation ▨ H. substitution ▨ L. substitution ▨ C. substitution

Figure 6.6 Creative Translation Strategies.

culture-specific humour. For instance, the use of cultural substitution is remarkable for translating jokes referring to cultural, social, and ideological themes, such as cultural references, fixed expressions, and taboo words. This strategy fulfils the same comical effect on the target audience, as they perceive the audiovisual product as if it were created within their own culture and language. Compensation is used to address cultural humour too – cultural references, national episodes, parody, and taboos – because it enables a fluent comprehension of the speech and avoids any loss of the comical effect. Discursive creation and linguistic substitution are the strategies that possibly involve the greatest creative effort by translators, as they must create a new text (in form) but recreate the same function. Both techniques have a notable presence when tackling language-based humour and nicknames.

On the other hand, it is noteworthy that conservative strategies such as universalisation and loan translation are occasionally applied to cultural humour that may not be shared by the target audience. Therefore, the loss of cultural load and meaning is unavoidable.

In the final step, I carried out a comparison between the number of samples found in both source and target texts for each type of humour, as illustrated in Figure 6.7.

Given the data above, I must bring out some changes occurring during the translation process. The number of jokes was reduced by one in the target text (97 to 96), meaning that a slight loss of comicalness was

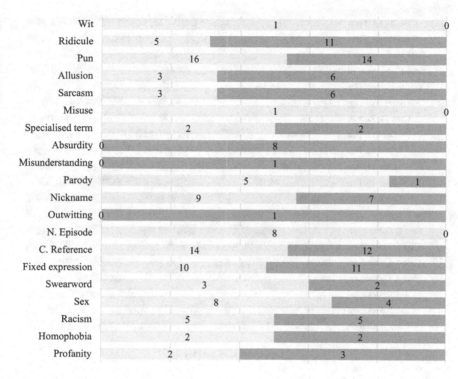

Figure 6.7 Samples for Each Type of Humour in ST and TT.[6]

produced. Moreover, there is an increase in the number of samples in language and logic categories, whereas the presence of humour based on national identity and culture is reduced. Translators opted for non-cultural, incongruent humour based on the lack of logic, linguistic jokes, and puns, which are not specific to any culture and can ensure a hilarious reaction among the audience. Nonetheless, a significant number of humorous excerpts are related to cultural and social humour, although most of them have been adjusted to the target culture for the purpose of achieving a better reception by the audience. Some cultural jokes were maintained because they refer to certain aspects of the original culture that are internationally known, or because they are linked to other semiotic signs that may act as supportive information. Concerning the humour based on taboo words, the number of samples barely varies, demonstrating that this unexpected use of language for humorous purposes in a professional context can be rendered accurately in comedies.

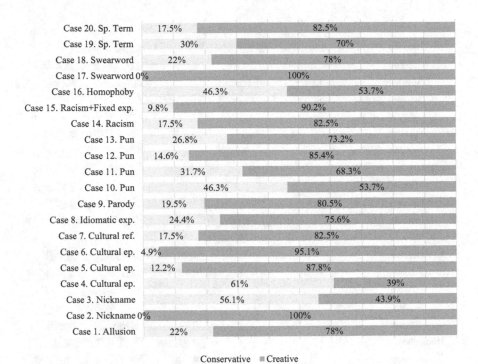

Figure 6.8 Viewers' Preferences for Creative or Conservative Translation. Source: HBO. *Veep*. S. 06 Ep. 05.

Moreover, their function prevails, and the linguistic forms can be easily accommodated to equivalent taboo words used in the target culture and language.

Results from Analysing Questionnaire Data

Figure 6.8 presents the data from the questionnaire on viewers' preferences of translation strategies of humour.

Furthermore, more than 50% of the respondents manifested problems understanding humour coded in the original text for all the examples selected. Therefore, it seems clear that humour exclusive to sociopolitical themes and cultural references which are not part of the viewers' cognitive encyclopaedia may cause difficulties in understanding (Denton & Ciampi, 2012). Only one fixed expression was fully understood by 58.5% of the respondents and they admitted that paralinguistic elements (i.e. gestures and facial expression) contributed to this fact (see Figure 6.9).

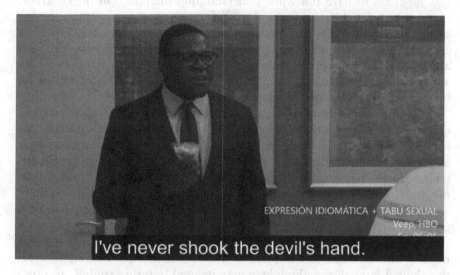

EXPRESIÓN IDIOMÁTICA + TABÚ SEXUAL
Veep, HBO

I've never shook the devil's hand.

Figure 6.9 Fixed Expression Linked to Visual Information.

Conclusions

One of the objectives of this case study was to identify the prevalence of different types of humour in this political satire, in terms of their bond to the source cultural and social background and their linguistic characteristics. For that purpose, I created a new typology that would allow researchers and audiovisual translators to classify humour and to prepare for dealing with certain difficulties inherent to each category. This typology proved to be useful in studying the forms of verbal humour found in *Veep*.

The presence of humour techniques was found to vary widely. In addition to this, I have corroborated that humour is versatile and complex, as the same humorous excerpt may involve more than just one type of humour. Therefore, humour studies in the framework of audiovisual translation must be flexible and dynamic, and they must heed any hint or sign that may affect the meaning and the function of the humorous component.

Given the results obtained in the analysis of the translation strategies applied, I believe that creativity plays a prominent role in translation and becomes even more prominent when multisemiotic signs and cultural aspects converge, as in the case of audiovisual comedies. The identification of translation strategies for humour was performed with the finding that a creative method maintains the semantic and humorous load and provides a satisfactory reception among viewers. The samples translated creatively and included in the experiment were assessed positively by the participants. This suggests that the desired effect among viewers was achieved, which and was for them to have fun while understanding the plot. On the contrary, excerpts translated by strategies classified as conservative were mostly discarded in favour of the alternative creative solutions proposed. This suggests that a creative approach provides optimal outcomes when dealing with audiovisual comedies pivoting on social and cultural themes, as an excessive attachment to the culture of origin can lead to a lack of comprehension by the audience and thus less amusement among them.

After the completion of the comparative analysis between both source and target texts, I come to the conclusion that the types of humour differ when transferring humour to the target language, but these variations are acceptable if the amount of humour conveyed is similar, albeit it is interpreted differently by the target audience. As mentioned at the beginning of this study, the primary objective of comedy consumers is to have fun (Chiaro, 2010), and for that reason, audiovisual translators may need to resort to their own creativity and imagination to meet the viewers' expectations.

I plan to provide a working model that could be used as a reference for training future audiovisual translators when practising and developing creative skills. I hope this methodology may be used in future studies, as a tool for observing the presence of different types of humour in comedies specific to a sociopolitical and cultural context, as well as for examining the adequate translation strategies to render audiovisual humour from a creative approach. Finally, I hope this study encourages future audiovisual translators to work on their creative skills to face challenges posed by humour associated with social and cultural matters and to ensure the best results.

Notes

1 Source: <https://www.indiewire.com/2012/05/why-veep-is-more-sitcom-than-po litical-satire-47598/>
2 Source: <https://www.vogue.es/moda/tendencias/articulos/veep-serie-hbo-disenado ra-de-vestuario-entrevista/39861>
3 Source: <https://www.vanityfair.com/hollywood/2017/04/veep-season-6-donald -trump-golden-shower>
4 Source: <https://www.rollingstone.com/tv/tv-lists/swearing-in-25-great-veep-ins ults-12907/>
5 Including one sex euphemism and one vulgar expression.
6 Among the 13 samples classified as "Cultural reference," seven alluded to the target culture, while five maintained the reference to the original culture.

References

Agnetta, M. (2015). Aproximaciones traductológicas a lo cómico en las comedias de situación estadounidenses. *Quaderns de Cine. Cine, Doblaje y Subtitulación*, 10(10), 13–21.

Barrena, S. (2014). La traducción como actividad creativa: El caso de Charles S. Peirce. In: Gómez Ramos, Antonio (Ed.), *Pensar la traducción: la filosofía de camino entre las lenguas* (pp. 241–249). Madrid: Actas del Congreso Universidad Carlos II.

Botella Tejera, C. (2017). La traducción del humor intertextual audiovisual. Que la fuerza os acompañe. *MONTI*, 9(9), 77–100.

Buijzen, M. & Valkenburg, P. (2004). Developing a typology of humor in audiovisual media. *Media Psychology*, 6(2), 147–167.

Chaume Varela, F. (2004). *Cine y traducción*. Madrid: Cátedra.

Chaume Varela, F. (2005). Los estándares de calidad y la recepción de la traducción audiovisual. *Puentes*, 6, 5–12.

Chiaro, D. (2008). Issues of quality in screen translation. In: D. In, C. Chiaro, Heiss & C. Bucaria (Eds.), *Between Text and Image: Updating Research in Screen Translation* (pp. 241–256). Amsterdam: John Benjamins.

Chiaro, D. (2010). Translation and humour, humour and translation. In: D. Chiaro (Ed.), *Translation, Humour and Literature*, Vol. 1 (pp. 1–29). London: Continuum.

Denton, J. & Ciampi, D. (2012). A new development in audiovisual translation studies: Focus on target audience perception. *LEA - Lingue e letterature d'oriente e d'Occidente*, 1(1), 399–422.

Díaz-Cintas, J. (2001). The value of the semiotic dimension in the subtitling of humour. In: L. Desblanche (Ed.), *Aspects of Specialised Translation* (pp. 181–191). Paris: La maison du dictionnaire.

Díaz-Cintas, J. & Remael, A. (2007). *Audiovisual Translation: Subtitling*. London: Routledge.

Franco-Aixelá, J. (1996). Culture-specific items in translation. In: R. Álvarez & M. Vidal (Eds.), *Translation, Power, Subversion* (pp. 52–78). Clevedon: Multilingual Matters.

Fuentes-Luque, A. (2003). An empirical approach to the reception of AV translated humor. *The Translator*, 9(2), 293–306.

Hernández Pérez, J. & Martínez Díaz, M. (2016). Nuevos modelos de consumo audiovisual: Los efectos del binge-watching sobre los jóvenes universitarios. *adComuni-ca. Revista Científica de Estrategias. Tendencias e Innovación en Comunicación*, 13, 201–221.

Hurtado Albir, A. (2001). *Traducción y Traductología. Introducción a la Traductología*. Madrid: Cátedra.

Iannucci, A. (Creator) (2012–2019). *Veep [HBO Spain Broadcast]*. USA: Dundee Productions.

Juckel, J., Bellman, S. & Varan, D. (2016). A humor typology to identify humor styles used in sitcoms. *Humor. International Journal of Humor Research*, 29(4), 583-603.

Kahane, E. (1990). Los doblajes cinematográficos. Trucaje lingüístico y verosimilitud. *Parallèles*, 12, 115-120.

Martínez Sierra, J. (2017). La traducción literal en el ámbito audiovisual. Método y técnica. *CLINA*, 3-1, 13–34.

McClarty, R. (2012). Towards a multidisciplinary approach in creative subtitling. *MONTI*, 4(4), 133–153.

O'Sullivan, C. (2013). Creativity. In: Y. Gambier & L. Van Doorslaer (Eds.), *Handbook of Translation Studies*, Vol. 4 (pp. 42–46). Amsterdam: John Benjamins.

Sorroche, S. (2010). El perfil del traductor audiovisual y de videojuegos: una mirada al mercado. *La linterna del traductor*, 4.

Ulrych, M. (2013). Diversity, uniformity and creativity in translation. In: S. Petrilli (Ed.), *Translation, Translation* (pp. 133–151). Amsterdam: Rodopi.

Zabalbeascoa, P. (1997). Dubbing and the nonverbal dimension of translation. In: F. Poyatos (Ed.), *Nonverbal Communication and Translation* (pp. 327–342). Amsterdam: John Benjamins.

Zabalbeascoa, P. (2001). La traducción del humor en textos audiovisuales. In: M. Duro (Ed.), *La traducción para el doblaje y la subtitulación* (pp. 251–263). Madrid: Cátedra.

7 Explicitations in Political Texts and the Translator's Rationale

Caiwen Wang

Introduction

This study responds to a call initiated by Chesterman (2004) and Halverson (2003, 2010) and later echoed by Jiménez-Crespo (2015) that the phenomenon of explicitations needs to be tested on different translation modalities and types, and on a cognitive basis. Our focus is explicitations in the out-of-mother-tongue translation of figures of speech ("FIGs" hereafter) in political texts. The aims are to examine explicitations and the cognitive process behind them, so as to contribute to our understanding of explicitations from a new angle.

Translation scholars often attribute the concept of explicitation to Blum-Kulka (1986), where the term is narrowly used to refer to the explication of implied cohesive ties. Some also went on to offer their own definition. For example, in their *Dictionary of Translation Studies*, Shuttleworth and Cowie (1997, p. 55) defined explicitation as "the phenomenon which frequently leads to TT stating ST information in a more explicit form than the original." Our literature review shows that later definitions of explicitations such as this are close to theorisations of the concept earlier than Blum-Kulka. For example, Vinay and Darbelnet (1958/1995, p. 342), the first scholars to propose the concept, defined it as:

> A stylistic translation technique which consists of making explicit in the target language what remains implicit in the source language because it is apparent from either the context or the situation.

For another example, Nida (1964, p. 227) used the term "addition" rather than "explicitation" when referring to the incorporation of elements that "may legitimately be incorporated into a translation." According to Murtisari (2016), Nida's notion is similar to Vinay and Darbelnet's explicitation. Murtisari's reading of Nida's addition is that such additions are "restricted to information that is clearly recoverable from the text or context," may be "grammatical, such as filling out elliptical expressions, or use of classifiers and connectives to create 'structural alteration,'" and may also involve amplification, i.e., "the explicitation of meaning derivable from context, which may be related to the text's socio-cultural context, in order to enhance readability or to avoid misunderstanding when there is ambiguity" (2016, p. 68).

We take the stance that Nida's "addition," Murtisari's understanding of it, Vinay and Darbelnet's concept of explicitations, and Shuttleworth and Cowie's new definition are all synonymous, and they cover a wide range of issues in the phenomenon, thus are more suitable for research looking for translation universals (Baker, 1993).

In an often-cited encyclopaedia article, Klaudy (1998, p. 107) distinguished between four kinds of explicitation in translation, as below:

- Obligatory explicitation: Caused by lexicogrammatical differences between the source language (SL) and the target language (TL).
- Optional explicitation: Motivated by differences in stylistic preferences between SL and TL.
- Pragmatic explicitation: Motivated by differences in cultural and/or world knowledge shared by members of SL and TL communities.
- Translation-inherent explicitation: Caused by "the nature of the translation process itself."

These categories all seem self-explanatory and thus far most studies in the literature (see Tables 7.1 and 7.2) focus on optional explicitation, which we believe serves the purpose of studying explicitations as a candidate for translation universals. There is one study on obligatory explication (Južnič, 2013) and one on pragmatic/cultural explicitation (Perego, 2003). Regarding translation-inherent explicitation, Becher (2010) proposes that this concept should be abandoned as there is no evidence for its existence. Becher (2010) also points out that Klaudy's four categories are not mutually exclusive, as optional explicitation and pragmatic explicitation typically overlap. In the current study, we align with this view and understand the first three of Klaudy's categories along with Vinay and Darbelnet's generic definition of explicitation as follows:

- Obligatory explicitation. This occurs when a translator has no other options except for making explicit the ST implicit meaning due to the differences between a source language/culture and a target language/culture, as the implicit way of translation is not acceptable in a TL. Klaudy relates these differences to lexicogrammatical ones. In the current research, the differences between an SL and TL are extended to cultural ones, which may lead to either obligatory or optional explicitation in translation.

- Optional explicitation. This occurs when a translator chooses one of two available/acceptable options – one explicit and the other implicit. The translator's choice of the explicitation strategy could be due to stylistic preferences or their non-knowledge of the implicit option, to be confirmed by evidence.
- Pragmatic explicitation. This can be obligatory or optional, depending on whether or not the meaning of a pragmatic concept can only be made explicit or can optionally be made explicit, due to the cultural and/or world knowledge shared by members of SL and TL communities.

The source political texts for our study, all written by academics in political science and comprising the book titled 中国周边安全形势评估 (English title: *China's Belt and Road Initiatives and Its Neighbouring Diplomacy*, 2016; also see the section of Methodology), belong to the category "politically relevant texts by non-politicians" as defined by Shäffner (1997, p. 132):

> These are speeches or essays and articles by writers and intellectuals. At a first glance, these texts may not seem to belong to the category of political texts at all. They probably are not prototypical exemplars of political texts, but they are nevertheless politically relevant.

As one of the different translation modalities and types in Jiménez-Crespo's terminology (2015), politically relevant texts by non-politicians have not been studied yet for explicitations, though there are studies of texts by politicians, such as Tong (2013a, 2013b), where works by China's former chairman Deng Xiaoping were studied, and Li (2014), where works by China's former premier Wen Jiabao were studied.

In discussing the translation strategies for political texts, Shäffner (*ibid.*, p. 138) contends that

> the most important factor determining the particular textual make-up of the TT is its function in the TL community – taking into account the necessity to reflect anew about the status of SL culture and TL culture as well as of ST and TT in view of internationalisation processes.

In a similar vein, Tong (2013a) refers to the differences between SL and TL cultures as translation difficulties in translating political texts by political figures and further hypothesises that explicitation is the solution. Nelson (2018) has found that political texts are closely bound to the source culture and consequently require a high degree of explication for the target-text addressee.

Tong (2013a, 2013b) and Li (2014) have both found explicitations in translations of political texts by politicians. Such explicitations occur with cohesive ties, thus merely in the lexicogrammatical sense. Evidence of explicitations in the sociocultural or pragmatic sense is yet lacking.

We seek to look into the translation of FIGs in political texts so as to investigate explicitations in the socio-cultural or pragmatic sense. Two research questions are asked:

(1) Do explicitations occur with the translation of FIGs in out-of-mother-tongue translation of political texts?
(2) Why do translators decide to use the explicitation strategy?

Explicitations: The Current Status Quo

Approaches to Studying Explicitations

Methodologically, there have been two lines of research into explicitation in literature. The first line of research uses comparable corpora, which consist of "two separate collections of texts in the same language: one corpus consists of original texts in the language in question and the other consists of translations in that language from a given source language or languages," and both "cover a similar domain, variety of language and time span, and [are] of comparable length" (Baker, 1995, p. 234). The aim of comparable corpus study is to investigate whether or not "translations tend to be more explicit on a number of levels than original texts" (Olohan, 2002, p. 154), thus (dis-)confirming translation universals or even translation language (Alasmri & Kruger, 2018). The second line of research employs parallel corpora where translations are compared with their source texts to examine what has been made explicit. Parallel corpus study shares the aim of comparable corpus study with respect to explicitations.

Our reviews of existing empirical studies employing the above two approaches are presented in Tables 7.1 and 7.2, respectively. The studies listed in Table 7.1, i.e. those adopting the comparable corpus approach, have confirmed that explicitation is a universal feature for translation, at least as far as cohesive ties, lexical items, and syntactic usage are concerned. The exceptions are Konšalová's (2007) and Van Beveren, De Sutter, and Colleman's (2018) studies. As is also clear, pragmatic explicitations have not been studied yet. Existing parallel corpus studies, i.e. those presented in Table 7.2, have also confirmed that explicitation may be a universal phenomenon, except for Molés-Cases (2019). Like in comparable corpus studies, cohesive ties and syntactic usages are common research objects, but not pragmatic explicitations.

Table 7.1 Existing Comparable Corpus Studies of Explicitations

Empirical Study	Research Object	Field/Register	Are Explicitations the Main Feature Found (Yes or No)
Olohan and Baker (2000)	Optional *that*	Various	Y
Olohan (2002)	• Optional relative pronoun *wh-/that* • Optional *while* in **ing* and *after* in **having + participle* • Optional *in order* in **in order to*	Various	Y
Pápai (2004)	• Personal pronouns • Shifts in cohesion • Instances of disambiguation • Additions of linguistic and extra-linguistic information etc. (The guiding principle for the selection being to "find steps towards an easy-to-understand, better structured, better organized and disambiguated text" [2004, p. 148])	Literary and non-literary texts	Y
Konšalová (2007)	• Finite verbs in main and subordinate clauses • Participial phrases and infinitive constructions • Deverbative nouns and adjectives	Popular texts on history	Y for German translations; N for Czech translations
Jiménez-Crespo (2011)	• Personal pronouns • Navigation menus	Localised corporate websites from the largest US companies addressed to customers in Spain	Y
Marco (2012)	• Substituting pronoun (one[s])	Literary texts	Y when clarity or even intelligibility are at stake
Zufferey and Cartoni (2014)	Backward causal connectives (consequence–reason connectives)	Minutes from the European Parliament	Variable
Li (2014)	Pronouns	Political texts	Y

(Continued)

Table 7.1 Continued

Empirical Study	Research Object	Field/Register	Are Explicitations the Main Feature Found (Yes or No)
Jiménez-Crespo (2015)	Navigation menus	Web localisation of social networking sites	Y[1]
Jiménez-Crespo (2017)	Medical terminology	Translated US medical websites addressed at laymen Spanish	Y
Jiménez-Crespo and Tercedor Sánchez (2017)	Medical terminology	US websites translated into Spanish	Y
Van Beveren, De Sutter and Colleman (2018)	Optional *om* (the explicit prepositional complementiser for infinitive complements)	Various	N
Marco (2018)	Connectives indicating result/consequence and those signalling contrast/concession	Literary texts	N in general, but Y with connectives expressing consequence
Feng, Crezee, & Grant (2018)	Collocation	Business texts	Y
Alasmri & Kruger (2018)	Conjunctive markers	Creative fictional narratives and legal writing	Y, but this is strongly conditioned by register
Molés-Cases (2019)	Manner-of-motion expressions	Narrative texts	Y

Table 7.2 Existing Parallel Corpus Studies of Explicitations

Empirical Study	Research Object	Field/Register	Are Explicitations the Main Feature Found (Yes or No)
Øverås (1998)	Cohesion	Fiction	Y
Perego (2003)	Cultural, channel-based and reduction-based explicitations	Film subtitling	Y when translators dealt with objects or events unknown in the target culture and pertaining to the realms of history and politics; Y when elicited by a shift from the visual non-verbal channel or from the auditive non-verbal channel to the visual verbal channel, namely, the written language, and Y when some information is made more important and focal by reduction
Pápai (2004)	• Shifts in cohesion • Instances of disambiguation • Additions of linguistic and extra-linguistic information etc.		Y
Konšalová (2007)	• Finite verbs in main and subordinate clauses • Participial phrases and infinitive constructions • Deverbative nouns and adjectives	Popular texts on history	Y
Denturck (2012)	Expression of causal relations	Novels	Y
Tong (2013a)	Pronouns	Political texts	Y
Tong (2013b)	Connectives of reason and result	Political texts	Y
Južnič (2013)	Nominalised infinitive	Literary and non-literary texts	Y, and obligatory due to differences between Italian and Slovene
Li (2014)	Pronouns	Political texts	Y
Krogsgaard (2017)	• Nominalisations • Passives • System-bound terms • Elliptical phrases	Legal texts	Y
Molés-Cases (2019)	Manner-of-motion expressions	Narrative texts	Y

Reasons for Explicitations

Literature discussions on the grounds for explicitation are very much from a third-party point of view, rather than from translators themselves. Studying subtitles, Perego (2003) suggested that the reason for explicitation is to facilitate comprehension by viewers. Explaining why translators tend to add (and sometimes remove) connectives in translation, Becher (2011, p. 32) listed five reasons: to comply with the communicative norms of the target language community; to exploit specific features of the target language system; to deal with specific restrictions of the target language system; to avoid stylistically marked ways of expression; and to optimise the cohesion of the target text. Theorising translation management, Pym (2015, p. 76) proposed that "explicitation simply reduces the risk of 'end-user misunderstanding.'" Discussing their findings, Van Beveren et al. (2018; see Table 7.1) pointed out that the reason that Dutch translators use the less explicit grammatical form in question is that in Dutch this is the more established/acceptable usage.

Our contestation is that these third-party assumptions need to be supported by evidence from a cognitive perspective, especially by investigating what happens in translators' minds when they decide to implement or not to implement explicitation. Among the three research questions Tong (2013a) asked, one is "Why are the strategies of explicitation employed by professional translators under such circumstances?" This question would be a good attempt, if asked to translators, to find out what translators think of their implementation. Nevertheless, Tong (2013a, p. 284) explained, from the stance of a third party, that this is because "[p]rofessional translators are able to process the source text in more depth owing to their translation expertise and thus will utilize the explicitation strategies to convey the underlying meaning of the source text." Similarly, Tong (2013b, p. 301) suggested that

> [a]s for the reasons why the explicitation strategies are used in the first place, the factors are many-fold, which involve the translator's conscious efforts to overcome linguistic constraints, the translator's conscious efforts to overcome socio-cultural constraints, the translator's subjectivity and the translation process per se.

Directionality of Translation

Directionality is not clear in all but one of the studies listed in Tables 7.1 and 7.2. The one exception is Perego (2003), where the researcher made it clear that the subtitle translators translating from Hungarian to Italian are Hungarian, "thus performing a very unusual and delicate task, whose impact on the quality and on the validity of the results cannot be neglected" (2003, p. 72). Perego goes on to state that:

Certainly, the ideal condition calls for a perfect bilingual and bicultural translator, although the 'traditional' position and hidden assumption that translators cannot translate into a non-mother tongue is shared by most of the contemporary theoreticians. Nevertheless, in 'peripheral language communities', the prevailing practice sees translators often working into a language that is non-native to them.

(p. 72)

We agree that whether translations are conducted into or out of one's mother tongue matters for research in explicitation and may be significant for the validity of relevant research results. It is therefore important for researchers to make directionality a clear point of departure. For the English and Mandarin Chinese pair, translation from Chinese to English is mostly done by Chinese natives, and it is not a peripheral language community given the large population of both English and Chinese and active translation business from Chinese to English (Xu & Wang, 2011). It follows that studying translations from Chinese to English by Chinese native speakers will contribute to our knowledge of explicitation as a candidate for translation universals.

It should be noted that this issue of directionality is different from the also important issue of direction in the asymmetry hypothesis by Klaudy and Károly (2005, p. 14). Klaudy and Károly's asymmetry hypothesis states that explicitations in the L1 → L2 direction are not always counterbalanced by implicitations in the L2 → L1 direction because translators, if they have a choice, prefer to use operations involving explicitation, and often fail to perform optional implicitation. In their hypothesis, Klaudy and Károly implicitly foreground into-mother-tongue translation, whether the direction is L1 → L2 or L2 → L1. We take the stance that if the study of explicitation is to find translation universals, then it is important to study translations by both native and non-native speakers of a target language.

Methodology

To answer the first of our research questions, we employed the parallel corpus approach and studied the Chinese book titled 中国周边安全形势评估 and its English version titled *China's Belt and Road Initiatives and Its Neighboring Diplomacy*.[2] To answer the second of our research questions, the commissioned translator, a Chinese native, was sent a questionnaire and interviewed afterwards. Details of our methodology are as follows.

Step 1
All cases of FIGs in the source book (ST) were manually identified along with their English translations (TT). These translations were then examined by following Vinay and Darbelnet's definition in order to identify cases of explicitation, be it optional or obligatory. Referring

to the coding criterion, Séguinot said that "[t]o prove that there was explicitation, there must have been the possibility of a correct but less explicit or less precise version" (1988, p. 108). In our study, this conception is for coding optional explicitations, and cases where the less explicit or less precise version is not possible and thus the explicit form is the only option are coded as obligatory explicitations.

Step 2

A questionnaire was designed according to the data analysis results from Step 1 and sent to the translator. The translator was asked six questions as in Table 7.4. The first four questions are related to the translation strategies identified for translating FIGs and are accompanied by examples. The other two questions are related to the general translation process. The translator was asked to recall her translation process and wrote down what came to her mind and what she did when she was translating. We believed that these questions would generate data that reveals the "characteristics or skills of the actual performer of the translation" (Zahedi, 2013, p. 43), thus sharpening our understanding of explicitations from a cognitive perspective. The questionnaire was prepared and replied to in Chinese, followed by an interview over the social media WeChat in our attempt to seek the translator's clarifications of what she said in the questionnaire. Table 7.4 shows our translation of both our questions and the translator's answers. The translation incorporates the translator's clarifications from our interviews and is kept as literal as possible in our attempt to keep the data as when they were collected, thus may read as being redundant.

Of note is that the questionnaire was not implemented immediately after the translation as is the usual case for retrospective questionnaire surveys, but was implemented after the translation had been despatched to the client. Since this relatively large book was translated by one professional translator alone, we think the translator's memory of the translation process for big recurrent translation problems like FIGs has not faded in a way that would affect our research. The translator herself also reported that her memory of the translation process was fresh and was pleased that someone "bothered" to ask her about her translation process, which involved a lot of hard work.

Data and Data Analysis

Data of Explicitations and Analysis Results

Explicitations

Our parallel corpora consist of 163,329 Chinese characters for the ST (equivalent to approximately 108,886 English words) and their English translations.[3]

130 cases of FIGs were identified in the ST. These FIGs were then transferred into an Excel spreadsheet. Their English translations were transferred into the same Excel spreadsheet into a different column. Forty-three cases of explicitation in the translations were identified as optional and three cases as obligatory. Below are two examples for optional explicitations.

Example 1

ST: 目前，俄罗斯在中亚推动"欧亚联盟"有心无力，尤其是资金投入上的巨大缺口，是影响俄罗斯与中亚合作的最大**瓶颈**。

TT: As to promote its Eurasian Union, Russia is strong in will but weak in power at present, especially when its shortage in funds becomes the biggest *obstacle* to making progress in its cooperation with Central Asia.

In this example, the ST metaphor "瓶颈" (literal translation: bottleneck) is translated as "obstacle."

Example 2

ST: 为了防止中国利用亚投行的建立影响和改变国际金融秩序，美日有可能会加大对东盟外交的力度以使东盟国家对亚投行产生**离心力**。

TT: In order to prevent China from influencing and changing the international financial order through the establishment of the AIIB, USA and Japan are likely to intensify the relationship with ASEAN to make member countries *not to unite* for the AIIB.

In this example, the ST metaphor "离心力" ("centrifugal force," a term borrowed from the field of physics) is translated as "not to unite."

Apart from explicitation, the translator also used the following three translation methods.

Translating the ST FIG as a FIG

Example 3

ST: 中国应在与中亚国家的具体合作中顾及俄罗斯的传统影响，尽量避免与俄罗斯主导的"欧亚经济联盟"产生利益竞争，巧妙利用俄罗斯与这些国家的"历史遗产"，让"丝路资金"成为盘活中亚经济的"润滑剂"。[4]

TT: China should consider Russia's conventional influence on these countries and try to avoid interest competing with Eurasians Economic Union when cooperating with five Middle Asian countries. China should subtly use history legacy from Russia and these countries so that

Silk Road could be *lubricants* of the economic engine in Middle Asia.

In this example, the ST metaphor "润滑剂" is translated as a metaphor, namely, "lubricants".

There are 75 such cases. These include six cases where the FIGs are back-translated into a TL FIG, as illustrated below.

Back Translation

Example 4

ST: 人们担心，一旦中国采取扩张型战略，与美国争夺影响力，世界就会陷入 "修昔底德陷阱"，发生大国争端，进而引发大的战争。

TT: People are worrying that the world will fall into *the Thucydides's trap*, conflicts among big powers arise, and that larger wars will be triggered once China adopts expansionary strategy and starts to vie with the USA for global influence.

The ST metaphor "修昔底德陷阱" is a loan metaphor. The translator back-translated it literally.

Omitting the ST FIG

Example 5

ST: 利用俄罗斯、蒙古国和中亚国家经济发展需要**搭乘**中国"顺风车"的良好机遇期，中国完全可以运用资金、技术和人力资源等优势，有效利用俄罗斯在中亚和蒙古国合作中的积极因素，在"亲、诚、惠、容"外交理念指导下，借助准备启动的"亚投行"和"丝路基金"加强基础设施建设。

TT: China can take advantage of its capital, technology and human resource, make full use of all active factors in cooperation among Russia, Middle Asian countries and Mongolia, follow the guidance of neighborhood diplomacy featuring amity, sincerity, mutual benefit, inclusiveness, and strengthen infrastructure construction under the framework of Asian Infrastructure Investment Bank and Silk Road Fund at the time when China is needed during economic development of Russia, Mongolia, and Middle Asian countries.

The ST metaphor "搭乘"…"顺风车" literally means "take a lift/free ride from…." It is omitted from the TT together with the adverbial phrase containing it.

Nine cases of omission were identified in the TT.
Table 7.3 shows the general picture of how FIGs in the ST were treated by the translator.

Table 7.3 Data of Explicitations

Total Number of ST FIGs	Translation Strategies	
130	Optional explicitation	43 (43/130 = 33.08%)
	Obligatory explicitation	3 (3/130 = 2.31%)
	FIG, including back translation	75 (75/130 = 57.69%)
	Omission	9 (9/130 = 6.92%)

It can be concluded that optional explicitation occurs at a high frequency though it is not the most frequently used translation strategy, and that in the vast majority of cases, FIGs are translated as FIGs.

As FIGs belong to cultural issues and thus would be expected to be treated with explicitation more often, we hope the questionnaire will reveal the reasons behind the translator's choices of strategy.

Data from Questionnaire and Analysis Results

The translator's answers to the six questions are presented in Table 7.4 below.

Table 7.4 Data from Questionnaire

Question	Answer
1. In your [the translator's] first method, you translated a FIG as a FIG, as illustrated [examples omitted]. Could you recall the moments when you translated this way and provide the reasons for your action?	If there is an equivalent TL FIG, I would translate the source FIG as a FIG, e.g. "瓶颈" vs. "bottleneck," both meaning "obstacle" for the context, "搭便车" vs. "take/offer a free ride," both meaning "take the advantage of," and "润滑剂" vs. "lubricants," both meaning "something that lessens or prevents friction or difficulty." Sometimes, I also amplified the context a bit for the TL readers to recognise a particular FIG. For example, I would say "the lubricant of the economic engine" instead of merely "the lubricant."
2. In your second method, you back-translated a FIG by using the TL FIG, as illustrated [examples omitted]. Could you recall the moments when you translated this way and provide the reasons for your action?	The Chinese for the FIG is borrowed for the TL. A back translation will be easier to understand and more acceptable for the TL readers.

(Continued)

Table 7.4 Continued

Question	Answer
3. In your third method, you did not translate a FIG as a FIG, but instead used plain language to convey the meaning intended, as illustrated [examples omitted]. Could you recall the moments when you translated this way and provide the reasons for your action?	Although I didn't think translating the FIG as a FIG is a problem, I was either worried about translationese, such as "开花结果" vs. "blossom and bear fruits" or "yield good results," or worried about the inadequacy of contextual information for TL readers to fully appreciate the source FIG, such as 蝴蝶效应" vs. "butterfly effect." Another reason is I wanted to vary my expressions to make my translation read more interesting for TL readers. For example, at one time, I translated "瓶颈" as "bottleneck," but at another time I translated it as "obstacle," because this metaphor occurs very frequently in the source book. In my translation of FIGs, my major concern is whether or not my way will be intelligible and acceptable for the TL readers given that they are in a different culture, thus potentially having different perceptions of the same image.
4. In your fourth method, you omitted an ST FIG, as illustrated [examples omitted]. Could you recall the moments when you translated this way and provide the reasons for your action?	Firstly, I believed the context is enough for conveying the meaning intended by a FIG in question, thus if I translated it, the TT would read redundant. Secondly, the rhetorical effect of some FIGs, e.g. "高歌猛进" ("with pomp and pageantry") in the context of China–Korean relation, is that they highlight something political that I believed would cause unfounded speculations or even misunderstandings among TL readers who are particularly sensitive to the specific political issues.
5. Could you recall the reference resources you used when you translated this book? Please tick as many as you used from the list below and add more as appropriate: a. Paper dictionaries b. E-dictionaries c. Corpora d. ST authors e. TL experts, including native speakers of English	I used all the resources listed and used more. Below is the full list: a. Paper dictionaries, such as *The English–Chinese Dictionary* by Lu Gusun b. E-dictionaries incl. Chinese–English and English–Chinese ones, such as Youdao, Google c. Corpora, but I don't remember the specific corpora I referred to d. Source authors (I asked the source authors to explain what they meant by some of their expressions) e. Experts in English that I know, including native speakers f. Peer translators g. Online resources, such as English (e.g. China Daily) and Chinese (e.g. Xinhua Net, websites of government departments) media reports, Baidu, Wikipedia, CNKI, etc. h. English documents of which the Chinese translations are cited in relevant literature housed at the China National Library

(*Continued*)

Table 7.4 Continued

Question	Answer
6. Could you recall your general approach to translating political texts? In other words, what do you think matters most to ensure the best translation quality for the TT?	Be faithful to the source meanings and try my best to convey these meanings. On this basis, I weighed whether or not my expressions or strategies will be acceptable for the target readers in light of their cultural background. At the same time, for those issues that have to do with China's policies, strategies or international relations, I paid special attention so that my translations will not cause bad consequences.

The translator's replies to the questionnaire indicate that when translating FIGs, 1) the translator omitted those that have to do with sensitive political issues or those of which the translation may be read as redundant by TL readers, and 2) for the FIGs not omitted, the translator switched between different translation methods and in so doing, her first and foremost concern was intelligibility and acceptability.

Conclusions

It has become clear to us that during her translation process, the translator drew upon all recommended resources and carefully weighed between different translation strategies, including explicitation, so as to achieve intelligibility and acceptability. In her words, she wanted to make sure that her translation does not sound "translationese," does not read "redundant," and is "acceptable for the target readers in light of their cultural background." This confirms what literature has hypothesised on why explicitation occurs. Our study shows that explicitation is more about abstaining from causing non-understanding or sounding translationese than about avoiding misunderstanding in Pym's (2015) sense. Our study strongly indicates that the translator's translation process for explicitation is a very conscious one and her decision-making on how to translate FIGs is deliberate or purposeful. This supports Tong's view (2013b), but contrasts with Olohan (2002, p. 166) where it is suggested that the "tendency not to omit optional syntactic elements may be considered subliminal or subconscious, rather than a result of deliberate decision-making of which the translator is aware."

It has also become clear to us that the operation of explicitation has to do with a translator's competence in the target language. Where the translator was confident that translating a FIG as a FIG would not cause non-understanding/misunderstanding or would not sound translationese, she would not resort to the option of explicitation, but instead would translate a FIG as a FIG. This resonates with Van Beveren, De Sutter, and Colleman (2018) where a less explicit grammatical usage is preferred by native Dutch translators because it is more conventional in Dutch. On the other hand, if the translator was not aware of an available FIG, she would choose to make the meaning explicit. An example is "开花结果" vs. "blossom and bear fruits" or "yield good results," where she chose "yield good results" instead of translating the FIG as a different FIG (e.g. as a pun "turn/become/be fruitful").

Hitherto, pragmatic explicitations have not been studied much, nor explicitations in political texts, nor explicitations in out-of-mother-tongue translation. Neither has there been research on explicitations that employs retrospective questionnaires to examine translators' translation process. Our current study intends to throw some light on optional pragmatic explicitation by studying the translation of FIGs in out-of-mother-tongue translation of political texts, and by examining translators' cognitive process during translation. Our results have shown that explicitations occur at a high frequency, that this reflects a translator's conscious efforts to produce a TT that is easy to understand and culturally/linguistically appropriate for TL readers, and that the implementation of explicitations appears to be related to translators' translation competences in dealing with cultural/pragmatic issues. We call for more evidence to support these conclusions and hope our study will contribute to the theorisation surrounding explicitations (e.g. Becher, 2010; Zufferey & Cartoni, 2014; Pym, 2015) and to translator training in terms of translation competences.

Notes

1 According to the researcher, this research tests explicitation in the collaborative environment (i.e. a specific translation version is selected from available options) and in translation modality (e.g. web localisation) and register (e.g. social networking sites) that did not exist when translation studies set off to systematically study the phenomenon.
2 We thank the Social Sciences Academic Press, Beijing, China for providing us with the source text and its translation. The publisher is one of China's biggest academic publishers. Special thanks go to Ms Ran Zhao at the Academic Press for her kind assistance in liaising with the commissioned translator.
3 From the author's experience as a professional translator, translation agencies often cite the ratios 1:(1.5–1.8) to be equivalent between English words and Chinese characters. In the current study, the ratio used for calculation is 1:1.5.
4 One of the two anonymous reviewers pointed out an omission in the TT here, where "丝路资金" ("Silk Road Fund") is translated only as "Silk Road."

References

Alasmri, I. and Kruger, H. (2018). Conjunctive markers in translation from English to Arabic: A corpus-based study. *Perspectives*, 26(5): 767–788.
Baker, M. (1993). Corpus linguistics and translation studies. Implications and applications. In: Baker, M., Francis, G. and Tognini-Bonelli, E. (Eds.) *Text*

and Technology. In Honor of John Sinclair (pp. 233–250). Amsterdam: John Benjamins.

Baker, M. (1995). Corpora in translation studies: An overview and some suggestions for future research. *Target*, 7(2): 223–243.

Becher, V. (2010). Abandoning the notion of "translation-inherent" explicitation: Against a dogma of translation studies. *Across Languages and Cultures*, 11(1): 1–28.

Becher, V. (2011). When and why do translators add connectives? *Target*, 23(1): 26–47.

Blum-Kulka, S. (1986). Shifts of cohesion and coherence in translation. In: House, J. and Blum-Kulka, S. (Eds.) *Interlingual and Intercultural Communication. Discourse and Cognition in Translation and Second Language Acquisition Studies* (pp.17–35). Tübingen: Narr.

Chesterman, A. (2004). Beyond the particular. In: Mauranen, A. and Kujamäki, P. (Eds.) *Translation Universals: Do They Exist?* (pp. 33–50). Amsterdam: John Benjamins.

Denturck, K. (2012). Explicitation vs. implicitation: A bidirectional corpus-based analysis of causal connectives in French and Dutch translations. *Across Languages and Cultures*, 13(2): 211–227.

Feng, H., Crezee, I. and Grant, L. (2018). Form and meaning in collocations: A corpus-driven study on translation universals in Chinese-to-English business translation. *Perspectives*, 26(5): 677–690.

Halverson, S. (2003). The cognitive basis of translation universals. *Target*, 15(2): 197–241.

Halverson, S. (2010). Cognitive translation studies: Developments in theory and method. In: Shreve, G. M. and Angelone, E. (Eds.) *Translation and Cognition* (pp. 349–369). Amsterdam: John Benjamins.

Jiménez-Crespo, M. A. (2011). The future of general tendencies in translation explicitation in web localization. *Target. International Journal of Translation Studies*, 23(1): 3–25.

Jiménez-Crespo, M. A. (2015). Testing explicitation in translation: Triangulating corpus and experimental studies. *Across Languages and Cultures*, 16(2): 257–283.

Jiménez-Crespo, M. A. (2017). Combining corpus and experimental studies: Insights into the reception of translated medical texts. *The Journal of Specialised Translation*, 28: 2–22.

Jiménez-Crespo, M. A. and Sánchez, M. T. (2017). Lexical variation, register and explicitation in medical translation: A comparable corpus study of medical terminology in US websites translated into Spanish. *Translation and Interpreting Studies*, 12(3): 405–426.

Južnič, T. M. (2013). Bridging a grammar gap with explicitation: A case study of the nominalised infinitive. *Across Languages and Cultures*, 14(1): 75–98.

Klaudy, K. (1998). Explicitation. In: Baker, M. (Ed.) *Routledge Encyclopaedia of Translation Studies* (pp. 80–84). London: Routledge.

Klaudy, K. and Károly, K. (2005). Implicitation in translation: Empirical evidence for operational asymmetry in translation. *Across Languages and Cultures*, 6(1): 13–28.

Konšalová, P. (2007). Explicitation as a universal in syntactic de/condensation. *Across Languages and Cultures*, 8(1): 17–32.

Krogsgaard, V. A. (2017). Explicitation in legal translation — A study of Spanish-into-Danish translation of judgments. *The Journal of Specialised Translation*, 27: 104–123.

Li, J. [李娟] (2014). 政论文的英译本中代词的显化现象--- 以政府工作报告为例 [The explicitation of pronouns in Chinese-English translation of political texts--- a case study of the Government Work Report. *Overseas English* [海外英语] 12: 130–132.

Marco, J. (2012). An analysis of explicitation in the COVALT corpus: The case of the substituting pronoun one(s) and its translation into Catalan. *Across Languages and Cultures*, 13(2): 229–246.

Marco, J. (2018). Connectives as indicators of explicitation in literary translation: A study based on a comparable and parallel corpus. *Target. International Journal of Translation Studies*, 30(1): 87–111.

Molés-Cases, T. (2019). Why typology matters: A corpus-based study of explicitation and implicitation of manner-of-motion in narrative texts. *Perspectives*, 27(6): 890–907.

Murtisari, E. T. (2016). Explicitation in translation studies: The journey of an elusive concept. *The International Journal for Translation & Interpreting Research*, 8(2): 64–81.

Nelson, I. (2018). *What's Hiding behind France's New National Front? Translating French Political Discourse for an English-Speaking Reader* (Doctoral dissertation, University of Geneva).

Nida, E. (1964). *Toward a Science of Translating: With Special Reference to Principles and Procedures Involved in Bible Translating*. Leiden: Brill.

Olohan, M. (2002). Leave it out! Using a comparable corpus to investigate aspects of explicitation in translation. *Cadernos de Tradução*, 9: 153–169.

Olohan, M. and Baker, M. (2000). Reporting that in translated English. Evidence for subconscious processes of explicitation? *Across Languages and Cultures*, 1(2): 141–158.

Øverås, L. (1998). In search of the third code: An investigation of norms in literary translation. *Meta*, 43(4): 571–588.

Pápai, V. (2004). Explicitation. A universal of translated text? In: Mauranen, A. and Kujamäki, P. (Eds.) *Translation Universals. Do They Exist?* (pp. 143–164). Amsterdam: John Benjamins.

Perego, E. (2003). 'Evidence of explicitation in subtitling: Towards a categorisation. *Across Languages and Cultures*, 4(1): 63–88.

Pym, A. (2015). Translating as risk management. *Journal of Pragmatics*, 85: 67–80.

Séguinot, C. (1988). Pragmatics and the explicitation hypothesis. *TTR Traduction, Terminologie, Rédacton*, 1(2): 106–111.

Shäffner, C. (1997). Strategies of translation political texts. In: Trosborg, A. (Ed.) *Text Typology and Translation* (pp. 120–142). Amsterdam: John Benjamins.

Shuttleworth, M. and Cowie, M. (1997). *Dictionary of Translation Studies*. Manchester: St. Jerome Publishing.

Tong, Y. (2013a). Corpus-based study on explicitation of personal pronouns in Chinese-English translation. *Applied Mechanics and Materials*, 411–414: 283–286.

Tong, Y. (2013b). Corpus-based study on the explicitation strategies in political text translation. *Applied Mechanics and Materials*, 411–414: 298–301.

Van Beveren, A., De Sutter, G. and Colleman, T. (2018). Questioning explicitation in translation studies: A multifactorial corpus investigation of the om-alternation in translated and original Dutch. Accessed October 2018 from: http://hdl.handle .net/1854/LU-8559947.

Vinay, J. and Darbelnet, J. (1958/1995). *Comparative Stylistics of French and English: A Methodology for Translation*. Amsterdam: John Benjamins.

Xu, M. and Wang, C. (2011). Translation students' use and evaluation of online resources for Chinese-English translation at the word level. *Translation and Interpreting Studies*, 6(1): 62–86.

Zahedi, S. (2013). L2 translation at the periphery: A meta-analysis of current views on translation directionality. *TranscUlturAl*, 5(1–2): 43–60. Accessed from: http: //ejournals.library.ualberta.ca/index.php/TC.

Zufferey, S. and Cartoni, B. (2014). A multifactorial analysis of explicitation in translation. *Target. International Journal of Translation Studies*, 26(3): 361–384.

8 A Corpus-Driven Multi-Dimensional Analysis of Interpreted Discourses in Political Settings

Bing Zou and Binhua Wang

Introduction

International communication of political discourses from governments and institutions has recently been drawing much attention from academia. Researchers of different disciplinary backgrounds, including cultural studies, communication studies, and translation studies, have shown their growing interest in the forms, approaches, patterns, methods, and effects of international communication of political discourses. In the field of Translation Studies, interesting findings have been made in terms of the operational norms of interpreted political discourses as well as the interpreters' behavioural norms and communication strategies. Further questions that are worthy of exploration include: what are the linguistic styles of translated texts and/or interpreted discourses in political settings? How are the translated English texts and interpreted English discourses in political settings different from each other, as well as from original English political texts and/or discourses? These questions serve as an important driving force for the current study, which aims at exploring the typical styles and common patterns as well as distinctive features of interpreted discourses in political settings by means of a corpus-driven multi-dimensional approach.

Interpreted Discourses in Political Settings

Interpreted discourses have become a growing focus of research with the rise of descriptive interpreting studies in recent years (Wang, 2013). Previous studies have focused on norms in interpreting, interpreting strategies, and translation universals in interpreting products, but there is a lack of investigation to reveal the global linguistic features of interpreted discourses, i.e. *interpretese* (Shlesinger, 2008) or the linguistic and/or paralinguistic features that are typical of interpreting discourses and that can make interpreting discourses distinct from other types of discourses such as non-interpreted discourses and/or translated texts. Descriptive studies of the global linguistic features of interpreted discourses will surely add further insights to our understanding of the complex nature of interpreting activities.

Interpreting in political settings, or political interpreting, also mentioned by other scholars as diplomatic interpreting (Roland, 1982; Buri, 2015) or public service interpreting (De Pedro Ricoy et al., 2009; Munyangeyo et al., 2016; Valero-Garcés & Tipton, 2017), provides much information not only about the interpreting activity but also about the political practice. Among all types of political settings, the political press conference is a typical one and also a good "example of institutionalised forms of political discourse" (Schäffner, 2017, p. 154). Specifically, in the English–Chinese language pair, Chinese premiers' press conferences during the NPC and CPPCC sessions have aroused much attention from scholars of interpreting studies. Many (parallel) corpora have been built by collecting and disposing the bilingual (original Chinese and interpreted English) discourses of Chinese premiers' press conferences, including the Chinese–English Conference Interpreting Corpus (CECIC) (Hu & Tao, 2010), the Corpus of Chinese–English Interpreting for Premiers' Press Conferences (CEIPPC) (Wang, 2012; Wang & Zou, 2018), the Chinese–English Political Discourse Corpora (CE-PolitDisCorp) (Gu, 2018), the Chinese/English Political Interpreting Corpus (CEPIC) (Pan, 2019), etc. Based on these corpora, previous studies contribute much to the discussion about such issues as explicitation (Hu & Tao, 2009), norms (Wang, 2012), modal verbs (Li & Hu, 2013), communication norms (Wang & Qin, 2015), indefinite quantifiers (Xie & Hu, 2015), collocation and semantic prosody (Pan & Li, 2017), hedging (Pan & Zheng, 2017; Pan, 2020), self-referential items and the use of present perfect (continuous) structures (Gu, 2018), gender difference (Hu & Meng, 2018), lexical chunks (Shao, 2018), stance-taking (Wang & Feng, 2018), uncertainty management (Shen et al., 2019), and explicitation of modality (Fu & Chen, 2019). These mentioned previous studies help disclose in a detailed way some specific aspects of the linguistic features of interpreted political press conference discourses. While these studies are mainly based on parallel corpora and focused on the interpreted discourses, they did not touch upon the issue of what makes the interpreted political discourses different from other types of political discourses (especially original English political discourses). Thus, we propose that it would be of much interest to utilise a comparable corpus and take a comparative standpoint so as to single out the distinctive linguistic features which are typical of interpreted political discourses and can differentiate interpreted political discourses from non-interpreted political discourses. To achieve this goal, the corpus-driven multi-dimensional approach is adopted as a useful methodological tool.

The Corpus-Driven Multi-Dimensional Approach

The multi-dimensional (MD) approach, also called the multi-feature/multi-dimensional (MF/MD) approach, was first developed by Douglas Biber "to describe textual relations among spoken and written genres" (Biber, 1988, pp. 55–56). It is in nature "a corpus-driven methodological approach that identifies the frequent linguistic co-occurrence patterns in a language, relying on inductive empirical/quantitative analysis" (Biber, 2015, p. 212).

By means of this multivariate statistical method, Biber not only redefined the different register characteristics of written texts and spoken discourses, but also provided a methodological model that can be applied to analysing more specialised discourses with different genres and text types (Friginal, 2013, p. 137). Biber's model has been widely accepted by researchers from a variety of fields, and mostly employed to analyse register variations in American English, Brazilian Portuguese, Internetregisters, movie discourses, pop songs, magazine texts, L2 Spanish, etc. (Sardinha & Pinto, 2014). Other researchers have adopted the multi-dimensional approach to conducting research on the distinctive linguistic styles and features of outsourced call centre discourses (Friginal, 2008), world English varieties (Xiao, 2009), moves of English abstracts (Xiao & Cao, 2014), discipline-specific writing (Crossley et al., 2019), etc.

In the field of translation studies, the multi-dimensional approach has also been applied by a few scholars to explore the register features of translated texts and/or interpreted discourses. For instance, Hu (2010) used the multi-dimensional approach to analyse the typical stylistic features of translated Chinese texts, and successfully generated two factors/dimensions with a group of linguistic features respectively: one factor/dimension could help differentiate translated Chinese texts from texts originally written in Chinese, while the other could help differentiate translated literary Chinese texts from translated non-literary Chinese texts. By utilising both monolingual (comparable) and bilingual (parallel) corpora of translational and native Chinese texts, Xiao and Hu (2015) conducted a comprehensive study on the linguistic features of translational Chinese, and found that, along the literate–oral continuum, the oral forms of reformulation markers "are substantially more common in translational than native Chinese" (Xiao & Hu, 2015, p. 114). Xiao (2015) made use of the multi-dimensional approach to investigate the oral–literate continuum of *interpretese*, reflected in interpreted discourses, as "a genre in its own right" (*ibid.*: i); she concluded with the finding that on the dimensions of involvedness and context-boundedness, *interpretese* tends to boast a distinctive feature of literateness on the oral–literate continuum. The previous studies conducted by Hu (2010), Xiao and Hu (2015), and Xiao (2015) show that the corpus-driven multi-dimensional approach is an effective methodological tool for researching the *translatese* of translated texts and/or the *interpretese* of interpreted discourses. These studies also serve as exemplary methodological demonstrations of how to apply the corpus-driven multi-dimensional approach to generating some key factors/dimensions of linguistic features that could represent the distinctive linguistic style of translated texts or interpreted discourses in the Chinese–English language pair. The factors or dimensions (translational/translated vs. non-translational/non-translated, interpreted vs. non-interpreted, literate vs.

oral, etc.) disclosed by these studies offer many implications for our study in singling out some factors or dimensions that are representative of interpreted political discourses.

Research Design

The current study explores the typical linguistic features of interpreted discourses in political settings. With such a research purpose, the study starts by adopting a corpus-driven approach. Specifically, the authors employ the approach proposed by Biber (1988) to analyse linguistic variations between different genres and types of texts/discourses, that is, the multi-dimensional approach. By following Biber's approach in conducting such a corpus-driven study, we want to answer the following two research questions: 1) What factors or dimensions can be identified for differentiating interpreted political discourses from other types of political discourses? 2) What are the genres and text types for interpreted political discourses and other types of political discourses that are closest to Biber's findings?

The multi-dimensional approach devised by Biber (1988) is in nature a corpus-driven method integrated with the inferential statistical method, exploratory factor analysis. For the corpus part, we based our study on the analysis of a comparable Chinese–English interpreting corpus of around 400,000 English words in total. The corpus consists of four sub-corpora of different types of discourses in political settings, each of which has about 100,000 English words. The four types of discourses are:

1) *Interpreted discourses* – the consecutively interpreted English discourses of China's premier's press conferences during the NPC & CPPCC sessions from 1998 to 2012.
2) *Government work report* – the English versions of China's premier's government work reports from 2006 to 2012.
3) *Daily press briefing* – the original English discourse of daily press briefings of the US Department of State during the first half month of January 2014.
4) *State address* – the original English versions of the US president's State of the Union Addresses from 1996 to 2012.

The corpus used for this study was POS-tagged by Treetagger and annotated with 67 linguistic features (as shown in Table 8.1) proposed by Biber (1988) for a multi-dimensional analysis. In line with Biber's methodological design of the multi-dimensional analysis, the 67 linguistic features of the four types of discourses are first identified and tagged according to the tagging scheme also proposed by Biber (1988). The frequency of these linguistic features is counted in the current study with the help of AntConc (3.4.3w) and standardised. Table 8.2 shows the standardised frequency (millesimal ratio) of the 67 linguistic features in the corpus.

Table 8.1 The 67 Linguistic Features Proposed by Biber (1988, pp. 223–245)

Abbr.	Linguistic Features	Abbr.	Linguistic Features
VBD	Past tense	CAUS	Causative adverbial subordinators
PEAS	Perfect aspect	CONC	Concessive adverbial subordinators
VPRT	Present tense	COND	Conditional adverbial subordinators
PLACE	Place adverbials	OSUB	Other adverbial subordinators
TIME	Time adverbials	PIN	Total prepositional phrases
FPP1	First-person pronouns	JJ	Attributive adjectives
SPP2	Second person pronouns	PRED	Predicative adjectives
TPP3	Third-person pronouns	RB	Total adverbs
PIT	Pronoun it	TTR	Type-token ratio
DEMP	Demonstrative pronouns	AWL	Word length
INPR	Indefinite pronouns	CONJ	Conjuncts
PROD	Pro-verb do	DWNT	Downtoners
WHQU	Direct WH-questions	HDG	Hedges
NOMZ	Nominalizations	AMP	Amplifiers
GER	Gerunds	EMPH	Emphatics
NN	Total other nouns	DPAR	Discourse particles
PASS	Agentless passives	DEMO	Demonstratives
BYPA	By-passives	POMD	Possibility modals
BEMA	Be as main verb	NEMD	Necessity modals
EX	Existential there	PRMD	Predictive modals
THVC	That verb complements	PUBV	Public verbs
THAC	That adjective complements	PRIV	Private verbs
WHCL	WH-clauses	SUAV	Suasive verbs
TO	Infinitives	SMP	Seemlappear
PRESP	Present participial clauses	CONT	Contractions
PASTP	Past participial clauses	THATD	Subordinator that deletion
WZPAST	Past participial WHIZ deletion relatives	STPR	Stranded preposition
WZPRES	Present participial WHIZ deletion relatives	SPIN	Split infinitives
TSUB	That relative clauses on subject position	SPAU	Split auxiliaries
TOBJ	That relative clauses on object position	PHC	Phrasal coordination
WHSUB	WH relative clauses on subject position	ANDC	Independent clause coordination
WHOBJ	WH relative clauses on object position	SYNE	Synthetic negation
PIRE	Pied-piping relative clauses	XX0	Analytic negation
SERE	Sentence relatives		

Table 8.2 The Standardised Frequency of the 67 Linguistic Features in the Corpus

Abbr. of the Features	Interpreted Discourses	Daily Press Briefing	Government Work Report	State Address
VBD	11.21	20.54	15.42	13.44
PEAS	11.15	5.61	1.51	7.51
VPRT	56.84	95.79	18.75	64.30
PLACE	2.59	2.23	2.18	3.26
TIME	3.90	6.58	0.62	6.80
FPP1	44.65	49.29	33.64	54.34
SPP2	9.24	16.96	0.18	6.75
TPP3	7.31	19.71	4.41	15.09
PIT	6.66	13.58	2.11	7.90
DEMP	5.98	12.95	0.84	4.64
INPR	0.13	0.50	0.02	0.28
PROD	1.02	2.33	0.53	1.97
WHQU	0.80	0.90	0.00	0.09
NOMZ	42.02	29.05	69.15	31.39
GER	5.19	3.59	9.38	4.33
NN	210.16	172.36	237.51	232.04
PASS	6.52	6.15	6.36	4.61
BYPA	0.60	0.53	0.38	0.68
BEMA	14.46	15.01	3.50	11.43
EX	2.07	5.96	0.51	1.18
THVC	5.03	6.24	1.17	2.57
THAC	0.77	0.69	0.16	0.35
WHCL	0.39	1.47	0.01	0.46
TO	25.11	24.86	21.94	27.91
PRESP	0.84	0.95	1.67	1.12
PASTP	0.07	0.15	0.08	0.22
WZPAST	1.36	0.68	2.19	0.84
WZPRES	1.82	1.99	2.56	1.84
TSUB	1.03	2.09	1.80	4.56
TOBJ	1.66	3.09	0.18	1.07
WHSUB	0.94	0.87	0.41	2.34
WHOBJ	0.10	0.20	0.16	0.11
PIRE	0.18	0.38	0.31	0.25
SERE	0.60	1.23	0.41	0.36
CAUS	1.16	1.94	0.08	1.68
CONC	0.34	0.34	0.06	0.09
COND	1.31	4.71	0.08	2.03
OSUB	1.59	1.28	0.80	1.42
PIN	107.31	88.98	108.49	97.95
JJ	76.25	51.20	119.56	68.73
PRED	6.57	4.77	2.04	5.03
RB	32.38	42.47	23.48	27.10
TTR	62.73	47.53	52.86	70.50
AWL	4.7	0.04	0.05	0.04
CONJ	2.99	0.47	0.97	0.68
DWNT	1.64	0.63	0.24	1.77
HDG	0.26	0.92	0.02	0.05

(Continued)

Table 8.2 Continued

Abbr. of the Features	Interpreted Discourses	Daily Press Briefing	Government Work Report	State Address
AMP	4.14	2.80	1.92	0.79
EMPH	5.81	10.39	3.46	7.95
DPAR	0.68	5.11	0.03	1.23
DEMO	13.95	16.33	3.16	12.31
POMD	4.70	6.24	0.74	5.92
NEMD	3.79	1.06	2.79	6.70
PRMD	13.40	7.32	22.60	9.71
PUBV	4.81	10.04	1.45	3.76
PRIV	14.46	22.59	5.11	10.50
SUAV	4.09	5.28	3.57	6.36
SMP	0.13	0.43	0.00	0.11
CONT	4.32	0.17	0.00	0.00
THATD	2.63	5.75	0.29	1.95
STPR	0.36	1.91	0.22	0.50
SPIN	0.38	0.30	1.32	0.22
SPAU	6.10	2.27	5.71	3.38
PHC	13.33	4.01	30.75	12.17
ANDC	9.26	10.05	15.72	15.43
SYNE	1.20	1.42	0.15	1.63
XX0	5.53	8.18	0.79	5.04

Findings and Discussion

Factors and Dimensions Identified

Following Biber's methodological procedures, an exploratory factor analysis with the help of SPSS 17.0 is conducted to find out major factors/dimensions that can differentiate the four types of discourses. Each of the factors/dimensions is represented by a cluster of linguistic features that have a similar explanatory function and can jointly explain one major aspect of difference among different types of discourses. The factors/dimensions are extracted with the method of principal component analysis and are then rotated to better fit the data with the method of varimax with Kaiser normalisation.

After the statistical analysis, three major factors/dimensions of global linguistic features are identified. As is shown in Table 8.3, the cumulative percentage of variance accounted for by all three factors generated via the factor analysis is 100%, which means the three factors altogether account for 100% of the total variance. In other words, the generated three factors can explain all the differences between the four types of discourses in terms of their linguistic features and styles. Figure 8.1 is the scree plot of the factor analysis, which also shows that the three factors identified represent 100% of all linguistic features.

Table 8.4 presents the rotated factor loadings of the generated three factors. The factor loading represents how each linguistic feature is weighted

Table 8.3 Total Variance Explained

Factor	Initial Eigenvalues			Rotation Sums of Squared Loadings		
	Total	% of Variance	Cumulative %	Total	% of Variance	Cumulative %
1	39.767	59.354	59.354	34.775	51.903	51.903
2	15.459	23.073	82.427	19.647	29.324	81.227
3	11.774	17.573	100.000	12.578	18.773	100.000

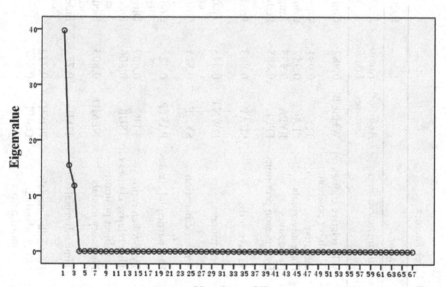

Figure 8.1 Scree Plot of the Factor Analysis.

for each factor, and it also shows the correlation (of values ranging from −1 to +1) between the linguistic feature and the corresponding factor. For instance, the factor loading of the linguistic feature "Seemlappear" with a value of 0.998 means this feature is heavily weighted for and is strongly correlated in a positive way with Factor 1, indicating that the very feature should be an effective variable or indicator of Factor 1. This feature and other linguistic features with a factor loading value above a certain level (set at 0.6 in its absolute value in the current study) can unite as a group or a cluster of variables/indicators – this group or cluster is thus labelled as Factor 1 – which can explain one aspect of the differences between different

Table 8.4 Factor Loadings of the Generated Three Factors

Factor 1			Factor 2			Factor 3		
Linguistic Features	Abbr. of Features	Factor Loadings	Linguistic Features	Abbr. of Features	Factor Loadings	Linguistic Features	Abbr. of Features	Factor Loadings
Seemlappear	SMP	0.998	WH relative clauses on subject position	WHSUB	0.987	Contractions	CONT	0.995
Existential there	EX	0.997	Infinitives	TO	0.981	Word length	AWL	0.991
Public verbs	PUBV	0.993	Place adverbials	PLACE	0.957	Conjuncts	CONJ	0.953
WH-clauses	WHCL	0.991	By-passives	BYPA	0.935	Amplifiers	AMP	0.847
Subordinator that deletion	THATD	0.987	First person pronouns	FPP1	0.885	Perfect aspect	PEAS	0.823
Demonstrative pronouns	DEMP	0.986	Suasive verbs	SUAV	0.883	Predicative adjectives	PRED	0.762
Hedges	HDG	0.986	Downtoners	DWNT	0.845	That adjective complements	THAC	0.74
Discourse particles	DPAR	0.981	Synthetic negation	SYNE	0.825	Other adverbial subordinators	OSUB	0.686
Total adverbs	RB	0.978	Past participial clauses	PASTP	0.82	Concessive adverbial subordinators	CONC	0.673
Stranded preposition	STPR	0.978	Type-token ratio	TTR	0.809	Direct WH-questions	WHQU	0.606
That relative clauses on object position	TOBJ	0.971	That relative clauses on subject position	TSUB	0.806	Present participial clauses	PRESP	−0.648
Sentence relatives	SERE	0.97	Necessity modals	NEMD	0.803	Pied-piping relative clauses	PIRE	−0.724
Conditional adverbial subordinators	COND	0.965	Time adverbials	TIME	0.77	Independent clause coordination	ANDC	−0.739
Private verbs	PRIV	0.963	Possibility modals	POMD	0.713			
Second person pronouns	SPP2	0.954	Other adverbial subordinators	OSUB	0.667			

Pronoun it	PIT	0.944	Causative adverbial subordinators	CAUS	0.662
Indefinite pronouns	INPR	0.912	Predictive modals	PRMD	−0.649
Present tense	VPRT	0.903	Gerunds	GER	−0.662
Analytic negation	XX0	0.879	Past participial WHIZ deletion relatives	WZPAST	−0.685
Emphatics	EMPH	0.875	Nominalizations	NOMZ	−0.716
That verb complements	THVC	0.871	Present participial WHIZ deletion relatives	WZPRES	−0.763
Third person pronouns	TPP3	0.821	Split infinitives	SPIN	−0.766
Direct WH-questions	WHQU	0.789	Agentless passives	PASS	−0.879
Pro-verb do	PROD	0.775			
Demonstratives	DEMO	0.77			
Past tense	VBD	0.751			
Causative adverbial subordinators	CAUS	0.746			
Concessive adverbial subordinators	CONC	0.733			
Be as main verb	BEMA	0.714			
Possibility modals	POMD	0.676			
That adjective complements	THAC	0.664			
Time adverbials	TIME	0.638			
WH relative clauses on object position	WHOBJ	0.638			
Independent clause coordination	ANDC	−0.661			
Nominalizations	NOMZ	−0.684			
Gerunds	GER	−0.715			
Past participial WHIZ deletion relatives	WZPAST	−0.728			

(Continued)

Table 8.4 Continued

Factor 1			Factor 2			Factor 3		
Linguistic Features	*Abbr. of Features*	*Factor Loadings*	*Linguistic Features*	*Abbr. of Features*	*Factor Loadings*	*Linguistic Features*	*Abbr. of Features*	*Factor Loadings*
Split auxiliaries	SPAU	−0.745						
Predictive modals	PRMD	−0.754						
Attributive adjectives	JJ	−0.805						
Phrasal coordination	PHC	−0.826						
Total prepositional phrases	PIN	−0.868						
Total other nouns	NN	−0.975						

types of discourses. Factor 1 thus serves as an umbrella term to represent the whole group or cluster of linguistic features heavily weighted for and strongly correlated with it. The same explanation goes to Factor 2 and Factor 3, respectively. These three factors are exactly what we are most interested in. The next step is to take all the linguistic features under the umbrella of each factor as a whole and try to name these factors by the aspect of difference that this factor can tell between one type of political discourse and another.

A close observation of the three factors generated by means of the factor analysis and the linguistic features grouped by these factors can shed light on the naming of the factors. After a close examination of the data about the factors and linguistic features as are presented in Table 8.4, we find that the three factors, namely Factor 1, Factor 2, and Factor 3, seem to be capable of explaining three respective aspects of differences among the four types of discourses in political settings.

Based on Biber's definition of the 67 linguistic features used for the factor analysis, we find that the cluster of linguistic features of Factor 1 tends to represent the characteristics of oral discourses, making Factor 1 a dimension that might help differentiate the type of written political texts (with distinct written language features) from the type of oral political discourses (with explicit oral language features). The proposal of naming or labelling Factor 1 as an "oral vs. literate" dimension is based on the functions of the cluster of linguistic features grouped under the umbrella of Factor 1. Such linguistic features as seem/appear, hedges, WH-clauses, subordinator that deletion, discourse particles, stranded preposition, sentence relatives, private verbs, second-person pronouns, third-person pronouns, and direct WH-questions are fairly typically used in interpersonal discourses (including both inter-actional conversations and informational speeches), and occur far less frequently in (edited) written texts. By contrast, such linguistic features (with negative factor loading values) as independent clause coordination, gerunds, attributive adjectives, phrasal coordination, total prepositional phrases, and total other nouns are representative of written texts and appear extremely less frequently in oral discourses.

Regarding Factor 2, the cluster of linguistic features under the umbrella of this factor tends to represent the characteristics of interpreted discourses, making Factor 2 a dimension that might help differentiate the type of inter-preted English political discourses (with salient inter-language features induced by the interpreting activity) from the type of original English politi-cal discourses. Thus we propose to name it as an "interpreted vs. non-inter-preted" dimension. The reason why we make such a proposal is based on two considerations. First, many linguistic features under the umbrella of Factor 2 like infinitives, first-person pronouns, suasive verbs, downtoners, and necessity modals are exactly mere renderings of the original Chinese politi-cal discourses, since they are very typical of China's premier's press confer-ence discourses and function with an obvious political appeal. Second, most of the linguistic features with a heavy factor loading accounted for Factor 2 represent both an oral characteristic and a literate characteristic: the orality is represented by such linguistic features as first-person pronouns, suasive verbs, and downtoners, while the literateness is represented by such linguistic features as infinitives, by-passives, synthetic negation, past participial clauses, that relative clauses on subject position, other adverbial subordinators, and causative adverbial subordinators. In other words, Factor 2 seems to imply that interpreted discourses are an intermediate type of discourse, lying somewhere between the two ends along the oral–literate continuum of *interpretese* (Xiao, 2015). It should be noticed that although Factor 2 implies that the interpreted political discourses embody the characteristics of both orality and literateness, such linguistic features (with negative factor loading values) as gerunds, nominalisations, and agentless passives which are typical of literate or written texts could be rarely seen in interpreted political discourses.

As for Factor 3, the cluster of linguistic features with a heavy factor loading accounted for this factor tends to represent the characteristics of well-prepared or well-planned discourses, making Factor 3 a dimension that might help differentiate the type of planned discourses from the type of unplanned discourses. Under the umbrella of Factor 3, such linguistic features as conjuncts, perfect aspect, other adverbial subordinators, and concessive adverbial subordinators are commonly and typically used in the type of planned discourses with an informational or stance-making purpose. That is to say, the type of discourse with a frequent use of these linguistic features tends to be a type of well-planned or well-prepared discourse. As a result, we propose to name Factor 3 as a "planned vs. unplanned" dimension.

Considering that we are analysing the styles and features of texts and discourses in political settings, no matter whether they are interpreted or non-interpreted/original, oral or literate/written, planned or unplanned/spontaneous, it should be noted that some of the linguistic features, heavily weighted for and strongly correlated with the three factors identified, are fairly typical of political texts and discourses. For instance, such features as public verbs, hedges, suasive verbs, downtoners, necessity modals, amplifiers, and predicative adjectives are commonly and frequently used in political texts and discourses.

Genres and Text Types Compared

The above exploratory factor analysis following Biber's multi-dimensional approach helps to identify three factors and dimensions, including: Factor 1 – the "oral vs. literate" dimension, Factor 2 – the "interpreted vs. non-interpreted" dimension, and Factor 3 – the "planned vs. unplanned" dimension. These three factors and dimensions help to reveal the aspects of difference among the four types of discourses in political settings, namely the "interpreted discourses" (of China's premier's press conferences), the (China's premier's) "government work report," the "daily press briefing" (of the US Department of State), and the "state address" (i.e. the US president's State of the Union Address).

The three factors and dimensions seem to indicate three aspects of properties of the interpreted discourses in political settings. First, Factor 1 shows us that the interpreted political discourses are moving along the oral–literate continuum; second, Factor 2 tells us that the interpreted political discourses are surely different from the non-interpreted political discourses; third, Factor 3 reveals to us that the interpreted discourses of China's premier's press conferences might also be moving along the planned–unplanned continuum. These findings shed some new light on the nature of interpreted discourses in political settings. In Biber's study on the variation across speech and writing, Biber (1988) not only proposed via the multi-dimensional approach several factors and dimensions that could help to differentiate speech from writing but also further explored what genre and text type a specific speech discourse or written text belongs to. Biber's exploration motivates us to think about a further question: what genre and text type are the interpreted political discourses closest to?

In order to explore this question, we made a comparison between our research findings and those of Biber's study (1988). With the help of this comparison by means of the Multidimensional Analysis Tagger (v. 1.1) (Nini, 2014), the genres and text types of the four types of political discourses that are closest to those of the texts/discourses identified by Biber (1988) are determined.

With regard to genre, Figure 8.2, Figure 8.3, Figure 8.4, and Figure 8.5 show us the genres that the genres of the four types of discourses in the current study are closest to. It is found that the "interpreted discourses" are closest to the genre of professional letters, while the closet genres for the "daily press briefing," "government work report," and "state address" are respectively prepared speeches, official documents, and professional letters.

Table 8.5 presents a description of the typical features of professional letters, prepared speeches, and official documents according to Biber (1988). Through a comparison between the current study and Biber's study, we determined that the interpreted discourses in political settings are more likely to be categorised into the genre of professional letters rather than the genre of speeches, which is a very interesting finding. When it comes to the activity of interpreting, generally we tend to take it for granted that the interpreted version of a speech should closely, or at least largely, resemble orally presented discourses. What makes the style of the interpreted discourses of China's premier's press conferences so unique? A reasonable explanation would be that in political settings, the interpreting activity is highly sensitive and the interpreters tend to follow consciously or unconsciously the basic principles and norms of political interpreting: be cautious about the choice of diction and stick to the original wording as literally as possible in their

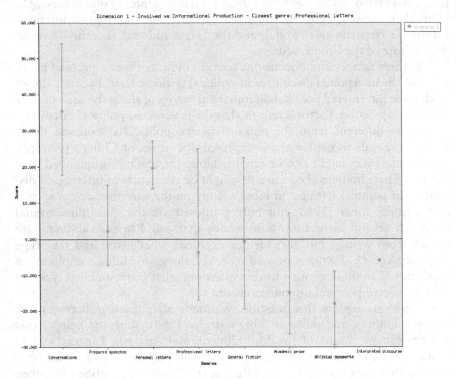

Figure 8.2 The Closest Genre to Interpreted Discourses: Professional Letters.

rendition. As a result, the style of the interpreted political discourses is usually very formal and rigorous. Another explanation comes from the fact that
China's premier's press conferences take the form of questions and answers,
which means the original discourses and the corresponding interpreted discourses should be both informational and interactional. The combination
of these two features leads to the unique style of the interpreted political
discourses.

As an equivalent of the "interpreted discourses," the "daily press briefing" (i.e. the daily press briefings of the US Department of State) discourses
are closest to the genre of prepared speeches. This is understandable because
the US daily press briefings are thought to be well planned and well prepared, and meanwhile, they are close to the oral side along the oral–literate continuum. The "government work report" and the "state address"
are respectively closest to the genre of official documents and the genre of
professional letters – this is also quite understandable because the former
is actually a translated version while the latter is originally a written text.

As regards text types, Figure 8.6 shows the text types that the four types
of discourses involved in the current study are closest to. The statistical

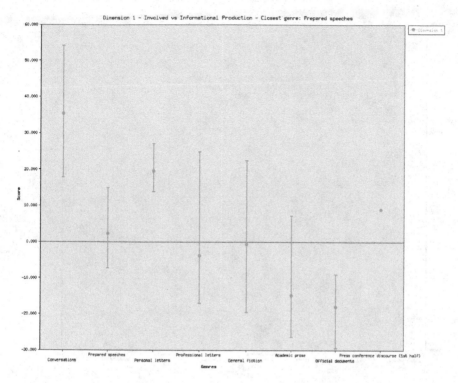

Figure 8.3 The Closest Genre to Daily Press Briefing: Prepared Speeches.

tool Multidimensional Analysis Tagger (v. 1.1) (Nini, 2014) reveals that the "interpreted discourses" are more likely to be labelled as the text type of general narrative exposition, while the closet genres for the "daily press briefing," "government work report," and "state address" are respectively involved persuasion, learned exposition, and involved persuasion.

Figure 8.6 presents a comparison between our data and Biber's data in terms of the five dimensions discovered by Biber (1988). In Dimension 1 – Involved vs. Informational Discourse, the "daily press briefing" discourses are the only type of political discourse among the four that boasts a positive value (above 0.0) along the vertical axis; this indicates that the "daily press briefing" discourses are an involved type of discourse, while the other three types, namely the "interpreted discourses," "state address," and "government work report," have an informational focus. In Dimension 2 – Narration vs. Non-Narrative Concerns, all four types of political discourses, including the "interpreted discourses," belong to a non-narrative type, and among the four types, the "government work report" discourses have the smallest quantity of narrative features. In Dimension 3 – Explicit vs. Situation-Dependent Reference, all four types

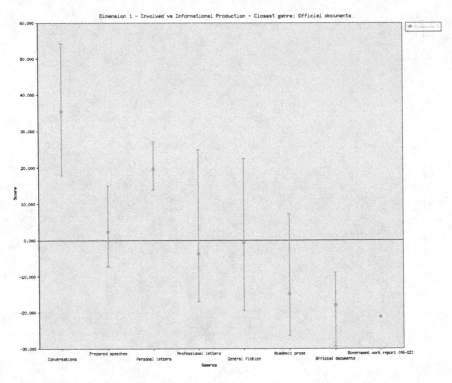

Figure 8.4 The Closest Genre to Government Work Report: Official Documents.

of discourses in political settings take on the style of explicit reference by using overt referential measures to achieve logical cohesion; among the four types, the "government work report" discourses present extremely salient characteristics in extensively using overt cohesive devices, which is very typical of spoken registers (Biber, 1988, p. 193). This should be an interesting point that awaits future in-depth investigation. In Dimension 4 – Overt Expression of Persuasion and Argumentation, all four types of political discourses possess a certain characteristic of explicit persuasion and argumentation. It seems that this finding is in contrast with the conclusive statistical finding (made by the Multidimensional Analysis Tagger) that only the "daily press briefing" and "state address" discourses belong to the text type of involved persuasion. But it should be noted that this conclusive finding is made on the basis of considering all five dimensions in a comprehensive way. In Dimension 5 – Abstract vs. Non-Abstract Information, the "interpreted discourses," with a lot of passive expressions, tend to be the most abstract among the four types of political discourses, while the "daily press briefing" discourses are the least abstract type.

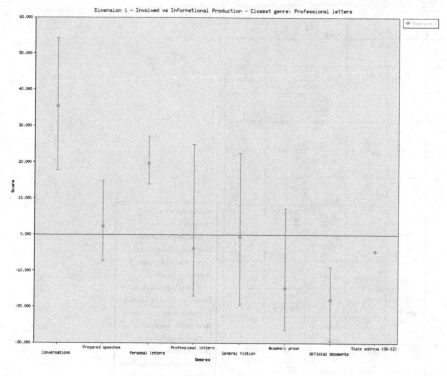

Figure 8.5 The Closest Genre to State Address: Professional Letters.

Table 8.5 Typical Features of the Genres That the Four Types of Discourses Are Closest To

Closest Genres	Typical Features (Biber, 1988)
Professional letters	• written in academic contexts • dealing with administrative matters • formal and directed to individuals • both informational and interactional
Prepared speeches	• planned but without a written text • taken from sermons, university lectures, legal speeches (like final statements in court), political speeches, etc. • highly informational • produced under strict real-time constraints
Official documents	• primarily government documents, also including foundation reports and industry reports • largely non-narrative • extremely abstract • requiring highly explicit and elaborated text-internal reference

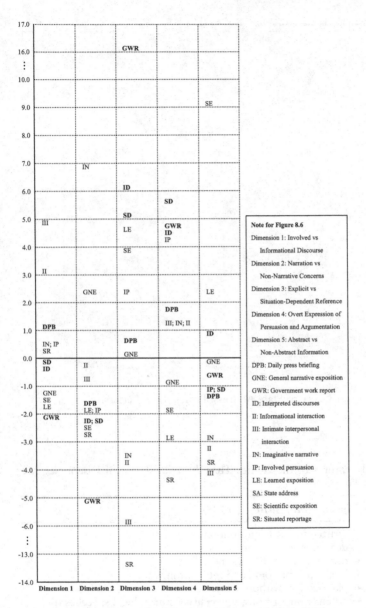

Figure 8.6 Text Types That the Four Types of Political Discourses Are Closest To.

Table 8.6 presents a description of the typical features of general narrative exposition, involved persuasion, and learned exposition according to Biber (1988). It is also very interesting to find that the two types of political discourses produced by the Chinese government, namely the "interpreted discourses" and the "government work report," are closest to the text

Table 8.6 Typical Features of the Text Types That the Four Types of Discourses Are Closest To

Closest Text Types	Typical Features (Biber, 1988)
General narrative exposition	• integrated
	• narrative
Involved persuasion	• non-narrative
	• moderately elaborated
	• very persuasive
Learned exposition	• extremely integrated
	• non-narrative
	• very elaborated
	• non-persuasive
	• moderately abstract

type of exposition, which is a text type that comprehensively describes and explains a theory, a plan, or an idea. As political discourses or texts, both of them are generally believed to have the mission of influencing, persuading, and involving their target audience or readers to accept a policy or a political idea, just as the "daily press briefing" and the "state address" do. The latter two types of discourses produced by the American government are both closest to the text type of involved persuasion, which closely accords with their political intention. This contrast might shed light on a further exploration about the reasons why the interpreted ("interpreted discourses") and translated ("government work report") political discourses or texts possess little function of influencing, persuading, and involving. The very myth exposed by this phenomenon might be of great interest for future studies and might bring some new knowledge about political interpreting and political translation.

Conclusion

In the current study, the authors conducted a corpus-driven analysis of interpreted discourses in political settings by following the multi-dimensional approach proposed by Biber (1988). We have found three factors and dimensions that could help to differentiate oral political discourses from literate or written political discourses, interpreted political discourses from non-interpreted political discourses, and planned political discourses from unplanned political discourses. By comparing our research findings with those of Biber's (1988), we have found that the interpreted political discourses are more likely to be categorised into the genre of professional letters rather than oral speeches. Our findings may shed new light on the understanding of the linguistic features of Chinese–English interpreted discourses in political settings.

As for limitations of the current study, our corpus size is not big enough, so some of the linguistic features and their frequencies might not be salient enough; in our corpus, the tagging and annotation were done only for the 67 features proposed by Biber (1988), so there might be some other interesting linguistic features about interpreted political discourses undiscovered yet. Future studies may continue to explore the representative style of other types of interpreted discourses by applying the corpus-driven multi-dimensional approach.

Acknowledgements

We would like to express our sincere gratitude to the anonymous reviewers and to the editors for their helpful suggestions. Our acknowledgement also goes to the following grants: the 13th Five-Year Project funded by the Guangdong Planning Office of Philosophy and Social Science (Grant No. GD20WZX01–09), the Guangdong Provincial Higher Education Innovative Universities Support Project for Young Innovative Research Talents (Grant No. 2017WQNCX045), and the Research Funds of Academic Programmes Division and Academic Research Division of Guangdong University of Foreign Studies (Grant No. GWJY2017020; 17QN24).

References

Biber, D. (1988). *Variation across Speech and Writing*. New York: Cambridge University Press.

Biber, D. (2015). Corpus-based and corpus-driven analyses of language variation and use. In: B. Heine & H. Narrog (Eds.) *The Oxford Handbook of Linguistic Analysis* (pp. 193–224). Oxford: Oxford University Press.

Buri, M. R. (2015, October 29). Interpreting in diplomatic settings. Accessed January 20, 2020, from http://aiic.net/p/7349.

Crossley, S. A., Kyle, K., & Römer, U. (2019). Examining lexical and cohesion differences in discipline-specific writing using multi-dimensional analysis. In: T. B. Sardinha & M. V. Pinto (Eds.) *Multi-Dimensional Analysis Research Methods and Current Issues* (pp. 127–143). London: Bloomsbury Academic.

De Pedro Ricoy, R., Perez, I. A., & Wilson, C. W. L. (Eds.) (2009). *Interpreting and Translating in Public Service Settings: Policy, Practice, Pedagogy*. London: Routledge.

Friginal, E. (2008). Linguistic variation in the discourse of outsourced call centers. *Discourse Studies*, 10(6), 715–736.

Friginal, E. (2013). Twenty-five years of Biber's multi-dimensional analysis: Introduction to the special issue and an interview with Douglas Biber. *Corpora*, 8(2), 137–152.

Fu, R., & Chen, J. (2019). Negotiating interpersonal relations in Chinese-English diplomatic interpreting: Explicitation of modality as a case in point. *Interpreting. International Journal of Research and Practice in Interpreting*, 21(1), 12–35.

Gu, C. (2018). Forging a glorious past via the 'present perfect': A corpus-based CDA analysis of China's past accomplishments discourse mediat(is)ed at China's interpreted political press conferences. *Discourse, Context and Media*, 24, 137–149.

Hu, K., & Meng, L. (2018). Gender differences in Chinese-English press conference interpreting. *Perspectives*, 26(1), 117–134.

Hu, K., & Tao, Q. (2009). Explicitation in the Chinese -English conference interpreting and its motivation: A study based on parallel corpus. *Journal of PLA University of Foreign Languages*, 4, 67–74.

Hu, K., & Tao, Q. (2010). The compilation and application of Chinese-English conference interpreting corpus. *Chinese Translators Journal*, 5, 49–56.

Hu, X. (2010). A corpus-based multi-dimensional analysis of the stylistic features of translated Chinese. *Foreign Language Teaching and Research*, 6, 451–458.

Li, X., & Hu, K. (2013). A corpus-based study of modal verbs in Chinese-English government press conference interpretation. *Computer-Assisted Foreign Language Education*, 3, 26–32, 74.

Munyangeyo, T., Webb, G., & Rabadán-Gómez, M. (Eds.) (2016). *Challenges and Opportunities in Public Service Interpreting*. Cham: Palgrave Macmillan.

Nini, A. (2014). Multidimensional analysis tagger 1.1 – Manual. Retrieved September 10, 2019, from http://sites.google.com/site/multidimensionaltagger.

Pan, F. (2020). Norms and norm-taking in interpreting for Chinese Government press conferences: A case study of hedges. In: K. Hu & K. H. Kim (Eds.) *Corpus-Based Translation and Interpreting Studies in Chinese Contexts: Present and Future* (pp. 89–114). Cham: Palgrave Macmillan.

Pan, F., & Li, X. (2017). Collocation, semantic prosody and ideology in interpreting for Chinese Government press conferences: A case study of the keyword "development". *Foreign Languages in China*, 6, 90–95.

Pan, F., & Zheng, B. (2017). Gender differences of hedging in interpreting: A corpus-based study. *Across Languages and Cultures*, 18(2), 171–193.

Pan, J. (2019). *The Chinese/English Political Interpreting Corpus (CEPIC)*. Hong Kong: Hong Kong Baptist University Library. Accessed August 15, 2020, from https://digital.lib.hkbu.edu.hk/cepic/

Roland, R. (1982). *Interpreters as Diplomats: A Diplomatic History of the Role of Interpreters in World Politics*. Ottawa: University of Ottawa Press.

Sardinha, T. B., & Pinto, M. V. (Eds.) (2014). *Multi-Dimensional Analysis, 25 Years on: A Tribute to Douglas Biber*. Amsterdam: John Benjamins.

Schäffner, C. (2017). Self-awareness, norms and constraints: Dealing with metaphors in interpreter-meditated press conferences. In: M. Biagini, M. S. Boyd, & C. Monacelli (Eds.) *The Changing Role of the Interpreter: Contextualising Norms, Ethics and Quality Standards* (pp. 149–172). London: Routledge.

Shao, X. (2018). A corpus-based research on structural categories of lexical chunks and "stitching" mode in interpretation. *Shanghai Journal of Translators*, 6, 50–56.

Shen, M., Lv, Q., & Liang, J. (2019). A corpus-driven analysis of uncertainty and uncertainty management in Chinese premier press conference interpreting. *Translation and Interpreting Studies*, 14(1), 135–158.

Shlesinger, M. (2008). Towards a definition of interpretese: An intermodal, corpus-based study. In: G. Hansen, A. Chesterman, & H. Gerzymisch-Arbogast (Eds.) *Efforts and Models in Interpreting and Translation Research: A Tribute to Daniel Gile* (pp. 237–254). Amsterdam: John Benjamins.

Valero-Garcés, C., & Tipton, R. (2017). *Ideology, Ethics and Policy Development in Public Service Interpreting and Translation*. Bristol: Multilingual Matters.

Wang, B. (2012). A descriptive study of norms in interpreting—Based on the Chinese-English consecutive interpreting corpus of Chinese premier press conferences. *Meta*, 57(1), 198–212.

Wang, B. (2013). *A Descriptive Study of Norms in Interpreting: Based on the Analysis of a Corpus of On-Site Interpreting*. Beijing: Foreign Language Teaching and Research Press.

Wang, B., & Feng, D. (2018). A corpus-based study of stance-taking as seen from critical points in interpreted political discourse. *Perspectives*, 26(2), 246–260.

Wang, B., & Qin, H. (2015). Describing the target-language communication norms in Chinese-English interpreting. *Foreign Language Teaching and Research*, 47(4), 597–610.

Wang, B., & Zou, B. (2018). Exploring language specificity as a variable in Chinese-English interpreting: A corpus-based investigation. In: M. Russo, C. Bendazzoli, & B. Defrancq (Eds.) *Making Way in Corpus-Based Interpreting Studies* (pp. 65–82). Singapore: Springer Nature Singapore Pte Ltd.

Xiao, R. (2009). Multidimensional analysis and the study of world Englishes. *World Englishes*, 28(4), 421–450.

Xiao, R., & Cao, Y. (2014). A multi-dimensional contrastive move analysis of English abstracts by Chinese and English writer. *Foreign Language Teaching and Research*, 2, 260–272.

Xiao, R., & Hu, X. (2015). *Corpus-Based Studies of Translational Chinese in English-Chinese Translation*. Berlin: Springer-Verlag GmbH.

Xiao, X. (2015). *On the Oral-Literate Continuum: A Corpus-Based Study of Interpretese*. Xiamen: Xiamen University Press.

Xie, L., & Hu, K. (2015). The use of English indefinite quantifiers in Chinese-English conference interpreting. *Technology-Enhanced Foreign Language Education*, 1, 17–22.

Part IV
T&I and Technology

Part IV

Sci and Technology

9 Measuring the Impact of Automatic Speech Recognition on Number Rendition in Simultaneous Interpreting

Elisabetta Pisani and Claudio Fantinuoli

Introduction

Simultaneous interpretation (SI) is the process of translating speech in real-time, with a partial overlap between the listening and the production phase. From a cognitive perspective, SI is a highly demanding task that requires active listening, translating, and monitoring processes. Because of the high cognitive complexity that is involved while performing this task, many co-occurring aspects can contribute to reduced interpreting performance.

The aspects that may constitute a challenge during interpreting have been the focus of research for many years. Among others, much effort has been devoted to understanding detrimental aspects, such as the knowledge gap between speaker and interpreter (e.g. Will, 2007), the speed of delivery (e.g. Meuleman & Van Besien, 2009), and memory constraints (e.g. Moser-Mercer, 2000; Liu et al., 2004), to name just a few. In this context of cognitive complexity, computers have been proposed lately as an instrument that may support interpreters in alleviating some of the pre-process tasks (e.g. Stoll, 2009; Fantinuoli, 2012). Given the fact that computers are ideally suited for the task of recalling items and that they have the ability to store large amounts of information and process it very quickly, it has been hypothesised that, if properly integrated into the interpreting workflow, they may prove helpful not only for the activities that precede the interpreting process proper, such as event preparation (e.g. Fantinuoli, 2018; Xu, 2018), but also as an instrument to be used while interpreting, i.e. for in-process tasks. In particular, computer tools equipped with automatic speech recognition have been proposed as an ideal companion to support the interpreter with real-time suggestions for several problem triggers identified in the literature, such as numbers, terminology, and named entities (Fantinuoli, 2017).

The development of such tools is still in its infancy, and consequently, little is known about how they may perform in real-life applications or, more importantly, how well or badly they will fit into the complex cognitive process of SI. Many questions need to be answered. For example, will the integration of the visual suggestions require too much cognitive load and, consequently, will it lead to a deterioration of the overall performance? Or will the alleviation and the reduction of other cognitive tasks thanks to the suggestions rebalance the added cognitive load introduced by this technology, and lead to an improvement of performance? How will training and experience, i.e. the development of advanced strategies in how to use such suggestions, change such performance?

This research sets out to give some preliminary answers to some of these questions. In particular, the research empirically tests the influence of ASR in the performance of interpreters, analysing a particular kind of problem, the simultaneous interpretation of numbers. The experimental study compares the performance of two groups of participants interpreting a speech dense in numbers, one with the aid of a supporting tool, the other without any form of technological support. Contrary to similar studies conducted to date that were based on a simulated transcription (e.g. Desmet, 2018; Canali, 2019), in our experimental design, we use a real-life ASR-enhanced CAI tool. The experiments performed with a mockup system have the clear advantage of granting better control of the variables at stake since they can simulate a controlled and stable transcription, both in terms of error rates and latency. However, the use of a real-life tool has the advantage of improving the ecological validity of the experiment. In this context, the typical issues of ASR, such as mistranscriptions, latency, etc., which are not eliminated by the experimental design, allow us to draw some conclusions considering both the product of the interpreting process as well as the potential and limits of the state-of-the-art of ASR technology. The present experiment is similar to the one described by Defrancq and Fantinuoli (2020), except for the way suggestions are presented to the user. In Defrancq and Fantinuoli, they were presented as embedded in the complete transcription; in our experiment, they are shown isolated with no embedded context. Since the way results are presented is central in terms of usability in a cognitive-intense activity, this study adds on the findings of Defrancq and Fantinuoli and allows for a more complete picture of user–machine interaction in the context of real-time CAI support. For the analysis of the results, we use a mixed-mode approach, combining both quantitative data and introspections by means of a questionnaire.

Computer-Assisted Interpreting Tools and Automatic Speech Recognition

Computer-assisted or computer-aided interpreting (CAI) is commonly known as a form of human speech translation in which some aspects of the interpreting task are supported by a computer programme (Fantinuoli, 2018). The software used to augment the interpreter's work is named a CAI tool. In this context, CAI tools can be all sorts of programmes and mobile applications specifically designed and developed to support interpreters in at least one of the several sub-processes of interpretation, for example, knowledge acquisition and management, lexicographic memorisation, terminology lookup, and so forth.

One of the most peculiar features of CAI tools is the ability to support the search for specialised terminology in the booth. This functionality is generally designed as a backup strategy when other interpreting strategies, such as paraphrasing or the use of synonyms, are not viable and would lead to miscommunication and to a general degradation of the interpreter's performance. Interpreters may look up a term, generally in an event-specific database, while interpreting, while helping the boothmate or simply during the pauses, perhaps to find the translation of a recurring term used in a previous speech.

While CAI tools have been designed ergonomically and aim at reducing the cognitive effort needed to start a search and retrieve the results, one of the main limits of such tools is that they require the interpreter to allocate a specific amount of cognitive capacity to perform this task and to integrate the result of such operation into their delivery. Considering the fact that simultaneous interpretation is a cognitively demanding task that is in general performed at the limit of cognitive saturation, a technological means to automate the lookup mechanism could have the potential to reduce the cognitive load, benefiting the whole interpreting process. In this context, the integration of automatic speech recognition to automatise the lookup process may increase the usability of CAI tools. ASR has been regarded as a technology "with considerable potential for changing the way interpreting is practiced" (Pöchhacker, 2016, p. 188). Different to classic CAI tools that require manual input to get a translation for a given terminological unit, an ASR-enhanced CAI tool is able to automatise this process, with obvious advantages at the level of human–machine interaction.

InterpretBank ASR (Fantinuoli, 2017) is a prototype of a web-based ASR-enhanced CAI tool that transcribes in real-time a speech delivered by a speaker and automatically provides the interpreter with translation candidates of terminology as well as with numerals and their units of measurement. The tool's workflow is straightforward: firstly, the acoustic signal that the interpreter receives in the headset is sent to the sound card of the computer equipped with the ASR-CAI tool. The audio signal is then sent to the server with the speech recognition engine which returns the real-time transcript of the speech. At the moment of writing, InterpretBank uses the Google Cloud Speech-to-Text API, since experimental tests have shown that, compared to other competitors, it provides the best transcription quality for features useful for CAI integration, such as specialised terminology and numbers (Brüsewitz, 2019). Secondly, the transcription stream is processed. This phase involves chunking the text stream into units of n-words of a fixed size and normalising it. Thirdly, for each n-words window, the units of interest (UI) are extracted: single- and multiword grams are looked up in the terminological database loaded in the tool or translated by means of machine translation and numbers and their units of measurement are detected. In this phase, predictive algorithms can be used to intelligently select the UI and increase the usability of the tool (cf. Vogler et al., 2019). Finally, the extracted data is visualised on the computer's monitor.

In order to empirically study different approaches to human–machine interaction, InterpretBank ASR has been designed with two main models of data visualisation. The first model spots terminological units and numbers and displays the entire speech transcript with highlighted UI. The rationale behind this is that the informational context of the UI may help the interpreter to disambiguate the information, for example, in terms of co-references. The second model, instead, suppresses the text stream and visualises only the extracted UI (terminology and numbers + units of measurement) in a vertical prompt, with the newest information highlighted on top. As a tradeoff for this loss of contextual information, the user is presented with less information load, which can potentially decrease the distraction factor and the risk of cognitive overload.

The quality of an ASR-enhanced CAI tool depends on the quality of the transcription provided by the ASR and the ability of the CAI tool to retrieve and identify the necessary information (Fantinuoli, 2017). Ideally, the system should be characterised by high recall, i.e. it should be able to recognise all transcribed units of interest (regardless of spelling variants, for example, in the case of terminology), and by high precision, i.e. it should have a low rate of wrong or unsolicited results. These factors aim to avoid overloading the interpreter with unnecessary or incorrect results which could be a potential source of distraction and of error.

Related Work

There is general consensus on the fact that numbers can cause performance losses in simultaneous interpreting and that interpreters require specific strategies and specific pedagogical approaches to cope with them (e.g. Gile, 2009; Setton & Dawrant, 2016; Frittella, 2019). In the past, several studies have been conducted on interpreters' performances in the context of number rendition, involving both professional interpreters and students (e.g. Braun & Clarici, 1996; Lamberger-Felber, 2001; Mazza, 2001; Pinochi, 2009; Timarová, 2012; Desmet et al., 2018; Collard, 2019). All seem to confirm that numbers are poorly rendered, with error rates ranging between 21% and 70%. The range of empirical results is wide and may depend on several factors: different experience level of the interpreter population (the worst performances are measured, as expected, with students, while the best performances with professional interpreters); text types and grade of difficulty; differences in the methodologies used to evaluate errors and evaluation discretionality (approximations, for example, may be counted as errors or not); the fact that studies are based on an experimental setup or on a corpus-based analysis of real-life data (i.e. interpreting conditions are intrinsically different), and so forth.

A notable factor that seems to play a crucial role in interpreters' performance with numbers is the possibility to rely on some sort of visual support during interpretation. For example, when interpreters are allowed to take notes while performing the interpretation, the number of errors decreases by about 10% (Mazza, 2001); when they are given documents in the booth, the error rate decreases by 50% (Lamberger-Felber, 2001); finally, when they can see the numbers synchronised with the original speech displayed on a screen, interpreters make 70% fewer errors than without any form of support (Desmet et al., 2018). These three studies seem to indicate two things. First, the availability of visual numerical input clearly improves interpreters' performance. Secondly, the degree of improvement is directly proportional to the reduction of the cognitive load needed to retrieve the numerical information, which is higher in the case of taking notes and lower in the case of synchronised support on-screen.

The first strain of empirical research in CAI support during the process of interpreting has focused on a relatively similar problem trigger, i.e. specialised terminology. Experimental studies have aimed at measuring how interactive visual support in the booth may improve interpreters' performance. The first set of empirical studies focused on manual terminology lookup (e.g. Prandi, 2015; Biagini, 2016). In these experiments, the probands were asked to interpret a speech and use a CAI tool to perform manual searches in an event glossary. The results of such studies seem to indicate that terminology lookup can help to increase the quality of the rendition, especially in terminology-dense texts. However, the level of the reported improvement seems modest. Reasons for this are the added cognitive load needed for the lookup operation, the perceived distracting influence of this dynamic activity and, on the most general term, the lack of familiarity and absence of training for such an added operation in the already demanding setting of simultaneous interpreting.

The introduction of the first prototype of an ASR tool for interpreters (Fantinuoli, 2017) has moved the interest of experimental research towards the analysis of the interpreter–machine interaction by means of automated lookup tools. Experiments on number rendition using mockup systems (Desmet et al., 2018; Canali, 2019) have indicated a clear reduction of error rates among probands, from 43.5% to 13.5% (gain 30%) in Desmet et al. (2018) and from 64% to 25% (gain 39%) in Canali (2019). In both experimental setups, the number transcription has been displayed either on a screen in the conference room or on a computer in the booth. The numbers were displayed without any information about context, reference, etc., following its delivery by the source speaker. In the first experiment, the speech was given live and the prepared numbers advanced manually, in this way generating a variable but minimal latency between spoken word and transcription. In the second, the text was recorded and the video edited with the transcriptions shown exactly after the term has been completely pronounced by the speaker. Another experiment by Defrancq and Fantinuoli (2020) used the same ASR system as in the current chapter, but implemented a different visualisation approach and highlighted numerals embedded in the complete transcription (see the second section of this chapter). With a complete transcription, a decrease of error rates from 32.3% to 9.8% (gain 22.5%) was reported.

Similar experiments with automated suggestion of other types of problem triggers, for example, terminological units, are underway (e.g. Prandi, 2018). Because of the high number of uncontrolled variables at stake in such experimental settings and the complexity of the simultaneous interpreting process, scholars have been animated to elaborate rigorous theoretical frameworks for the design of empirical studies in the area of ASR-supported CAI tools. Prandi (2018), for example, expands the cognitive load model for the "standard" simultaneous interpreting proposed by Seeber (2011) to accommodate the allocation of cognitive resources during the querying and retrieving of lexical information. Different from the traditional manual lookup, the integration of automatic speech recognition in a CAI tool would require no manual-spatial resources, thus lowering the total interference score (Prandi, 2018). This, again, seems to suggest that ASR may have the potential to integrate better into the interpreting workstation than a traditional CAI tool.

Another strain of research aims at improving CAI tools' suggestions by means of machine learning techniques. One of the main limitations of ASR-enhanced CAI tools, in fact, is that they show suggestions in a non-selective way. In the case of terminology, for example, they show all terminological units contained in the event database that match the transcription. In the case of numbers, no distinction is made between complex and simple ones (100 and 153.867 have different levels of difficulty), nor are different strategies applied based on the number density in a given speech segment, etc. This has several disadvantages. The most prominent one is that the interpreter will be prompted with an abundance of (unfiltered) suggestions, with the possible consequence of being distracted, experiencing a cognitive overload, and, ultimately, decreasing the overall quality of the rendition. Users' feedback stressing this shortcoming is introduced in the analysis of results later in this chapter.

With this in mind, Vogler et al. (2019) have proposed to use machine learning to anticipate the textual units that may cause difficulties for the interpreter and limit the number of suggestions only to these cases. The proposed approach is based on the comparison of a parallel corpus of translated and interpreted speeches in order to automatically identify the text features that led to a terminological issue (for example, omission) in the interpreted rendition. This approach is based on an ML-augmented corpus-based analysis and represents one of the first attempts at process-oriented research in technology-mediated interpreting.

Users' Study on the Use of ASR in SI

The goal of the experimental study was to analyse the impact of using automatic speech recognition on the simultaneous interpretation of numbers. Based on the empirical evidence described in the previous sections, the experiment hypothesised that the visualisation of numbers and their units of measurement by means of ASR would improve the rendition of numbers in simultaneous interpretation. The study aimed therefore to establish the extent to which participants benefitted from the support provided by a real-life CAI tool during the simultaneous interpretation of a text that was dense in numbers. In our experiment, we used the tool InterpretBank ASR with the visualisation of the units of interest without full transcription.

A quantitative analysis of the performance of interpreting students was carried out to verify the hypothesis. The results were then triangulated against the feedback given by the participants at the end of the experiment.

Participants

The experimental study analysed the performance, with or without the help of ASR, of 20 students (all Italian native speakers) at the end of the first and second year of the master's programme in Conference Interpreting at the University of Trieste. In order to take part in the experiment, participants needed to have passed at least the first-year exam in simultaneous interpretation from English into Italian. The participants were equally divided into two groups of ten people: one group interpreted using InterpretBank ASR, while the control group interpreted without support. The participants in the experiment did not undergo any targeted training and had never used CAI tools before.

Data

We set out to use a text dense in numbers. An English speech was selected from the European Commission website in order to keep the text typology as close as possible to the ones used during the interpreting classes. In order to achieve the set goal of number density, more sentences containing figures were added, after some research was conducted on the subject using the European Investment Bank website. The speech was then recorded by an English native speaker. The speech rate reached 123.8 words per minute, which is close to the ideal speed for the interpretation of improvised speeches (Riccardi, 2010).

Experimental Setup

The participants were divided into four batteries. The recorded video was played four times, one for each battery of probands. Before entering the booth, each group received a briefing on the topic of the speech and the group that used ASR was shown how the software worked. The participants did not actively try InterpretBank before the experiment or take part in any practice experiment beforehand. They were only introduced to the speech recognition function by means of a short explanation by the authors of the experiment and by watching a live demonstration with a video fragment taken from a different speech, also dense in numbers. This helped them get to grips with the way in which numbers were transcribed, their colour, and how the order of magnitude was shown. The control group was asked to bring a notepad into the booth as the use of traditional tools was allowed. The performances of the participants were audio-recorded. No information on gaze, fixations, and other features was taken into consideration in this experiment.

At the end of the assignment, the participants were asked to fill in a questionnaire including questions on their note-taking habits as well as on their perception of the speech and of their performance, and their opinion of the ASR functionality. The participants were used to working alone in the booth most of the time and usually without technological support. The interaction with a CAI tool could therefore have led to a perceived increase in cognitive effort for the participants and a feeling of distraction. These perceptions were then triangulated against the measured performance in terms of numbers rendition. Furthermore, they were supposed to give first insights on how the use of CAI tools is perceived by undergraduate users that have not undergone a specific training phase in their use.

Error Annotation

We applied the error categories defined in similar studies on the interpretation of numbers (Braun & Clarici, 1996; Pinochi, 2009). The error typologies considered for the study were the following: *omissions* (the numeral is left out or replaced by a generic expression such as "some," "a few"); *approximations* (the number is rounded off and sometimes a phrasal element such as "approximately," "about" is added); *lexical errors* (the order of magnitude is correct, but one or more figures were wrongly interpreted; i.e. 243 instead of 244); *syntactical errors* (the number is of a wrong order of magnitude); *errors of phonetic perception* (the error can be ascribed to a phonetically wrong perception of the number; i.e. 30 instead of 13); *errors of inversion* (the figures are correct, but in the wrong order; i.e. 1.7 instead of 7.1); *other errors* (all errors that do not completely correspond to any of the other typologies). In particular, for each stimulus (the number pronounced by the speaker in the source language) the following information was recorded: numerical class, whether the number was correctly interpreted, the actual number the interpreter pronounced, and, if applicable, the error typology. The total correct/wrong/partially wrong outputs and the distribution of every error typology were computed. For the data gathered from the group using InterpretBank, the following information was recorded: number transcribed by the software, whether the transcription was correct, and temporary versions of the transcriptions. Finally, the total amount of correct/incorrect transcriptions was determined.

It should be noted that, in order not to alter the results of the data analysis, all cases where two errors coexisted were counted as one error when computing the total number of errors. However, in order to produce a more complete picture of the error distribution, double errors were split during the analysis of the error typologies. Consequently, due to the phenomenon of double errors, discrepancies emerged between the sum of incorrectly interpreted numbers and the sum of errors by typology.

ASR Results

The source text included 56 numbers. The overall precision of the transcription was of 81.43%. This score also takes into account the cases where numbers were erroneously transcribed without any digit present in the original speech (for example, in the case of speaker hesitations recognised as numbers or pronouns transcribed as numbers).

Considering only the transcription quality of the numbers in the original speech, the precision reaches 82.6% which is well below evaluations conducted in similar experiments (e.g. Brüsewitz, 2019; Defrancq & Fantinuol, 2020). This result was mainly caused by a particular type of error that occurred repeatedly during the course of the text, namely lists of numbers. With adjacent numbers, such as "in 2000: 6.7%," the absence of a clear stop signal between the digits made the tool first transcribe "2000" correctly, then correct itself by changing the "2000" into "2006." This was even more true for long sequences of numbers which were present in the speech. Without considering this particular case of number proximity, the ASR performed similarly to the results of the above-mentioned experiments, with precision values around 94%.

The other errors made by the ASR can be ascribed to phonetic misinterpretations, such as "2" instead of "to," "6" instead of "success," and by number proximity. In some cases, the real-time correction ability of the ASR system caused the transcription to be changed several times until the final result stabilised. This is due to frequent phonetic perception errors found in the early stages of transcription, for example, 30 being transcribed as 30, then as 13, and finally as 30 again. For the purposes of this study, all cases in which the last transcription on the screen was incorrect or not displayed were categorised as errors, even when a previous correct transcription had been displayed. On the other hand, even when the final transcription was correct, the time constraints of simultaneous interpretation, however, may prevent the interpreter from making proper use of the suggestion provided or, conversely, create confusion and worsen his or her performance.

In other cases, the live correction of the transcribed number created confusion by quickly and repeatedly changing the displayed digit. In the case of "for the next financial period 2021–2027," for example, "2027" was interpreted as a correction of the previous number "2021," which was immediately substituted by "2027." In some isolated cases, the numbers were correctly transcribed in a temporary version (shown for a relatively long interval), but the final version transcribed on the screen was incorrect. In these cases, the participants often had the chance to read the correct temporary transcription, without letting the following incorrect transcription affect their performance.

An analysis of how wrong transcriptions were interpreted by the students highlighted that, on average, 0.8 errors committed by the student were to be ascribed to an incorrect/inexistent transcription by the software. The fact that participants correctly interpreted numbers even when the transcription displayed was wrong or lacking shows that the students were able to use InterpretBank as a supportive tool, rather than as a replacement of their skills.

Product-Based Results

The objective of this study is to assess whether the use of automatic speech recognition for the rendition of numbers can improve the performances of students who usually interpret without any aid. Overall, the data analysis revealed an error rate of 14.8% for the group using technological support and 39.8% for the control group. Therefore, the participants who used an ASR-enhanced CAI tool correctly interpreted 41.5% more numbers than the other group.

As far as a more fine-grained analysis is concerned, the control group registered a wider distribution of errors over several different typologies and in a more balanced way. In the following, a brief analysis of the single typologies of errors is presented. Overall, the support of the software led on average to 25% more correctly interpreted numbers in every numerical class.

Omissions

In both groups, the majority of errors were classified as omissions. On average, 4.5 numbers were omitted with ASR and 12.9 without technological support. As expected, the control group recorded a higher percentage of full omissions. It has to be noted that omissions, as a typology of errors, can be seen both as an error and a strategy, since interpreters often omit numbers strategically to avoid cognitive overload, preventing in this way a worsening of their overall rendition at the expense of a limited loss in numerical precision. In this context, both groups limited omissions to cases in which they did not entail any actual loss of meaning. Whenever possible they applied strategies to mitigate the omission, for example, by using determiners.

Comparing the two groups, the participants relying on the help of ASR omitted numbers by replacing them with a linguistic expression ("many," "few") on average only 0.3 times, while the control group resorted to this strategy more readily (on average 2.6 times). This seems to highlight the benefit of technological support not only in reducing the number of errors that lead to a complete loss in the meaning conveyed but also in improving the precision of the rendition.

Approximations

The students who used technological support resorted to approximations to a lesser extent (from an average of 2.1 numbers approximated without technological support to 0.3 with ASR), since they most frequently succeeded in retrieving the number transcribed on the screen and correctly interpreting all the digits. On the other hand, the students of the control group frequently rounded off a number in order to avoid a rendition which was either incorrect or too imprecise. To be specific, only two out of the ten students using ASR resorted to this strategy, compared to eight out of ten students of the control group. Hence, it can be inferred that the control group encountered more difficulties in correctly rendering all the digits that constitute a number. This result confirms the effectiveness of the software in providing support for interpreting numbers, including complex or very long ones.

Lexical and Syntactic Errors

Lexical errors – the order of magnitude is correct, but one or more digits are incorrect, i.e. 1998 instead of 1989 – were registered in both groups (on average 0.8 with ASR and 1.6 without), especially when it came to interpreting decimal numbers (for example, 6.7 interpreted as 6.2). Syntactic errors – the order of magnitude is incorrect, but the digits are correct – were found in both groups (on average 1.2 with ASR and 2.7 without). The greatest part of errors occurred while translating "billion" or "million" into Italian. Taking into consideration that the software always correctly transcribed the orders of magnitude and showed their full original form (i.e. "billion" and not "bl") in the source language, these data show that students still have doubts – at least when they are under pressure – about the translation of these words into Italian and often confuse one for the other (i.e. "billion" as "milione"). A solution to this challenge could lie in a translated transcription of the order of magnitude (_billion>_miliardo).

Phonetic Perception

The participants who used the support committed considerably fewer phonetic perception errors (from an average of 2.2 errors for the control group to 0.4 with ASR). Students in the control group not only made recurrent phonetic perception mistakes, such as 30 > 13, but also often wrongly inter-preted decimals (i.e. 8.7% > 7%). On the other hand, no participant using ASR made this kind of mistake with decimals because they had the possibil-ity to check the digits on the screen. The CAI tool therefore proved useful and effective for non-complex numbers too.

Errors of Inversion

In both groups, no error corresponding to such typology was identified. Since the language of the speech (English) has a linear numerical system, a low percentage of such errors was expected, even though they were expected to occur at least with decimals. However, regarding the category of decimals, the analysis often detected approximations, phonetic perception errors, or lexical errors, but never errors of inversion.

Other Typology

This additional typology was included to count all those errors that did not completely correspond to any of the other typologies, and all errors to be ascribed to incorrect transcriptions by the software. Some errors categorised as "other typology" turned out to be linked to the expectations of the inter-preter, such as the example of "it will have multiplied 15 times over," where "15 times" was often interpreted (in Italian) as "by 15%," even though the software did not transcribe "%," but only "15." Only 7% of the total errors committed by the control group were categorised as "other typol-ogy," whereas 15% is the case for the group using the technological sup-port. The higher number of errors for the group using ASR is also due to the fact that this typology included all errors caused by relying on incorrect transcriptions.

Perception-Based Results

At the end of the experiment in the booth, participants were asked to fill in a questionnaire regarding their habits of jotting down numbers on paper during the simultaneous interpretation of numbers, how they perceived the speech and their performance during the experiment, and how they perceived interaction with the automatic suggestions. The questionnaire included both open and closed questions to be answered by choosing the level of agreement to a statement (Likert scale). From these data (averaged for each group), the degree of difficulty perceived during the experiment can be deducted. In the following paragraph, some of the most telling results will be discussed.

Participants affirmed that they usually perceive the simultaneous rendi-tion of numbers as slightly difficult (average levels of agreement of 3.4/5 and 3.8/5 on the Likert scale for the two groups). In both groups, only half of the participants claimed to always jot a number down before interpreting it. Participants who do not have the habit of taking notes of numbers stated that they usually display them mentally and focus only on the number (often to the detriment of the general output in the target language).

Regarding the experiment in question, the number of numbers in the text was considered high (4.2/5) by the group using technological support and extremely high (5/5) by the control group. Hence, all the participants of the control group experienced many difficulties when interpreting this text dense in numbers. The control group considered the high frequency of numbers to be a source of high cognitive load (4.8/5), whereas the group using ASR only agreed to a medium extent (3.5/5). The distance between the numbers in the text was considered acceptable by the group using technological support, but too short by the control group. The statement *"the numerical density affected my output in Italian"* obtained a 3.5/5 level of agreement by the group using ASR and 4.6/5 by the control group. These answers are aligned to the performances measured in the empirical experiment.

Another interesting result is the perceived difficulty in understanding the exact number uttered, which is given 2.8/5 on the Likert scale by the group using technological support but reaches the value of 4.3/5 with the control group. These figures highlight the significantly higher degree of difficulty perceived by participants who did not use the software. The students in the group using ASR also claimed not to have encountered any particular difficulties in identifying the order of magnitude (2.1/5) or what the number referred to (2.9/5), while students of the control group encountered more difficulties (3.4/5 in both cases).

All participants were generally quite dissatisfied with their own performance (2.4/5 for those who used the software and 2.2/5 for the control group), even though the first group, in fact, interpreted more numbers correctly. However, it should be noted that an interpreting performance includes not only the correct rendition of numbers but also their context, the discursive parts, and a good output in the target language. Therefore, the results of the analysis of the rendition of numbers cannot be linearly compared to the satisfaction of the performance during the experiment, since the data analysed only examine one of the several aspects of satisfactory interpreting performance.

Participants also pointed out that when the software made mistakes in the transcription of a number, they often found it difficult to correct their rendition in a timely manner. Participants using ASR stated in the questionnaire that they believed they interpreted discursive parts well and demonstrated a strong ability to close sentences. However, when asked to provide examples of weaknesses in their performance, they listed poor accuracy, references not understood, the output in the target language, and the rendition of segments dense in numbers. The control group considered their strengths to be the application of strategies (approximation or omission) in the case of numbers not fully understood, the output in Italian, and the general understanding of the text. Under the weak points, almost all participants of the control group included difficulties related to quantity and density of figures in the text, especially as regards the rendering of references and of the order of magnitude.

The probands who used ASR during the experiment emphasised that they could have made better use of the tool if they had had the opportunity to practice beforehand. The statement *"the speed at which numbers appeared on the screen was appropriate for the purposes of interpreting"* was given a degree of agreement of 3.6/5. This value may suggest that participants encountered difficulties in interpreting a text dense in numbers, even when relying on the software. Future measurements with different values of latency should shed light on the ideal threshold of latency in order to increase the usability of the suggestions.

Regarding the formal aspects of ASR, the transcription of the number by the software was rated as averagely accurate (3.2/5), and the way numbers were shown was considered on average clear and understandable (3.1/5). This value indicates a misalignment between the perception of ASR accuracy and the measured precision of transcription. The probands suggested small improvements such as different demarcation signs between units and decimals and between thousands and hundreds (i.e. for Italian, comma and full stop). The answers to the question *"the use of the software was not a source of distraction"* are a useful indicator of the perceived difficulties encountered by the students in integrating this kind of tool while simultaneously interpreting: 50% agreed with a level of 4/5, 30% with 3/5, and only 20% with 2/5. In general, the probands that used the software described it as helpful, especially in segments rich in numbers (including complex numbers), but less so with dates or numbers with up to three zeros.

The added task of reading the transcribed numbers did not raise any particular difficulty, as the numbers were marked with different colours and the last number would always appear at the top. Nonetheless, reading the transcription on the screen proved to be a potential source of distraction, which is why some probands stressed the importance of getting to grips with the software before using it in a real-life situation. Of the probands who used technological support during the experiment, 40% stated they would use it in a work context, while 50% stressed that the choice would depend primarily on the type of text in question (namely, on its number density).

Finally, the integration of CAI tools into translation and interpretation technology courses was strongly recommended by both groups, since more practice with CAI tools would considerably decrease the distraction factor linked to such tools.

Conclusions

The experiment confirms that automatic speech recognition proved effective in providing support during the interpretation of a speech dense in numbers.

The results show a significant reduction of error rate, which drops from 39.8% without technological support to 14.8% with the support of automatic speech recognition (gain 25%). In particular, the support of the ASR led to a reduction in omissions (from an average of 12.9 without ASR to 4.5 with ASR) and helped to improve performance for complex or very long numbers, as shown by the decrease in cases of approximation (from an average of 2.1 errors without ASR to 0.3 with ASR). Furthermore, ASR helped participants avoid phonetic perception errors (from an average of 2.2 errors without ASR to 0.4 with ASR). The experimental group also registered a smaller percentage of double errors (for example, syntactic error and approximation at the same time), especially with long numbers (from an average of 0.6 double errors without ASR to 0.1 with ASR). This phenomenon could be partly explained by the larger quantity of elements to be processed in complex numbers: without technological support, this numerical class could entail more significant memorisation and elaboration difficulties.

Most of the software errors occurred with simple numerals. Being easier to process, they had no serious repercussions in the output, since the probands either did not rely on the ASR for that speech segment or they were able to correct the wrong suggestion.

Quite interestingly, the results of our experiment using state-of-the-art automatic speech recognition are very similar to the results of Desmet et al. (2018) using a simulated transcription and manual synchronisation between suggestions and original speech. In their experiment, the average error rate without technological support was 43.5% (compared to 39.8% in ours) while the average error rate with technological support was 13.5% (compared to 14.8% in ours). This seems to suggest that the quality of today's technological development, at least in a comparable setting and in the context of numbers, is already mature enough to be used in real-life applications.

The analysis of the questionnaire stresses some of the difficulties encountered by the probands, such as the feeling of distraction caused by the added visual stimulus and the need to coordinate it with the other co-occurring subprocesses of simultaneous interpretation. Such drawbacks could be mitigated by specific training in the use of the support. The fact that the probands were already able to do a selective use of the technological support, as demonstrated, for example, by the fact that they correctly interpreted numbers even when they were wrongly transcribed (hence indicating a use of the software as a supportive tool, rather than as a replacement for the listening and comprehension skill), leads us to think that training could develop a strategic approach to the use of CAI tools and, as a consequence, reduce the effect of distraction produced by them. Furthermore, the user feedback indicated some shortcomings in the way suggestions were presented. In this context, further research in data visualisation should be conducted and new methods tested.

One limitation of our experiment was that the test population did include only undergraduate interpreters. In order to generalise the validity of the results, a similar study should be replicated with professional interpreters. It is our hypothesis that professionals, especially after being trained on how to use the tool, will improve their performance on numbers too, but that the magnitude of improvement will be smaller because of the lower error rates that characterise professional renditions without technological support.

References

Biagini, G. (2016). *Printed glossary and electronic glossary in simultaneous interpretation: A comparative study.* Thesis: Università degli studi di Trieste.

Braun, S., & Clarici, A. (1996). Inaccuracy for numerals in simultaneous interpretation: Neurolinguistic and neuropsychological perspectives. *The Interpreters' Newsletter*, 7:85–102.

Brüsewitz, N. (2019). Simultandolmetschen 4.0: Ist automatische Spracherkennung der nächste Schritt? In: *Proceedings of the Conference on Übersetzen Und Dolmetschen 4.0. – Neue Wege im digitalen Zeitalter.* BDÜ Fachverlag.

Canali, S. (2019). *Technologie und Zahlen beim Simultandolmetschen: Utilizzo del riconoscimento vocale come supporto durante l'interpretazione simultanea dei numeri.* Università degli studi internazionali di Roma, unpublished MA thesis.

Collard, C. (2019). *A Corpus-Based Study of Simultaneous Interpreting with Special Reference to sex.* PhD diss. Ghent University.

Defrancq, B., & Fantinuoli, C. (2020). Automatic speech recognition in the booth: Assessment of system performance, interpreters' performances and interactions in the context of numbers. *Target*, 32(2), 73–102.

Desmet, B., Vandierendonck, M., & Defrancq, B. (2018). Simultaneous interpretation of numbers and the impact of technological support. In: Fantinuoli C. (Ed.) *Interpreting and Technology*. Berlin: Language Science Press, 13–27.

Fantinuoli, C. (2012). *InterpretBank—Design and Implementation of a Terminology and Knowledge Management Software for Conference Interpreters.* PhD diss. University of Mainz.

Fantinuoli, C. (2017). Speech recognition in the interpreter workstation. In: *Proceedings of the Translating and the Computer 39.* London.

Fantinuoli, C. (2018). Computer-assisted interpreting: Challenges and future perspectives. In: Durán Muñoz I. & Corpas Pastor G. (Eds.) *Trends in e-Tools and Resources for Translators and Interpreters.* Leiden: Brill, 153–174.

Frittella, F. (2019). "70.6 billion world citizens": Investigating the difficulty of interpreting numbers. *Translation & Interpreting*, 11(1):79–99.

Gile, D. (2009). *Basic Concepts and Models for Interpreter and Translator Training* (2nd ed.). Amsterdam: John Benjamins.

Lamberger-Felber, H. (2001). Text-oriented research into interpreting: Examples from a case-study. *Hermes - Journal of Language & Communication in Business*, 26(26):39–63.

Liu, M., Schallert, D. L., & Carroll, P. J. (2004). Working memory and expertise in simultaneous interpreting. *Interpreting. International Journal of Research & Practice in Interpreting*, 6(1):19–42.

Mazza, C. (2001). Numbers in simultaneous interpretation. *The Interpreters' Newsletter*, 11:87–104.

Meuleman, C., & VanBesien, F. (2009). Coping with extreme speech conditions in simultaneous interpreting. *Interpreting. International Journal of Research & Practice in Interpreting*, 11(1):20–34.

Moser-Mercer, B. (2000). Simultaneous interpreting: Cognitive potential and limitations. *Interpreting. International Journal of Research & Practice in Interpreting*, 5(2):83–94.

Pinochi, D. (2009). Simultaneous interpretation of numbers: Comparing German and English to Italian. An experimental study. *The Interpreters' Newsletter*, 14:33–57.

Pöchhacker, F. (2016). *Introducing Interpreting Studies* (2nd ed.). London: Routledge.

Prandi, B. (2015). The use of CAI tools in interpreters' training: A pilot study. In: *Proceedings of the 37 Conference Translating and the Computer*, 48–57.

Prandi, B. (2018). An exploratory study on CAI tools in simultaneous interpreting: Theoretical framework and stimulus validation. In: Fantinuoli C. (Ed.) *Interpreting and Technology*. Berlin: Language Science Press, 25–54.

Riccardi, A. (2010). Velocità d'eloquio e interpretazione simultanea. In: *Am Schnittpunkt von Philologie und Translationswissenschaft : Festschrift zu Ehren von Martin Forstner*, 281–299.

Seeber, K. G. (2011). Cognitive load in simultaneous interpreting: Existing theories – new models. *Interpreting*, 13, 176–204.

Setton, R., & Dawrant, A. (2016). *Conference Interpreting: A Complete Course*. Amsterdam: John benjamins.

Stoll, C. (2009). *Jenseits simultanfähiger Terminologiesysteme: Methoden der Vorverlagerung und Fixierung von Kognition im Arbeitsablauf professioneller Konferenzdolmetscher*. Trier: WVT Wissenschaftlicher Verlag Trier.

Timarová, S. (2012). *Working Memory in Simultaneous Interpreting*. PhD diss. KU Leuven.

Vogler, N., Stewart, C., & Neubig, G. (2019). *Lost in Interpretation: Predicting Untranslated Terminology in Simultaneous Interpretation*. arXiv:1904.00930v1.

Will, M. (2007). Terminology work for simultaneous interpreters in LSP conferences: Model and method. In: *Proceedings of the EU-High-Level Scientific Conference Series MuTra*, 65–99.

Xu, R. (2018). Corpus-based terminological preparation for simultaneous interpreting. *Interpreting. International Journal of Research & Practice in Interpreting*, 20(1):29–58.

10 Machine Translation Problems at Discourse Level

Pro-Drop Language and Large-Context Machine Translation

Xiaojun Zhang

Introduction

Language units (words, phrases, sentences, and paragraphs) are all orderly, hierarchically, and semantically organised as a whole (Asher & Lascarides, 2003). Like words in a sentence, sentences in a document (or utterances in a dialogue) are also closely related to each other. Therefore, high-quality translation of a document requires a thorough understanding of the source sentence based on discourse relation as well as good knowledge of the target language (Hardmeier, 2014).

Since 1954, MT has been significantly developed through rule-based MT (Nirenburg et al., 1986), traditional SMT (Koehn, 2009), and NMT (Kalchbrenner & Blunsom, 2013; Sutskever et al., 2014; Bahdanau et al., 2015) stages. Despite the success, MT systems usually translate a text sentence by sentence based on an assumption that the sentences in a text are strictly independent of one another. However, ignoring the property of context-connectedness leads to serious translation problems with regard to discourse. In response to this kind of problems, some researchers have explored integrating discourse information to improve translation quality. At early rule-based MT stage, the interlingual representations were used to store conversational states in a dialogue. With the developments of statistical modelling, discourse is widely investigated in SMT, such as language model (Foster et al., 2010), discourse connectives (Meyer & Poláková, 2013; Meyer & Webber, 2013), lexical cohesion (Xiong et al., 2013), and anaphora (Le Nagard & Koehn, 2010; Taira et al., 2012), and experiments from them show both qualitative and quantitative improvements. In recent years, the encoder-decoder architecture was proposed by Cho et al. (2014) and Sutskever et al. (2014), in which the encoder summarises the source sentence into a vector representation and the decoder generates the target sentence word by word from the vector representation. Using this framework as well as gating and attention techniques, it has been shown that the performance of NMT has surpassed the performance of traditional SMT on various language pairs (Luong et al., 2015). However, through the analysis of NMT outputs, we have found that gains mainly come from fluency while discourse problems still exist.

The first challenge of dealing with discourse in MT is that existing parallel corpora lack discourse information. As a result, few researchers have investigated how to improve the MT of conversational material by exploiting their internal structure. Therefore, we firstly explored corpus construction and propose a novel approach to parallel discourse corpus construction for dialogue MT (Wang et al., 2016). Dropped pronouns are one of specific discourse phenomena, in which certain classes of words can be omitted to make the sentence compact yet comprehensible. However, this poses difficulties for MT from pro-drop languages to non-pro-drop languages, since translation of such missing pronouns cannot be normally reproduced. To tackle the problem, we proposed to find a general and replicable method of improving translation quality (Wang et al., 2017).

In the rest of this chapter, the background of discourse and MT will be described first. Then the MT problems at discourse level will be analysed. After that, our approaches to addressing discourse problems for MT will be applied and experimented. Finally, conclusions and a research plan for future work will be discussed.

Discourse

From bottom to top, natural languages can be divided into six levels: word, phrase, clause, sentence, paragraph, and discourse (Longacre, 2013). In Table 10.1, we take two examples to illustrate what discourse is. Example 1 has four sentences, which are all grammatically correct and put together into a paragraph. However, it is not a discourse because the meaning of each sentence is independent and they bear no relation to one another. In contrast, the dialogue in Example 2 is a discourse. Speaker A makes a request for Speaker B to perform an action (answering the phone). Speaker B then states a reason why he/she cannot comply with the request. Finally, Speaker A undertakes to perform the action. Although some information is implicit to compact utterances, they are closely related to each other under a clear topic. Obviously, there are three main features of discourse and its

Table 10.1 Two Discourse Examples

No.	Example
1	It is very hot today. Cohen comes from Germany. HK launches first sightseeing bus to promote tourism. Natural language processing has been rapidly developed in recent years.
2	A: That's the telephones. B: I'm in the bath. A: O.K.

properties: 1) it is a continuous stretch of language longer than a sentence; 2) it involves conversation (e.g. dialogue) or text (e.g. a document); 3) it is meaningful, coherent, unified, and purposive.

Cohesion

De Beaugrande and Dressler (1981) proposed seven fundamental properties of discourse: cohesion, coherence, intentionality, acceptability, informativity, situationality, and intertextuality. Among them, cohesion and coherence are the two most basic properties that establish "connectedness" in a text (Sanders & Maat, 2006).

Cohesion is a surface property of the text that is realised by explicit clues. It occurs whenever "the interpretation of some element in the discourse is dependent on that of another" (Halliday & Hasan, 1976). The two main categories of cohesion are referential cohesion and lexical cohesion.

Referential cohesion is mainly realised by way of pronominal reference, including anaphora and coreference. Anaphora is the use of an expression whose interpretation depends specifically upon an antecedent expression. The anaphoric (referring) term is called an anaphor. Sometimes anaphor may rely on the postcedent expression, and this phenomenon is called cataphora. Taking Sentence (a) in Figure 10.1, for example, the pronoun *It* is an anaphor, which points to the left towards its antecedent, *Audi*. Zero anaphora (pronoun-dropping) is a more complex case of anaphora. In some languages such as Chinese and Japanese, certain classes of words can be omitted to make the sentence compact yet comprehensible when the identity of the pronouns can be inferred from the context. Taking a Chinese Sentence (c) in Figure 10.1 as an example, all the pronouns including 你 (*you*), 我 (*I*), 它 (*it*), and the second 你 (*you*) are all omitted in the conversation between Speakers A and B; however, speakers can still recall the missing pronouns

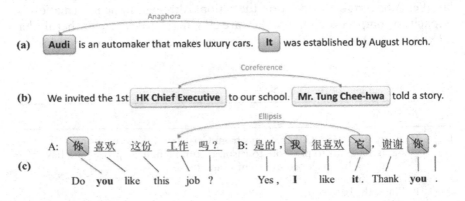

Figure 10.1 Examples of Cohesion.

from the context. Besides, the omitted object pronoun 它 (*it*) refers to the noun 工作 (*job*) while the other pronouns refer to the speakers themselves.

Coreference means two or more expressions (e.g. nouns) in a text which refer to the same referent. As the referents point to persons or things in the real world, the coreference relation can exist independently of the context. Taking Sentence (b) in Figure 10.1, for instance, the noun phrases *HK Chief Executive* and *Mr Tung Chee-hwa* point to the same person, although their surfaces are totally different.

Another term that has sometimes been used by fewer linguistic researchers is that of lexical or terminological consistency. The underlying assumption is that the same concepts should be consistently referred to with the same words in a translation. Consistency is another critical issue in document-level translation, where a repeated term should keep the same translation throughout the whole document (Xiao et al., 2011).

Coherence

To make a text semantically meaningful, coherence is related to the connectedness of the "mental representation of the text rather than of the text itself" (Sanders & Maat, 2006). It is created referentially, when different parts of a text refer to the same entities, and relationally, by means of coherence relations such as "Cause–Consequence" between different discourse segments. Researchers studied discourse structure mainly based on rhetorical structure theory (RST) (Mann & Thompson, 1988) and Penn Discourse Treebank (PDTB) annotation methodology (Marcu, 2000).

RST relations are applied recursively in a text until all units in that text are constituents in a predefined relation. As shown in Figure 10.2, the

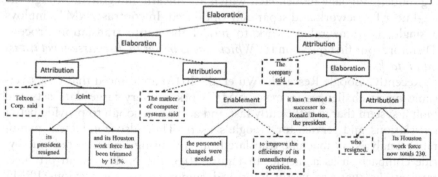

Figure 10.2 An Example of an RST Tree.

Table 10.2 PDTB Annotation Example

No.	Example (Argument 1 – **Connective** – Argument 2)
1	According to Lawrence Eckenfelder, "Kemper is the first firm to make a major statement with program trading." He added that "having just one firm do this isn't going to mean a hill of beans. <u>But</u> if this prompts others to consider the same thing, then it may become much more important."
2	According to Lawrence Eckenfelder, "Kemper is the first firm to make a major statement with program trading." He added that "having just one firm do this isn't going to mean a hill of beans. If this prompts others to consider the same thing, then it may become much more important."

result of such analysis is that RST structure is typically represented as trees, with one top-level relation that encompasses other relations at lower levels. Besides, the tree also contains a number of predefined relations such as "Attribution" (Cause–Consequence), "Elaboration," etc.

The PDTB annotation methodology is proposed based on RST but highlights the role of the connectives. According to whether they contain a connective or not, discourse relations can be divided into two categories: explicit and implicit. In Table 10.2, Example 1 shows an explicit discourse, which uses the coordinating conjunction *But* to bridge two text spans (i.e. arguments), and the relationship between them is "Comparison. Concession" (two-level relation category). However, Example 2 omitted the discourse connective and the implicit relation between two arguments is "Comparison.Contrast."

Machine Translation Problems at Discourse Level

SMT vs. NMT

SMT consists of several components including translation model, reordering model, language model, etc., which are linearly integrated through the log-linear framework and separately optimised. In contrast, NMT employs a single, large neural network to model the entire translation process. Therefore, our first question is "*Which one is better in discourse-level translation tasks?*"

Recently, Google Research (Wu et al., 2016) announced that they overcame many challenges to make NMT work on very large data sets and built a system that is sufficiently fast and accurate enough to provide better translations and service for Google's users. They also conducted quantitative analysis on machine-translated outputs using human-rated side-by-side comparison as a metric. In Figure 10.3, the NMT system produces translations that are vastly improved compared to the previous PBMT system in various language pairs, especially for English–Chinese. Based on

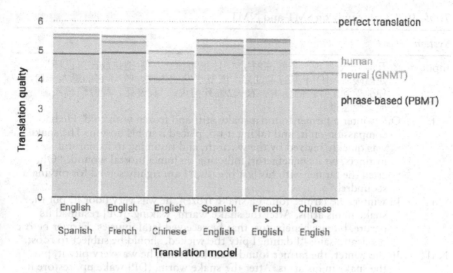

Figure 10.3 Google Research Translation Model.

the quantitative analysis, our second question is *"Why can NMT surpass SMT?"* The reasons can be summarised as follows:

1) The use of distributed word representations can facilitate the computation of semantic distance and alleviate the curse of dimensionality (Bengio et al., 2003).
2) There is no need to explicitly design features to capture translation regularities, which is quite difficult in SMT. Instead, NMT is capable of learning representations directly from the training data (Tu et al., 2016).
3) NMT algorithms such as Recurrent Neural Network (RNN) are better at capturing long-distance reordering, which is a significant challenge for SMT (Zhang et al., 2015).

Case Study

Although NMT has significantly improved translation quality, we are still wondering *"Have those problems been solved by NMT?"* In order to answer this question, we use an example to qualitatively analyse discourse problems in both SMT and NMT outputs. We employed the widely used Google Translate to translate a text from Chinese into English. We used the old version of Google Translate as an SMT system, and the latest version (Wu et al., 2016) as an NMT system.

The translation results are shown in Table 10.3. Overall, NMT translations are more fluent than those of SMT. For instance, *"When the*

Table 10.3 Case Study on SMT and NMT

System	Text
Input	冬天[1]，农夫[2]发现一条蛇冻僵了，[3]他很可怜它，便[6]把蛇放在自己怀里。蛇温暖后，[DP][4]苏醒了过来，恢复了它的本性，咬[5]了它的恩人一口，使他受到了致命的伤害。农夫2临死前说："我该死，我怜悯恶人，应该受恶报。"
Ref.	One winter a farmer found a snake stiff and frozen with cold. He had compassion on it, and taking it up, placed it in his bosom. The snake was quickly revived by the warmth, and resuming to its natural instincts, bit its benefactor, inflicting on him a mortal wound. "Oh," cried the farmer with his last breath, "I am rightly served for pitying a scoundrel."
SMT	In winter, the farmer found a snake frozen, he was very poor it, put the snake in his arms. After the snake warm, waking, [DP] resumed its nature, bite its benefactor, that he received fatal injuries. Farmer before his death, said: "I damn, I pity the wicked, should be subject to roost."
NMT	In the winter, the farmer found a snake frozen, he was very pity it, put the snake in his arms. After the snake warm, [DP] wake up, restore its nature, bite it benefactor, so that he suffered a fatal injury. When the farmer dies, he said, "I will die, and I will have mercy on the wicked."

farmer dies, he said..." is much better than "*Farmer before his death, said...*" and the connective phrase *so that* can better show a causal relation between preceding and following clauses. Besides, the lexical choice of NMT is also better, such as using the verb *pity* instead of the adjective *poor* and using *I will die* instead of *I damn*. This seems to qualitatively illustrate that NMT is better in a quite general sense. However, we drew quite distinct conclusions when analysing results from the perspective of discourse:

1) The Chinese word 冬天 (*winter*) has different translations according to its context. For general referencing, it can be translated into *in winter*. For specific referencing, we need to further consider whether it means an uncertain winter or a known winter. If the winter is uncertain, it should be translated into *once in a winter* or *one winter*, otherwise, *in the winter*. Obviously, at the beginning of the story, it means "one unknown winter." Both SMT and NMT made a mistake here.

2) The Chinese word 农夫 (*farmer*) should be translated into *a farmer* when it appears for the first time. In the following sentences, if the noun occurs again and refers to the same person, we should use *the farmer* instead. However, both instances of 农夫 in the source text were translated incorrectly by SMT. Although NMT correctly generated the translation for the second one, it seems to achieve it by chance because NMT always translates it in a general referencing way.

3) Like the first sentence of the input, a Chinese sentence in chronicle style represents a typical pattern and is usually rather long. It should be translated into several sentences in English. However, both NMT and SMT still translate them sentence by sentence and incorrectly connect two complete sentences with commas.

4) As discussed earlier, Chinese is a pro-drop language, in which certain classes of words can be omitted to make the sentence compact yet comprehensible when the identity of the pronouns can be inferred from the context. Taking the second sentence of the input, for example, since the subject 蛇 (*snake*) has already occurred in the subordinate clause 蛇温暖后 (*after the snake is warm*), it can be omitted in the main clause [DP] 苏醒了过来 (*the snake woke up*). However, the subject of the main clause is missing in both NMT and SMT translations.

5) NMT and SMT also have a tense inconsistency problem. The whole story happened in the past, thus it should be described in past tense. But the translated words *restore* and *bite* are still in present tense and NMT is even worse than SMT.

6) The Chinese word 便 （*and/then*） is a discourse connective, which shows a continuation or causality relation between its preceding and following parts. Without considering the discourse structure and relation, NMT and SMT generate grammatically incorrect translations and destroy the coherence.

Through qualitative analysis, we can draw a conclusion that discourse is a big challenge for NMT and SMT, and NMT output is more fluent than that of SMT. From the perspective of discourse, the translation quality is quite far away from a human-acceptable level. Therefore, we expect to integrate discourse knowledge into a strong NMT to alleviate the translation problems in coherence, cohesion, and consistency.

Proposed Approaches

In order to deal with the MT problems at discourse level, we propose two typical scenarios of pro-drop language translation and large-context NMT to show our methods in improving MT quality at discourse level, in SMT and NMT respectively.

Pro-Drop Language Translation

We analyse a one-million-word Chinese–English parallel corpus, and found that there are 6.5 million Chinese pronouns and 9.4 million English pronouns, which shows that more than 2.9 million Chinese pronouns are dropped. For example, as shown in Figure 10.1, among the subject pronouns 你 (*you*) and 我 (*I*) and the object pronoun 它 (*it*), the second subject pronouns 你 (*you*) are all omitted in the Chinese side. These omissions pose difficulties for MT from pro-drop languages to non-pro-drop languages, since translation of such missing pronouns cannot be normally reproduced.

Some researchers investigated dropped pronoun (DP) translation from different perspectives. For example, Taira et al. (2012) propose both simple rule-based and manual methods to add zero pronouns on the source side for Japanese–English translation. However, the BLEU scores (Papineni et al., 2002) of both systems are nearly identical, which indicates that merely considering the source side and forcing the insertion of pronouns may be less principled than tackling the problem head-on by integrating them into the SMT system itself. Le Nagard and Koehn (2010b) present a method to aid English pronoun translation into French for SMT by integrating a co-reference (CR) system. Unfortunately, their results are not convincing due to the poor performance of the CR method (Pradhan et al., 2012). Chung and Gildea (2010) systematically examine the effects of an empty category (EC) on MT with three methods: pattern, CRF (which achieves best results), and parsing. The results show that this work can really improve the end translation even though the automatic prediction of EC is not highly accurate. Tan et al. (2019) propose a method to both automatically detect the DPs and recover their translation equivalences rather than their original forms in source sentences. The detection and recovery are simultaneously performed as a sequence labelling task on source sentences. The recovered translation equivalences of DPs are incorporated into NMT as external lexical knowledge via a tagging mechanism.

Experiments

We carry out our experiments using Moses (Koehn et al., 2007) on a Chinese–English dialogue translation task. Furthermore, we train five-gram language models using the SRI Language Toolkit (Stolcke, 2002). To obtain a good word alignment, we run GIZA++ (Och & Ney, 2003) on the training data together with another larger parallel subtitle corpus that contains six million sentence pairs. We use minimum error rate training (Och, 2003) to optimise the weights.

We measure the accuracy (in terms of words) of our generation models in two phases. DP detection shows the performance of our sequence-labelling model based on RNN. We only consider the tag for each word (pro-drop or not pro-drop before the current word), without considering the exact pronoun for DPs. DP prediction shows the performance of the MLP classifier in determining the exact DP based on detection. Thus we consider both the detected and predicted pronouns. Table 10.4 lists the results of the above DP generation approaches. This indicates that predicting the exact DP in Chinese is a really difficult task. Even though the DP prediction is not highly accurate, we still hypothesise that the DP generation models are reliable enough to be used for end-to-end machine translation. Note that we only

Table 10.4 DP Detection and DP Prediction

DP	Set	P	R	F1
DP Detection	Dev	0.88	0.84	0.86
	Test	0.88	0.87	0.88
DP Prediction	Dev	0.67	0.63	0.65
	Test	0.67	0.65	0.66

Table 10.5 Results of Pro-Drop Language Translation

Systems	Dev Set	Test Set
Baseline	20.06	18.76
+DP-ins. TM	20.32 (+0.26)	17.37 (+0.61)
+DP-gen. Input		
1-best	20.49 (+0.43)	19.50 (+0.74)
2-best	20.15 (+0.09)	18.89 (+0.13)
4-best	20.64 (+0.58)	19.68 (+0.92)
6-best	21.61 (+1.55)	20.34 (+1.58)
8-best	20.94 (+0.88)	19.83 (+1.07)
Manual Oracle	24.27 (+4.21)	22.98 (+4.22)
Auto Oracle	23.10 (+3.04)	21.93 (+3.17)

show the results of 1-best DP generation here, but in the translation task, we use N-best generation candidates to recall more DPs.

As shown in Table 10.5, the baseline system uses the parallel corpus and input sentences without inserting/generating DPs. It achieves 20.06 and 18.76 in BLEU scores on the development and test data, respectively. The BLEU scores are relatively low because 1) we have only one reference; and 2) dialogue machine translation is still a challenge for the current SMT approaches. By using an additional translation model trained on the DP-inserted parallel corpus, we improve the performance consistently on both development (+0.26) and test data (+0.61). This indicates that the inserted DPs are helpful for SMT. Thus, the gain in the "+DPins TM" is mainly from improved alignment quality. We can further improve translation performance by completing the input sentences with our DP generation model. We test N-best DP insertion to examine the performance, where N = {1, 2, 4, 6, 8}. Working together with "DP-ins. TM," 1-best–generated input already achieves +0.43 and + 0.74 BLEU score improvements on development and test set, respectively. The consistency between the input sentences and the DP-inserted parallel corpus contributes most to these further improvements. As N increases, the BLEU score grows, peaking at 21.61 and 20.34 BLEU points when N = 6. Thus we achieve a final improvement of 1.55 and 1.58 BLEU points on the development and test data, respectively. However, when adding more DP candidates, the BLEU score decreases by 0.97 and 0.51. The reason for this may be that more DP candidates add more noise, which harms the translation quality. The oracle system uses the input sentences with manually annotated DPs rather than "DP-gen. Input." The performance gap between "Oracle" and "+DP-gen. Input" shows that there is still a large space (+4.22 or +3.17) for further improvement for the DP generator.

Analysis

We select sample sentences from the test set to further analyse the effects of DP generation on translation. In Figure 10.4, we show an improved case (Case A), an unchanged case (Case B), and a worse case (Case C) of translation using/not using DP insertion (i.e. "+DP-gen. Input 1-best"). In each case, we give (a) the original Chinese sentence and its translation, (b) the DP-inserted Chinese sentence and its translation, and (c) the reference English sentence. In Case A, *Do you* in the translation output is compensated by adding DP <你> (*you*) in (b), which gives a better translation than in (a). In contrast, in Case C, our DP generator regards the simple sentence as a compound sentence and inserts a wrong pronoun <我> (*I*) in (b), which causes an incorrect translation output (worse than [a]). This indicates that

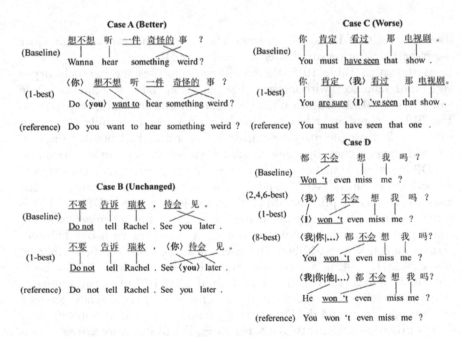

Figure 10.4 Analysis of Pro-Drop Language Translation.

we need a highly accurate parse tree of the source sentences for more correct completion of the antecedent of the DPs. In Case B, the translation results are the same in (a) and (b). This kind of unchanged case always occurs in "fixed" linguistic chunks such as preposition phrases (*on* my *way*), greetings (*see* you *later*, *thank* you) and interjections (My *God*). However, the alignment of (b) is better than that of (a) in this case. Case D shows an example of "+DP-gen. Input N-best" translation. Here, (a) is the original Chinese sentence and its translation; (b) is the 1-best DP-generated Chinese sentence and its MT output; (c) stands for 2-best, 4-best, and 6-best DP-generated Chinese sentences and their MT outputs (which are all the same); (d) is the 8-best DP-generated Chinese sentence and its MT output; (e) is the reference. The N-best DP candidate list is <我> (*I*), <你> (*you*), <他> (*he*), <我们> (*we*), <他们> (*they*), <你们> (*you*), <它> (*it*), and <她> (*she*). In (b), when integrating an incorrect 1-best DP into MT, we obtain the wrong translation. However, in (c), when considering more DPs (2-/4-/6-best), the SMT system generates a perfect translation by weighting the DP candidates during decoding. When further increasing N (8-best), (d) shows a wrong translation again due to increased noise.

Larger-Context Neural Machine Translation

The continuous vector representation of a symbol encodes multiple dimensions of similarity, equivalent to encoding more than one meaning of a word. Consequently, NMT needs to spend a substantial amount of its capacity in disambiguating source and target words based on the context defined by a source sentence (Choi et al., 2017). Consistency is another critical issue in document-level translation, where a repeated term should keep the same translation throughout the whole document (Xiao et al., 2011; Carpuat & Simard, 2012). Nevertheless, current NMT models still process a document by translating each sentence alone, suffering from inconsistency and ambiguity arising from a single source sentence. These problems are difficult to alleviate using only limited intra-sentence context.

The cross-sentence context, or global context, has proven helpful to better capture the meaning or intention in sequential tasks such as query suggestion (Sordoni et al., 2015) and dialogue modelling (Vinyals & Le, 2015; Serban et al., 2016). The leverage of global context for NMT, however, has received relatively little attention from the research community. In this chapter, we propose a cross-sentence context-aware NMT model, which considers the influence of previous source sentences in the same document. Specifically, we employ a hierarchy of Recurrent Neural Networks (RNNs) to summarise the cross-sentence context from source-side previous sentences, which deploys an additional document-level RNN on top of the sentence-level RNN encoder (Sordoni et al., 2015). After obtaining the global context, we design several strategies to integrate it into NMT to translate the current sentence. Zhang et al. (2020) propose a new framework to model cross-sentence dependencies by training neural machine translation (NMT) to predict both the target translation and surrounding sentences of a source sentence.

Experiments

We carried out experiments on a Chinese–English translation task. However, high-quality discourse-level MT training and test data are scarce (Liu & Zhang, 2020). As the document information is necessary when selecting the previous sentences, we collected all LDC corpora that contained a document boundary. The training corpus consisted of one million sentence pairs extracted from LDC corpora with 25.4 million Chinese words and 32.4 million English words. We chose the NIST05 (MT05) as our development set and NIST06 (MT06) and NIST08 (MT08) as test sets. We used a caseinsensitive BLEU score as our evaluation metric and a sign-test (Collins et al., 2005) for calculating statistical significance. We implemented our approach on top of an open-source attention-based NMT model, Nematus8 (Sennrich et al., 2016, 2017). We limited the source and target vocabularies to the most frequent 35,000 words in Chinese and English, covering approximately 97.1% and 99.4% of the data in the two languages respectively. We trained each model on sentences of length up to 80 words in the training data with early stopping. The word-embedding dimension was 600, the hidden layer size was 1,000, and the batch size was 80. All our models considered the previous three sentences' patterns (i.e. $K = 3$) as cross-sentence context.

Table 10.6 shows the translation performance in terms of BLEU score. Clearly, the proposed approaches significantly outperform the baseline in all cases. As far as the baseline (rows 1–2), Nematus significantly outperforms Moses, a commonly used phrase-based SMT system (Koehn et al., 2007b), by 2.3 BLEU points on average, indicating that it is a strong NMT baseline system.

Table 10.6 Evaluation of Translation Quality

#	System	MT05	MT06	MT08	Ave.	Δ
1	Moses	33.08	32.69	23.78	28.24	–
2	Nematus	34.35	35.75	25.39	30.57	–
3	$-\text{Init}_{enc}$	36.05	36.44[†]	26.65[†]	31.55	+0.98
4	$+\text{Init}_{dec}$	36.27	36.69[†]	27.11[†]	31.90	+1.33
5	$+\text{Init}_{enc+dec}$	36.34	36.82[†]	27.18[†]	32.00	+1.43
6	+Auxi	35.26	36.47[†]	26.12[†]	31.30	+0.73
7	+Gating Auxi	36.64	37.63[†]	26.85[†]	32.24	+1.67
8	$+\text{Init}_{enc+dec}$+Gating Auxi	36.89	37.76[†]	27.57[†]	32.67	+2.10

Table 10.7 Example of Large-Context NMT

Hist.	这 不 等于 明着 提前 告诉 贪官 们 赶紧 转移 罪证 吗 ?
Input	能否 遏制 和 震慑 腐官 ?
Ref.	Can it inhibit and deter corrupt officials?
NMT	Can we contain and deter the *enemy*?
Our	Can it contain and deter the *corrupt official*?

It is consistent with the results in Tu et al. (2017b) (i.e. 26.93 vs. 29.41) on training corpora of similar scale. For initialization strategy (rows 3–5), Initenc and Initdec improve translation performance by around +1.0 and +1.3 BLEU points individually, proving the effectiveness of warm-start with cross-sentence context. Combining them achieves a further improvement. For auxiliary context strategies (rows 6–7), the gating auxiliary context strategy achieves a significant improvement of around +1.0 BLEU points over its non-gating counterpart. This shows that, by acting as a critic, the introduced context gate learns to distinguish the different needs of the global context for generating target words. Finally, (see row 8), we combine the best variants from the initialisation and auxiliary context strategies, and achieve the best performance, improving upon Nematus by +2.1 BLEU points. This indicates the two types of strategies are complementary to each other.

Analysis

In Table 10.7, the word 腐官 (*corrupt officials*) is mistranslated as *enemy* by the baseline system. With the help of the similar word 贪官 (*corrupt officials*) in the previous sentence, our approach successfully corrects this mistake. This demonstrates that cross-sentence context indeed helps resolve certain ambiguities.

Conclusion

In this chapter, we have introduced the basics of both discourse and MT. We have also systematically analysed discourse problems in MT outputs. Targeting these problems, we presented novel approaches to improve translation qualities. Our main contributions to discourse-level machine translation cover both pro-drop language translation and large-context NMT.

We have presented an approach to recall missing pronouns for machine translation from a pro-drop language to a non-pro-drop language. Experiments show that it is crucial to identify the DP in order to improve the overall translation performance. In future work, we plan to validate the effectiveness of our approach on other text genres with different prevalence of DPs. For example, in formal text genres (e.g. newswire), DPs are not as common as in informal text genres, and the most frequently dropped pronoun in Chinese newswire is the third person singular 它 (*it*) (Baran et al., 2012), which may not be crucial to translation performance.

We proposed two complementary approaches to integrating cross-sentence context into NMT. We quantitatively and qualitatively demonstrated that the presented model significantly outperforms a strong attention-based NMT baseline system. Our models benefit from larger contexts and would be possibly further enhanced by other document-level information, such as discourse relations. We propose to study such models for full-length documents with more linguistic features in future work. In our future work, we expect several developments that will shed more light on utilising long-range contexts, i.e. designing novel architectures, such as employing discourse relations instead of directly using decoder states as cache values.

Future Work

We will explore the application of one particular aspect of discourse analysis, named argumentation theory, to evaluate machine translation quality at discourse level and develop an evaluation model to complement existing evaluation schemes, with specific reference to instrumental translation in a production context. A corpus of two million sentence pairs (Chinese–English) of parallel discourse has been set up as the base of discourse machine translation evaluation. Based on argument structure analysis and discourse modelling, the outputs of a novel machine translation evaluation system will be ready for discourse-level machine translation assessment. Specifically, the following three aspects will be included in our future work.

1) Discourse argument structure analysis. We will exploit the following aspects of argumentation theory: overall argument structure or superstructure of the textual discourse, propositional functions, conjunctives and inference indicators, types of argument, figures of speech, and narrative strategy. Based on these, we will show that evaluating transfer of argument necessarily leads to an examination of the messages conveyed in the discourse text, and of the reasoning on which they are based.

2) Argumentation parameters and evaluation grid. The components of an argument are essentially the same in all fields and types of text for any language. A set of elements (Toulmin et al., 1984) will be introduced and proposed for an argument in any field – claims, grounds, warrants, backings, qualifiers, and rebuttals – to form the argumentation schema. Based on this schema, we will add organisational relations, propositional functions, conjunctives and other inference indicators, argument types, figures, and narrative strategy to have a multi-parameter grid for an argumentation-centred translation evaluation model.

3) Dialogue information extracting and automatic scoring. The initial idea for formalising the above evaluation model is to match the target text

argumentation grid with the source text one and to score the target text accordingly. Extracting the dialogue argumentation information will be the priority to fulfil this evaluation system.

Acknowledgement

This work is supported by the XJTLU KSF project (Grant Number: KSF-E-24) and GDUFS open project (Grant Number: CTS201501). The authors also wish to thank the anonymous reviewers for many helpful comments.

References

Asher, N., & Lascarides, A. (2003). *Logics of Conversation*, Cambridge: Cambridge University Press.

Bahdanau, D., Cho, K., & Bengio, Y. (2015). Neural machine translation by jointly learning to align and translate. In: *Proceedings of the 3rd International Conference on Learning Representations* (pp. 1–15), San Diego, California, USA.

Baran, E., Yang, Y., & Xue, N. (2012). Annotating dropped pronouns in Chinese newswire text. In: *Proceedings of the 8th Language Resources and Evaluation Conference* (pp. 2795–2799), Istanbul, Turkey.

Bengio, Y., Ducharme, R., Vincent, P., & Jauvin, C. (2003). A neural probabilistic language model. *Journal of Machine Learning Research: JMLR*, 3:1137–1155, doi:10.5555/944919.944966.

Carpuat, M., & Simard, M. (2012). The trouble with SMT consistency. In: *Proceedings of the 7th Workshop on Statistical Machine Translation* (pp. 442–449), Montreal, Quebec, Canada.

Cho, K., van Merrienboer, B., Gulcehre, C., Bahdanau, D., Bougares, F., Schwenk, H., & Bengio, Y. (2014). Learning phrase representations using RNN encoder-decoder for statistical machine translation. In: *Proceedings of the 2014 Conference on Empirical Methods in Natural Language Processing* (pp. 1724–1734), Doha, Qatar.

Choi, H., Cho, K., & Bengio, Y. (2017). Context-dependent word representation for neural machine translation. *Computer Speech & Language*, 45:149–160, doi:10.1016/j.csl.2017.01.007.

Chung, T., & Gildea, D. (2010). Effects of empty categories on machine translation. In: *Proceedings of the 2010 Conference on Empirical Methods in Natural Language Processing* (pp. 636–645), Cambridge, Massachusetts, USA.

Collins, M., Koehn, P., & Kucerova, I. (2005). Clause restructuring for statistical machine translation. In: *Proceedings of the 43rd Annual Meeting of the Association for Computational Linguistics* (pp. 531–540), Ann Arbor, Michigan.

De Beaugrande, R., & Dressler, W. (1981). *Introduction to Text Linguistics*, London: Longman.

Foster, G., Isabelle, P., & Kuhn, R. (2010). Translating structured documents. In: *Proceedings of the 9th Conference of the Association for Machine Translation in the Americas*, Denver, Colorado, USA.

Halliday, M. A. K., & Hasan, R. (1976). *Cohesion in English*, London: Longman.

Hardmeier, C. (2014). *Discourse in Statistical Machine Translation*. PhD thesis, Acta Universitatis Upsaliensis.

Kalchbrenner, N., & Blunsom, P. (2013). Recurrent continuous translation models. In: *Proceedings of the 2013 Conference on Empirical Methods in Natural Language Processing* (pp. 1700–1709), Seattle, Washington, USA: Association for Computational Linguistics.

Koehn, P. (2009). *Statistical Machine Translation*, Cambridge: Cambridge University Press.

Koehn, P., Hoang, H., Birch, A., Callison-Burch, C., Federico, M., Bertoldi, N., Cowan, B., Shen, W., Moran, C., Zens, R., Dyer, C., Bojar, O., Constantin, A., & Herbst, E. (2007). Moses: Open source toolkit for statistical machine translation. In: *Proceedings of the 45th Annual Meeting of the Association for Computational Linguistics* (pp. 177–180), Prague, Czech Republic.

Le Nagard, R., & Koehn, P. (2010). Aiding pronoun translation with co-reference resolution. In: *Proceedings of the Joint 5th Workshop on Statistical Machine Translation and MetricsMATR* (pp. 252–261), Uppsala, Sweden.

Liu, S., & Zhang, X. (2020). Corpora for document-level neural machine translation. In: *Proceedings of the 12th Edition of the Language Resources and Evaluation Conference (LREC2020)* (pp. 3775–3781), Marseille, France.

Longacre, R. E. (2013). *The Grammar of Discourse*, Berlin: Springer.

Luong, T., Pham, H., & Manning, D. C. (2015). Effective approaches to attention-based neural machine translation. In: *Proceedings of the 2015 Conference on Empirical Methods in Natural Language Processing* (pp. 1412–1421), Lisbon, Portugal.

Mann, W. C., & Thompson, S. A. (1988). Rhetorical structure theory: Toward a functional theory of text organization. *Text-Interdisciplinary Journal for the Study of Discourse*, 8(3):243–281, doi:10.1515/text.1.1988.8.3.243.

Marcu, D. (2000). *The Theory and Practice of Discourse Parsing and Summarization*, Chicago: MIT Press.

Meyer, T., & Pol'akov'a, L. (2013). Machine translation with many manually labeled discourse connectives. In: *Proceedings of the 1st Workshop on Discourse in Machine Translation* (pp. 43–50), Sofia, Bulgaria.

Meyer, T., & Webber, B. (2013). Implicitation of discourse connectives in (machine) translation. In: *Proceedings of the 1st Workshop on Discourse in Machine Translation* (pp. 19–26), Sofia, Bulgaria.

Nirenburg, S., Raskin, V., & Tucker, A. (1986). On knowledge-based machine translation. In: *Proceedings of the 11th Conference on Computational Linguistics* (pp. 627–632), Bonn, Germany.

Och, F. J. (2003). Minimum error rate training in statistical machine translation. In: *Proceedings of the 41st Annual Meeting on Association for Computational Linguistics* (pp. 160–167), Sapporo, Japan.

Och, F. J., & Ney, H. (2003). A systematic comparison of various statistical alignment models. *Computational Linguistics*, 29(1):19–51, doi:10.1162/089120103321337421.

Papineni, K., Roukos, S., Ward, T., & Zhu, W.-J. (2002). BLEU: A method for automatic evaluation of machine translation. In: *Proceedings of the 40th Annual Meeting on Association for Computational Linguistics* (pp. 311–318), Philadelphia, Pennsylvania, USA.

Pradhan, S., Moschitti, A., Xue, N., Uryupina, O., & Zhang, Y. (2012). CoNLL-2012 shared task: Modeling multilingual unrestricted coreference in ontonotes.

In: *Proceedings of the 15th Conference on Computational Natural Language Learning: Shared Task* (pp. 1–27), Jeju Island, Korea.

Sanders, T., & Maat, H. P. (2006). Cohesion and coherence: Linguistic approaches. In: Brown K. (Ed.), *Encyclopedia of Language & Linguistics* (2nd edition). Berlin: Elsevier Science. doi:10.1016/B0-08-044854-2/00497-1.

Sennrich, R., Firat, O., Cho, K., Birch, A., Haddow, B., Hitschler, J., Junczys-Dowmunt, M., L''aubli, S., Barone, A. V. M., & Mokry, J. (2017). Nematus: A toolkit for neural machine translation. In: *Proceedings of the 15th Conference of the European Chapter of the Association for Computational Linguistics* (pp. 65–68), Valencia, Spain.

Sennrich, R., Haddow, B., & Birch, A. (2016). Edinburgh neural machine translation systems for WMT 16. In: *Proceedings of the First Conference on Machine Translation, Shared Task Papers 2* (pp. 371–376), Berlin, Germany.

Serban, I. V., Sordoni, A., Bengio, Y., Courville, A., & Pineau, J. (2016). Building end-to-end dialogue systems using generative hierarchical neural network models. In: *Proceedings of the 30th AAAI Conference on Artificial Intelligence Phoenix* (pp. 3776–3783), Arizona.

Sordoni, A., Bengio, Y., Vahabi, H., Lioma, C., Simonsen, J. G., & Nie, J. (2015). A hierarchical recurrent encoder-decoder for generative context-aware query suggestion. In: *Proceedings of the 24th ACM International Conference on Information and Knowledge Management* (pp. 553–562), Melbourne, Australia.

Stolcke, A. (2002). SRILM - An extensible language modeling toolkit. In: *Proceedings of the 7th International Conference on Spoken Language Processing* (pp. 901–904), Colorado, USA.

Sutskever, I., Vinyals, O., & Le, Q. V. (2014). Sequence to sequence learning with neural networks. In: *Proceedings of the Neural Information Processing Systems 2014* (pp. 3104–3112), Montreal, Canada.

Taira, H., Sudoh, K., & Nagata, M. (2012). Zero pronoun resolution can improve the quality of j-e translation. In: *Proceedings of the 6th Workshop on Syntax, Semantics and Structure in Statistical Translation* (pp. 111–118), Jeju, Republic of Korea.

Tan, X., Kuang, S., & Xiong, D. (2019). Detecting and translating dropped pronouns in neural machine translation. In: Tang J., Kan M. Y., Zhao D., Li S., & Zan H. (Eds.), *Natural Language Processing and Chinese Computing*. NLPCC 2019. Cham: Springer, doi:10.1007/978-3-030-32233-5_27.

Toulmin, S., Rieke, R., & Janik, A. (1984). *An Introduction to Reasoning*, New York: Macmillan.

Tu, Z., Lu, Z., Liu, Y., Liu, X., & Li, H. (2016). Modeling coverage for neural machine translation. In: *Proceedings of the 54th Annual Meeting of the Association for Computational Linguistics* (pp. 76–85), Berlin, Germany.

Vinyals, O., & Le, Q. (2015). *A Neural Conversational Model*. arXiv Preprint ArXiv:1506.05869.

Wang, L., Tu, Z., Zhang, X., Liu, S., Li, H., Liu, Q., & Liu, Q. (2017). A novel and robust approach for pro-drop language translation. *Machine Translation*, 31(1–2):65–87, doi:10.1007/s10590-016-9184-9.

Wang, L., Zhang, X., Tu, Z., Way, A., & Liu, Q. (2016). The automatic construction of discourse corpus for dialogue translation. In: *Proceedings of the 10th Language Resources and Evaluation Conference* (pp. 23–28), Portoro˘z, Slovenia.

Wu, Y., Schuster, M., Chen, Z., Le, Q. V., Norouzi, M., Macherey, W., Krikun, M., Cao, Y., Gao, Q., & Macherey, K. (2016). *Google's Neural Machine Translation System: Bridging the Gap between Human and Machine Translation.* arXiv Preprint ArXiv:1609.08144.

Xiao, T., Zhu, J., Yao, S., & Zhang, H. (2011). Document-level consistency verification in machine translation. In: *Proceedings of the 13th Machine Translation Summit 13* (pp. 131–138), Xiamen, China.

Xiong, D., Ben, G., Zhang, M., Lv, Y., & Liu, Q. (2013). Modeling lexical cohesion for document-level machine translation. In: *Proceedings of the 23rd International Joint Conference on Artificial Intelligence* (pp. 2183–2189), Beijing, China.

Zhang, J., & Zong, C. (2015). Deep neural networks in machine translation: An overview. *IEEE Intelligent Systems*, 30(5):16–25, doi:10.1109/MIS.2015.69.

Zhang, P., Zhang, X., Chen, W., Yu, J., Wang, Y., & Xiong, D. (2020). Learning contextualized sentence representations for document-level neural machine translation. In: *Proceedings of the 24th International Joint Conference on Artificial Intelligence*, Santiago de Compostela, Spain.

Part V
T&I Education

11 Taxing Brings Benefits
The Interpreter Advantage in Emotional Regulation

Yiguang Liu, Hailun Huang,
and Junying Liang

Introduction

In the domain of bilingual studies, there is a heated debate regarding whether "bilingual advantage" exists, that is, whether learning or using two or more languages results in cognitive advantages (e.g. Bialystok et al., 2003; Paap, 2019). As an intense bilingual experience, interpreting, especially simultaneous interpreting, is highly taxing in terms of cognitive demands (Frauenfelder & Schriefers, 1997, p. 55). In consecutive interpreting (CI), interpreters perceive and comprehend (typically assisted by note-taking) speech input and then render it into output in the target language, during which the cognitive load may accumulate before a stretch of language chunks have been interpreted (Liang et al., 2017). Simultaneous interpreting, however, is produced in synchrony with language perception and comprehension (Pöchhacker, 2011, p. 190), with the ear–voice spans ranging from two to three seconds (Christoffels et al., 2003, p. 202). In either mode of interpreting, interpreters work under great time pressure and are subject to strict executive demands. Similar to the hypothesised "bilingual advantage" deriving from bilingual experience, the issue of "interpreter advantage" has also been stimulated (for reviews, see García, 2014; Dong & Zhong, 2019; García et al., 2019) and forms the foci of the present study.

Interpreter Advantage in Executive Functions

The "interpreting advantage hypothesis" posits that "task-specific cognitive skills developed by interpreters generalize to more efficient linguistic and executive abilities in non-interpreting tasks" (García, 2014, p. 219). Compared to other common bilingual or monolingual processing tasks, interpreting induces extra difficulties, including storing and processing new information under extreme time constraints (Dong & Zhong, 2017), managing multitasks concurrently (Seeber & Kerzel, 2012), and resisting code mixing–related distractors caused by the concurrent activation of two different languages (Gerver, 1976; Liang et al., 2018). The characteristics of such challenges in interpreting seem to be closely associated with certain executive functions, such as inhibitory control and cognitive flexibility.

Executive functions (also called executive control or cognitive control) refer to a set of general-purpose control mechanisms to support self-control or self-regulation in daily life (Miyake & Friedman, 2012, p. 8). There is a general consensus that working memory (WM), inhibition, and cognitive flexibility constitute the core components of executive functions (Diamond, 2013, p.135). Work in this line of research has provided evidence supporting the existence of interpreter advantage in some aspects, including working memory (e.g. Tzou et al., 2011), inhibition (e.g. Yudes et al., 2011), and cognitive flexibility (e.g. Morales et al., 2015).

To achieve successful performance, interpreters are required to efficiently store and process continuous upcoming information, where the central role of memory, especially WM, is underscored (Padilla et al., 1995; Liang et al., 2017). In the Effort Model (Gile, 2009), it is claimed that the "memory effort," a concept similar to WM in many ways, affects all facets of interpreting, including comprehension, production, and coordination. Empirically, WM has been shown to be highly predictive of interpreting performance (Liu et al., 2004; Lin et al., 2018), and varied requirements on WM are also found to characterise different interpreting types (Liang et al., 2019; Lv & Liang, 2019; Jia & Liang, 2020). With regard to research on the interpreter advantage, the findings are mixed (for a review, see Liang & Lv, 2020). For example, an interpreter advantage in WM indexed by word span was found in Christoffels et al. (2006), but not replicated in Köpke and Nespoulous (2006). However, trained interpreters consistently show advantages in WM updating (Morales et al., 2015; Henrard & Van Daele, 2017), probably because continuous memory updating is quite important for successful interpreting.

Besides, interpreters need to switch between different tasks and reformulate inputs into outputs in the target language while inhibiting surrounding distractions. It can thus be speculated that the interpreting practice and training may benefit interpreters in terms of inhibitory control and cognitive flexibility. To test inhibitory control, participants typically need to respond to one source of information from stimuli while inhibiting the interference of distracting information displayed. However, except for the behavioural results from Timarová et al. (2014), findings from this line of research are yet to provide solid support for the potential interpreter advantage in inhibition (Morales et al., 2015; Babcock & Vallesi, 2017).

As to cognitive flexibility, empirical work commonly draws on the Wisconsin card sorting task (WCST) or dual tasks to test the switching ability. Among them, Yudes et al. (2011) recruited professional interpreters and non-interpreter controls to participate in WCST. The results demonstrated that the interpreters outperformed bilinguals because they needed fewer attempts to figure out the correct rules and made fewer errors. Nevertheless, two studies involving professional interpreters in the bivalent colour–shape task (Becker et al., 2016; Babcock & Vallesi, 2017) found an interpreter advantage in monitoring (indexed by smaller mixing cost) and faster information process (indexed by smaller global RT), but not in cognitive flexibility (indicated by switch cost).

To sum up, the hypothesised interpreter advantage seems to exist in some aspects, but the findings are inconclusive. Such findings seem to be task-dependent to some degree and characterised with a few limitations as well. As summarised by Dong and Zhong (2019), executive functions change as a function of age and L2 proficiency, which may function as two factors contributing to mixed results when they are not matched well. For example, professional interpreters are generally older than student interpreters or non-interpreter bilinguals recruited in those studies. The small sample size in some studies (e.g., ten in Padilla et al., 1995; nine in Tzou et al., 2011) is also a problem.

Psycho-Emotional Dimension of Interpreting

Most of the existing empirical efforts approach interpreter advantage from the cognitive perspective. However, many ubiquitous triggers in the authentic working environment, beyond pure cognitive ones, can impact interpreters' decision-making and other behaviours. It is reasonable to assume psycho-emotional factors may play a crucial role in interpreting. With the so-called "emotional turn" in the sciences and humanities, the psycho-emotional aspects in individual and social behaviour have drawn more attention (Rojo & Caro, 2016); though still scarce, studies on the psycho-emotional dimension of translation and interpreting studies are increasing (for a review, see Rojo, 2017).

In the face of extreme challenges, interpreters can be highly sensitive to the emotional triggers around them. Any seemingly subtle change from the normal working condition may induce more stress, which might weigh on interpreters' performance. For example, the participants in Moser-Mercer (2003) reported more physiological and psychological strains as well as a feeling of lack of control in the remote interpreting task relative to the normal conference setting. Anxiety and sustainable stress resulting from time pressure are also likely to compromise interpreting performance (Rojo, 2017). In addition, positive and negative feedback tends to impact processing styles and bias performance (Rojo & Caro, 2016).

With the impact of various emotional triggers recognised, it makes sense that professional and student interpreters acquire interpreting experience and learn to handle these emotional factors through certain strategies. Empirical work has been made to explore emotional regulation, which indicates that professional interpreters have a greater capacity to moderate the interference of emotions compared with novices, which is partly due to their work experience as well as the capacity to make use of metacognition

(Angelone & Shreve, 2011). Furthermore, Hild (2014) argued for the need to integrate emotion regulation as a component of interpreting expertise since professional interpreters have the ability to efficiently regulate emotions to maintain task focus. In this regard, training and practice may help interpreters become more free from emotional interference, particularly in the setting of a conference.

The Current Study

The current study aims to investigate whether the domain-specific emotional regulation advantages acquired through interpreting training can be generalised to domain-general settings. To this end, we recruited student interpreters and non-interpreter bilinguals who are matched in terms of age and L2 proficiency. Participants engaged in the Simon task (Experiment 1) and the digit switch task (Experiment 2) under different emotional conditions. The Simon task is frequently used to capture inhibitory control ability with a conflicting design, where participants must respond to one stimulus dimension (i.e. colour) while inhibiting the response tendency elicited by the other stimulus dimension (i.e. position). In the task, participants tend to respond more slowly when there is a mismatch between the position of the displayed stimulus on the screen (left or right) and that of the response key on the keyboard (left or right), which is called the Simon effect. The smaller reaction time (RT) difference between the incongruent and the congruent condition can be indicative of better inhibitory ability. As for the digit switch task, we followed the version used in Sudevan and Taylor (1987) to test switching ability. According to the task cue in each trial, participants are instructed to evaluate the displayed digit as even/odd or lower/higher than five. The switch cost, which is calculated as the RT difference between the repetition trial and switch trial, can be used to measure cognitive flexibility. In addition to the RT difference, global RT is also worthy of attention in both of the tasks because it is an index of monitoring ability, another essential component of executive functions (Mishra, 2018, p. 55). In detail, it is in charge of evaluating changes and then the need for inhibitory control or response switches (Bialystok, 2006; Costa et al., 2009).

   With regard to the emotion induction, we selected music clips to induce and maintain certain emotional states during the whole procedure, which was inspired by a relevant work (Guo et al., 2019). Given that a line of research suggests that the level of approach motivation instead of valence mainly alters the breadth of attention as well as executive functions (Gable & Harmon-Jones, 2008; Liu & Wang, 2014), the present study focuses on the dimension of approach motivation. In this regard, Liu and Wang (2014) found that there is a balance between cognitive flexibility and stability, with low-approach-motivated positive affect promoting cognitive flexibility but also resulting in higher distractibility. Therefore, it is expected that our participants generally show performance advantage in the Simon task under the high-approach-motivated emotion condition, while in the digit switch task better performance is anticipated for the low-approach-motivated emotion condition.

Taken together, by using two executive function tasks and manipulating participants' approach motivation, the current study sought to answer the following two research questions:

Q1: Will interpreters gain advantages in executive functions through interpreting training?
Q2: Will interpreters gain advantages in emotional regulation through interpreting training?

The first question is intended to enrich the existing studies on the interpreter advantage in executive functions. If the answer to the first question were "yes," the student interpreters would exhibit better performance in the two tasks. The second question is the main focus of the current study that is anticipated to extend the interpreter advantage studies to the psycho-emotional dimension. If the interpreter advantage in emotional regulation existed, the student interpreters in the present study would perform more stably under different emotional conditions.

Experiment 1

Method

PARTICIPANTS

A total of 32 students (22–24 years old) from Zhejiang University participated in the experiment and were rewarded by cash. All participants reported normal or correct-to-normal vision with no history of psychiatric or neurological disorders. The participants provided their written informed consent before the experiment and all details of the experiment conformed to and were also approved by the Research Ethics Board of Zhejiang University.

All participants were divided into two groups, the bilingual group and the interpreter group. The bilingual group consisted of 16 students (seven females) without translation or interpreting training experience. The interpreter group consisted of 16 students (11 females) who had received one year of in-class interpreting training. Before the main experiment, they participated in the Quick Placement Test (QPT), a quick test to evaluate English proficiency (Geranpayeh, 2003). QPT has been frequently used in bilingual studies and the score is highly correlated with participants' language proficiency in terms of listening (e.g. Namaziandost et al., 2018), speaking (e.g. Mahdavirad, 2015), vocabulary (e.g. Ma et al., 2016), reading (e.g. Gürergene, 2019), and writing (Peng et al., 2020). According to the score, these participants can be recognised as advanced English learners (M = 48.97, SD = 2.33), without statistically significant difference between the two groups (t [30] = 0.76, p = 0.451, d = 0.16).

EMOTION INDUCTION AND ASSESSMENT

For emotion manipulation, two pieces of music (*Espana Cani* and *Kiss the Rain*) were selected to induce high- and low-approach-motivated emotional states, respectively. These two pieces of music are both clips without lyrics so that the possible interference caused by word meaning could be avoided. To ensure the effectiveness of arousing respective emotions, another ten students from Zhejiang University participated in a rating pre-test. The results showed that corresponding emotional states (in terms of approach motivation rather than valence) can be induced by the selected music.

In order to measure the induced emotional states of participants, a 6 × 6 affect grid was used in the main experiments, which is an adjusted version of the 9 × 9 grid graph used by Russell et al. (1989) and can assess emotion in the dimension of approach motivation (extremely high at the top to extremely low at the bottom) and valence (extremely positive on the right to extremely negative on the left). By selecting the 6 × 6 affect grid, there were only three levels (low, medium, high) of emotional strength for each emotional tendency, which made it easier for the participants to understand the rules and make a clear self-evaluation.

PROCEDURE AND DESIGN

The participants were first given instructions to both the emotion assessment and the Simon task. After that, they rated their emotional state through the affect grid, which provided their emotional baseline. Then they listened to one music clip for one minute and the music continued throughout the rest of the experiment at half volume. After the experiment, they were required to complete the second emotion assessment.

In the Simon task, the participants were asked to respond to the colour information of stimuli while ignoring the irrelevant spatial location of stimuli. Specifically, each trial began with a fixation "+" at the centre of the screen presented for 350 ms. Then, a blank screen was displayed for 350 ms. After that, a coloured dot was displayed on either the left or right side of the fixation and the participants were instructed to respond to the stimuli colour by pressing one of the two target keys ("A" key for blue stimuli, "K" key for green stimuli); see Figure 11.1. To note, there could be the congruent (the location of the stimulus coincided with the position of the response key, e.g. green dot on the right) or incongruent condition (the above-mentioned locations did not match, e.g. green dot on the left). The participants were required to respond as quickly as possible within a time window of 500 ms. There were 80 trials in total, 16 for practice.

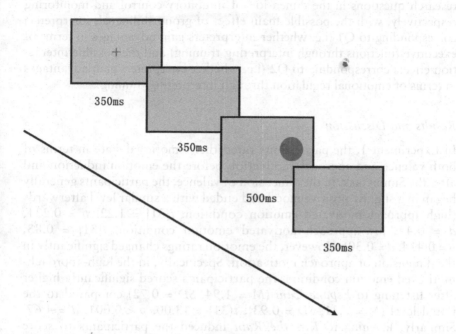

Figure 11.1 The Procedure of the Simon Task in Experiment 1.

After the first Simon task, all participants repeated the whole procedure above but listened to the other music clip for inducing the other emotional state. The sequence of the music played was counterbalanced, that is, half of the participants were randomly assigned to be induced by *Espana Cani* first and *Kiss the Rain* later, and the other half *Kiss the Rain* first and *Espana Cani* later.

Data Analyses

To evaluate the effectiveness of emotion induction, paired sample *t*-tests were used to analyse the emotional ratings. For the statistical analyses for the Simon task, we did the data trimming first. Specifically, for each participant, the outliers in which the RTs deviated more than three SD from the mean were excluded. With a focus on the RT difference between the congruent and incongruent conditions, ANOVA was used with the trial type (congruent, incongruent) and emotional state (high-approach-motivated, low-approach-motivated) as within-subject factors and group (bilingual, interpreter) as a between-subject factor. In addition, we did an additional 2 (group: interpreters vs. bilinguals) × 2 (emotional state: high-approach-motivated vs. low-approach-motivated) mixed two-way ANOVA for analysing global RT. The two ANOVA analyses can provide answers to the research questions in the dimension of inhibitory control and monitoring respectively, with the possible main effect of group (bilingual, interpreter) corresponding to Q1 (i.e. whether interpreters gain advantages in terms of executive functions through interpreting training) and the possible interaction effects corresponding to Q2 (i.e. whether interpreters gain advantages in terms of emotional regulation through interpreting training).

Results and Discussion

In Experiment 1, the participants rated their emotional state in terms of both valence and approach motivation before the emotion induction and after the Simon task. In the dimension of valence, the participants generally began in a slightly positive mood and ended with a similar level afterwards (high-approach-motivated emotion condition: $t[31] = 1.22$, $p = 0.231$, $d = 0.44$; low-approach-motivated emotion condition: $t[31] = 0.83$, $p = 0.414$, $d = 0.30$). However, the emotion ratings changed significantly in the dimension of approach motivation. Specifically, in the high-approach-motivated emotion condition, the participants scored significantly higher after listening to *Espana Cani* ($M = 1.94$, $SD = 0.72$) compared to the initial level ($M = 0.31$, $SD = 0.93$), $t(31) = 13.00$, $p < 0.001$, $d = 4.67$. Similarly, listening to *Kiss the Rain* induced the participants to score lower ($M = -0.22$, $SD = 0.32$) relative to their baseline level ($M = 0.97$, $SD = 0.97$), $t(31) = 6.73$, $p < 0.001$, $d = 2.42$. The results indicate the success of emotion induction in terms of approach motivation while the level of valence is controlled.

With respect to data analysis for the Simon task, the three-way ANOVA on RTs revealed a main effect of trial type, $F(1, 30) = 103.99$, $p < 0.001$, $\eta_p^2 = 0.78$, with faster responses in the congruent condition ($M = 436.16$ ms, $SD = 41$) than the incongruent condition ($M = 474.09$ ms, $SD = 39$). This is consistent with our intuition and the Simon effect. The main effect of emotional state was statistically significant, $F(1, 30) = 6.71$, $p = 0.015$, $\eta_p^2 = 0.18$, but not the main effect of group, $F(1, 30) = 0.79$, $p = 0.382$, $\eta_p^2 = 0.03$. Besides, there was a significant trial type × emotional state × group interaction effect, $F(1, 30) = 5.81$, $p = 0.022$, $\eta_p^2 = 0.16$. To further analyse the different Simon effects in each condition, we conducted the simple effect analysis, with the magnitude of Simon effect measured through the RT differences between the congruent and incongruent conditions. The results demonstrated that bilinguals showed a significantly stronger Simon effect in the high-approach-motivated emotion condition ($M = 40.78$ ms, $SD = 24$) relative to the low-approach-motivated emotion condition ($M = 22.70$ ms, $SD = 29$), $t(15) = 3.32$, $p = 0.005$, $d = 1.71$. However, no statistically significant difference was observed for the student interpreters under the different emotional states, $t(15) = 0.68$, $p = 0.505$, $d = 0.35$, indicating the student interpreters showed more stable Simon effect in magnitude under the different emotional states; see Figure 11.2. Taken together, emotional triggers affected

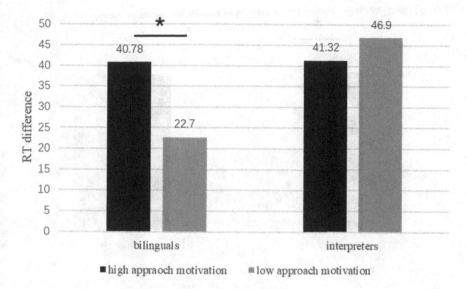

Figure 11.2 The Average RT Difference Between the Congruent and Incongruent Condition in the Simon Task Across the Two Different Groups (* $p < 0.05$).

the participants' performance in the Simon task when inhibitory control was involved, and meanwhile interpreting training helped the student interpreters mitigate the emotional modulation.

Furthermore, the other two-way ANOVA was conducted with global RT as the dependent variable. The results revealed a significant main effect of emotional state, $F(1, 30) = 4.56$, $p = 0.041$, $\eta_p^2 = 0.13$, and the participants performed better in the high-approach-motivated condition ($M = 455.16$ ms, $SD = 37$). But the main effect of group was insignificant, $F(1, 30) = 1.79$, $p = 0.191$, $\eta_p^2 = 0.06$. The interaction effect between group and emotional state was significant, $F(1, 30) = 4.20$, $p = 0.049$, $\eta_p^2 = 0.12$. The simple effect analysis showed that for bilinguals, they performed significantly better in the high-approach-motivated emotion condition ($M = 459.69$ ms, $SD = 41$) than in the low-approach-motivated emotion condition ($M = 477.74$ ms, $SD = 48$), $t(15) = 3.26$, $p = 0.005$, $d = 1.68$. However, the student interpreters did not show significantly different performance across the two conditions (high-approach-motivated condition: $M = 450.62$ ms, $SD = 32.83$; low-approach-motivated condition: $M = 451.00$ ms, $SD = 35.82$), $t(15) = 0.06$, $p = 0.955$, $d = 0.03$; see Figure 11.3.

The results partly replicated the results presented in the previous paragraph concerning the main effect of emotional state and group, also indicating the existence of the interpreter advantage in emotional regulation in terms of monitoring ability.

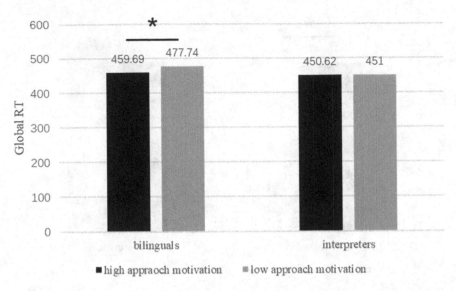

Figure 11.3 The Average Global RT in the Simon Task Across the Two Different Groups (* $p < 0.05$).

Experiment 2

Method

PARTICIPANTS

Another 32 students (22–24 years old) from Zhejiang University participated in the experiment, consisting of 16 Chinese–English bilinguals (seven females) without any translation or interpreting training experience, as well as 16 student interpreters (11 females) who had received one year of in-class interpreting training. All participants reported normal or correct-to-normal vision with no history of psychiatric or neurological disorders. The participants provided their written informed consent before the experiment and all details of the experiment conformed to and were approved by the Research Ethics Board of Zhejiang University. They also participated in the Quick Placement Test (QPT), with the results showing they were advanced English learners ($M = 48.97$, $SD = 2.33$), without statistically significant difference between the bilingual group and the interpreter group, $t(30) = 0.13$, $p = 0.895$, $d = 0.05$.

PROCEDURE AND DESIGN

Experiment 2 was the same as Experiment 1 except that the participants performed the digit switch task. Specifically, they were instructed to respond to stimuli based on two different task cues in each trial.

Each trial started with a fixation "+" at the centre of the screen presented for 350 ms, with a blank screen following for 350 ms. After that, a task cue (i.e. 奇偶判断 "jioupanduan" meaning "odd–even evaluation" or 大小判断 "daxiaopanduan" meaning "lower–higher evaluation") was presented for 1,000 ms, informing the participants to evaluate the following integer (from 1 to 9 without 5) as odd/even or lower/higher than 5. When the odd–even task cue was given, the participants pressed the "A" key for odd digits or "K" for even ones. Similarly, if they saw the lower–higher cue, they needed to press the "A" key when the displayed digit was lower than 5 or the "K" key when higher than 5; see Figure 11.4. The participants were required to respond as quickly as possible and each digit would remain on the screen for 500 ms at most. There were 100 trials in total, 20 for practice.

Data Analyses

Experiment 2 followed a similar data trimming and analysis procedure to Experiment 1. A three-way ANOVA was used to investigate performance related to cognitive flexibility, with the trial type (repetition, switch) and emotional state (high-approach-motivated, low-approach-motivated) as within-subject factors and group (bilingual, interpreter) as a between-subject factor. Focusing on the global RT, we also performed an additional 2 (group: interpreters vs. bilinguals) × 2 (emotional state: high-approach-motivated

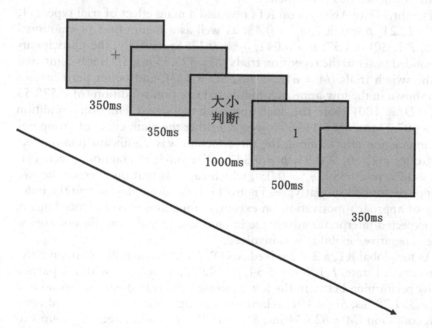

Figure 11.4 The Procedure of the Digit Switch Task in Experiment 2.

vs. low-approach-motivated) mixed two-way ANOVA given that the global RT can indicate the monitoring efficiency for changes. The two ANOVA analyses can provide answers to the research questions in the dimensions of cognitive flexibility and monitoring, respectively, with the possible main effect of group (bilingual, interpreter) addressing Q1 and the possible inter-action effects addressing Q2.

Results and Discussion

The participants rated their emotional states in terms of both valence and approach motivation before the emotion induction and after the digit switch task. In the dimension of valence, the participants generally began in a slightly positive mood and ended with a similar level later on (high-approach-motivated emotion condition: $t[31] = 0.30$, $p = 0.768$, $d = 0.11$; low-approach-motivated emotion condition: $t[31] = 0.85$, $p = 0.402$, $d = 0.31$). However, in the high-approach-motivated emotion condition, the participants scored significantly higher after listening to *Espana Cani* ($M = 1.88$, $SD = 0.87$) compared to the initial level ($M = 0.34$, $SD = 0.90$), $t(31) = 10.29$, $p < 0.001$, $d = 3.70$. Similarly, listening to *Kiss the Rain* induced the participants to score lower ($M = -0.19$, $SD = 1.33$) relative to their baseline level ($M = 0.88$, $SD = 1.10$), $t(31) = 5.75$, $p < 0.001$, $d = 2.07$. The results suggest that the participants were successfully assigned to the corresponding motivated emotion condition while the emotional level in terms of valence was controlled.

The three-way ANOVA on RTs revealed a main effect of trial type, $F(1, 30) = 22.21$, $p < 0.001$, $\eta_p^2 = 0.43$, as well as a main effect of emotional state, $F(1, 30) = 4.57$, $p = 0.041$, $\eta_p^2 = 0.13$. Specifically, the participants responded faster in the repetition trials ($M = 573.33$ ms, $SD = 90$) compared to the switch trials ($M = 612.49$ ms, $SD = 113$), and better performance was shown in the low-approach-motivated emotion condition ($M = 578.55$ ms, $SD = 100$) than the high-approach-motivated emotion condition ($M = 607.27$ ms, $SD = 113$). However, neither the main effect of group nor the interaction effect among the three factors was significant (main effect of group: $F[1, 30] = 0.91$, $p = 0.347$, $\eta_p^2 = 0.03$; interaction effect: $F[1, 30] = 0.79$, $p = 0.380$, $\eta_p^2 = 0.03$), which suggests that on average the two groups performed similarly; see Figure 11.5. Accordingly, though the influ-ence of approach motivation on executive functions was evidenced again, the expected interpreter advantage in emotional regulation did not appear when cognitive flexibility was involved.

As for global RT, a 2 × 2 mixed ANOVA found a significant main effect of emotional state, $F(1, 30) = 5.54$, $p = 0.025$, $\eta_p^2 = 0.13$, with the partici-pants performing better in the low-approach-motivated emotion condition ($M = 591.78$ ms, $SD = 101$) relative to the high-approach-motivated emo-tion condition ($M = 623.54$ ms, $SD = 112$). The main effect of group was insignificant, $F(1, 30) = 0.50$, $p = 0.485$, $\eta_p^2 = 0.02$. The group × emotional

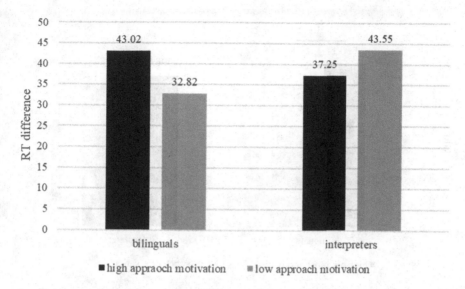

Figure 11.5 The Average RT Difference Between the Repetition and Switch Condition in the Digit Switch Task Across the Two Different Groups.

state interaction effect was significant, $F(1, 30) = 4.36$, $p = 0.045$, $\eta_p^2 = 0.13$. The simple effect analysis showed that for the bilinguals, the low-approach-motivated emotion ($M = 590.15$ ms, $SD = 111$) contributed to their better performance compared to the high-approach-motivated emotion ($M = 650.10$ ms, $SD = 120$), $t(15) = 2.91$, $p = 0.011$, $d = 1.50$. However, the student interpreters did not present any statistically significant performance difference under the two emotional states (high-approach-motivated emotion condition: $M = 596.98$ ms, $SD = 104$; low-approach-motivated emotion condition: $M = 593.41$ ms, $SD = 89$), $t(15) = 0.20$, $p = 0.841$, $d = 0.10$; see Figure 11.6. This indicates that interpreting training benefits the student interpreters in fighting emotional interference in the process of monitoring for changes.

Above all, it is suggested that emotional state, rather than interpreting training experience, can modulate the participants' performance in the digit switch task. Furthermore, we found that the student interpreters showed better emotional regulation when monitoring efficiency (but not cognitive flexibility) was required.

General Discussion

This chapter focuses on the possible interpreter advantage in emotional regulation and investigates whether the domain-specific emotional regulation advantages resulting from interpreting training can transfer to

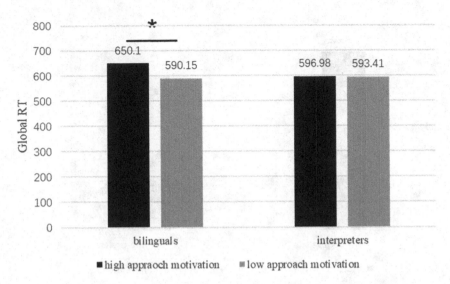

Figure 11.6 The Average Global RT in the Digit Switch Task Across the Two Different Groups (* $p < 0.05$).

domain-general settings. To this end, we recruited student interpreters and well-matched non-interpreter bilinguals to participate in two common tasks taxing different executive functions, namely, the Simon task (Experiment 1) and the digit switch task (Experiment 2), with their emotional state manipulated. No group differences in executive functions were found but the student interpreters outperformed the bilinguals in emotional regulation because they performed more stably under different emotional conditions. To note, the interpreter advantage in emotional regulation was shown when inhibitory control and monitoring were required, but not cognitive flexibility.

Interpreter Advantage in Executive Functions

According to the hypothesis of the "interpreting advantage," interpreters acquire more benefits in executive function skills than bilinguals and monolinguals because WM capacity, inhibitory control, and cognitive flexibility are thought to be necessary for successful interpreting. Empirical effort has been made to explore the interpreter advantages in various tasks but mixed findings have been shown. Based on the experiment design in the present study, the first research question is intended to generate additional evidence for this body of research.

In Experiment 1, the null main effect of group (interpreter, bilingual) reveals no difference between student interpreters and bilinguals in inhibitory control measured by the Simon task. The result is in line with most behavioural studies, in which either student interpreters (Köpke & Nespoulous, 2006) or professional interpreters (Morales et al., 2015) were involved. The reason for the lack of inhibitory control advantage in these studies, along with the present one, may be due to the limitation of behavioural experiments because the results could be a coordination of several processes (Luck, 2014). According to an ERP study conducted by Dong and Zhong (2017), the advantage may have appeared but declined before participants responded by pressing a certain button.

Similarly, Experiment 2 reveals that interpreting training did not benefit student interpreters in switch cost, which is an important indicator for cognitive flexibility. The results are inconsistent with the studies where expertise in interpreting was found to enhance cognitive flexibility through the WCST task (Yudes et al., 2011), but consistent with a study reporting a null effect of switch cost and a marginally significant effect of mixing cost (Babcock & Vallesi, 2017), as well as a study in which students without much interpreting training participated (Rosiers et al., 2019). In this regard, there may be two explanations for the current absence of between-group effect in terms of cognitive flexibility. One explanation is that the positive results are somehow task-dependent. Several studies employing the WCST task provide support for the interpreter advantage (Yudes et al., 2011), but not the studies where the task-switching paradigm was used (Babcock & Vallesi, 2017; Rosiers et al., 2019). For the other explanation, it may be reasonable to assume that switching skills are developed during training and practice but the acquisition takes time. According to the prior work, various neurocognitive effects in interpreters are associated with their hours of practice (Elmer et al., 2014) and years of experience (Santilli et al., 2018). In this sense, one year of in-class training may not be enough for novices to acquire significant advantages in cognitive flexibility.

Interpreter Advantage in Emotional Regulation

Despite the absence of interpreter advantage in executive functions, here our major focus is the possible interpreter advantage in emotional regulation. In Experiment 1, the significant interaction effect between emotional state and group affiliation indicates that the student interpreters showed statistically significant difference relative to non-interpreters in the magnitude difference of the Simon effect under different emotional conditions. Thus, we can safely say that interpreting training benefits interpreters in the capacity to free themselves from the modulation of emotion on inhibitory control.

Recently, an increasing number of translation and interpreting studies have acknowledged the essential role of psycho-emotional factors (Rojo, 2017). The consideration of emotion contributes to the ecological validity of interpreting studies because in the authentic stressed-out working and learning environment, many triggers, including untypical working mode (Moser-Mercer, 2003), time pressure (Rojo, 2017), feedback (Rojo & Caro,

2016), etc., can modulate interpreters' emotional states and thus affect their interpreting performance. According to the rationale of the interpreter advantage, it is natural to assume that interpreting experience can be beneficial to emotional regulation in certain aspects because of its potential role as an important component of interpreting expertise (Hild, 2014).

In the present study, the more stable performance of student interpreters in the Simon task is consistent with our prediction. The Simon task is a classic paradigm for measuring inhibitory control. Inhibitory control plays a crucial role in producing successful interpretation because interpreters must focus only on the things that are relevant to their task and try to avoid the influence of many distractions from the learning or working environment. It is also evidenced by an ERP study as an aspect of interpreter advantage (Dong & Zhong, 2017). Thus, with the emotion × cognition interaction presented, this study furthers our understanding of inhibitory control in interpreting as well as the benefit of interpreting training to help people inhibit distractions from the emotional perspective. Given that the recruited participants with interpreting training were novices, it suggests that emotional regulation advantage can be acquired at an early stage of interpreting training. Albeit student interpreters may still be inexperienced, interpreting training might have helped them to be confident and avoid anxiety in the face of challenges.

Nevertheless, no similar interaction effect was found in Experiment 2, where cognitive flexibility was measured by the digit switch task. The unexpected results indicate that the emotional regulation advantage deriving from interpreting training may not transfer to general cognitive flexibility. Based on the view that only those distinctively taxed and specific executive functions during interpreting tend to be boosted (García et al., 2019), cognitive flexibility may not be that specific to interpreting compared to general bilingual communication, which is in line with some empirical research (e.g., Henrard & Van Daele, 2017). However, regarding why the interpreter advantage in emotional regulation was shown in the task related to inhibitory control but not cognitive flexibility, the data in the present study are not able to provide a thorough explanation and further efforts are needed.

Besides, as two cognition-related tasks to measure inhibitory control and cognitive flexibility respectively, the Simon task and the digit switch task share something in common. There are different trial types in both of them, namely, the congruent/incongruent condition in the Simon task and the repetition/switch condition in the digit switch task. In this sense, the global RT is also worthy of attention because it is indicated as an index of another important component of executive functions, that is, monitoring for changes. According to the above-mentioned results in terms of global RT, the two experiments showed the same pattern. Specifically, under the different emotional conditions in terms of approach motivation, student interpreters generally performed more stably in the Simon task and the digit switch task, regardless of the trial type. The monitoring system is in charge of evaluating changes and the need for inhibitory control or switching (Costa et al., 2009), and monitoring in a task includes both alertness and vigilance (Mishra, 2018). Compared with the monitoring in the bilingual context (Mishra, 2018), monitoring for interpreters could include determining the distractions and then inhibiting them on the one hand, and evaluating and even predicting the pauses and ends of input speech to switch between multiple processes efficiently on the other hand. In this sense, it is an extremely cognitively taxing process under great time pressure and possibly interfered by emotional triggers. It makes sense that interpreting training can help interpreters to mitigate the modulation of emotion in terms of monitoring.

We have to admit that the current study has potential limitations. First, we drew on only one task to measure one certain component of executive functions. To provide more solid evidence, it is worthwhile to include multiple tasks simultaneously for testing one aspect of executive functions. Moreover, one might argue that the emotional regulation advantages may not be unique to interpreters but fueled by other factors. For this issue, an experimental design with more precisely controlled populations may be a good solution, e.g. contrasting student interpreters and matched bilinguals who have been trained in public speaking or debating.

Conclusions

The present study is the first empirical effort that extends the interpreter advantage studies to the psycho-emotional dimension. The findings suggest that interpreting training can be beneficial to emotional regulation in domain-general settings. Specifically, the advantage in emotional regulation deriving from interpreting training was shown in the task taxing cognitive functions specifically required by interpreting, i.e. inhibitory control and monitoring, but not cognitive flexibility. The explanations of the findings as well as the limitations of the present study have been discussed. Future investigations are required to dig deeper into emotional factors in interpreting as well as their interaction with interpreting-specific cognitive functions.

References

Angelone, E., & Shreve, G. M. (2011). Uncertainty management, metacognitive bundling in problem solving, and translation quality. In: S. O'Brien (Ed.), *Cognitive Explorations of Translation* (pp. 108–130). London: Continuum.

Babcock, L., & Vallesi, A. (2017). Are simultaneous interpreters expert bilinguals, unique bilinguals, or both? *Bilingualism: Language and Cognition*, 20(2), 403–417. doi:10.1017/S1366728915000735

Becker, M., Schubert, T., Strobach, T., Gallinat, J., & Kühn, S. (2016). Simultaneous interpreters vs. professional multilingual controls: Group differences in cognitive control as well as brain structure and function. *NeuroImage*, 134, 250–260. doi:10.1016/j.neuroimage.2016.03.079

Bialystok, E. (2006). Effect of bilingualism and computer video game experience on the Simon task. *Canadian Journal of Experimental Psychology/Revue Canadienne de Psychologie Expérimentale*, 60(1), 68–79. doi:10.1037/cjep2006008

Bialystok, E., Majumder, S., & Martin, M. M. (2003). Developing phonological awareness: Is there a bilingual advantage? *Applied Psycholinguistics*, 24(1), 27–44. doi:10.1017/S014271640300002X

Christoffels, I. K., de Groot, A. M. B., & Kroll, J. F. (2006). Memory and language skills in simultaneous interpreters: The role of expertise and language proficiency. *Journal of Memory and Language*, 54(3), 324–345. doi:10.1016/j.jml.2005.12.004

Christoffels, I. K., De Groot, A. M. B., & Waldorp, L. J. (2003). Basic skills in a complex task: A graphical model relating memory and lexical retrieval to simultaneous interpreting. *Bilingualism: Language and Cognition*, 6(3), 201–211. doi:10.1017/S1366728903001135

Costa, A., Hernández, M., Costa-Faidella, J., & Sebastián-Gallés, N. (2009). On the bilingual advantage in conflict processing: Now you see it, now you don't see it, now you don't. *Cognition*, 113(2), 135–149. doi:10.1016/j.cognition.2009.08.001

Diamond, A. (2013). Executive functions. *Annual Review of Psychology*, 64, 135–168. doi:10.1146/annurev-psych-113011-143750

Dong, Y., & Zhong, F. (2017). Interpreting experience enhances early attentional processing, conflict monitoring and interference suppression along the time course of processing. *Neuropsychologia*, 95, 193–203. doi:10.1016/j.neuropsychologia.2016.12.007

Dong, Y., & Zhong, F. (2019). The intense bilingual experience of interpreting and its neurocognitive consequences. In: J. W. Schwieter & M. Paradis (Eds.), *The Handbook of the Neuroscience of Multilingualism* (pp. 685–700). Hoboken: Wiley-Blackwell.

Elmer, S., Klein, C., Kühnis, J., Liem, F., Meyer, M., & Jäncke, L. (2014). Music and language expertise influence the categorization of speech and musical sounds: Behavioral and electrophysiological measurements. *Journal of Cognitive Neuroscience*, 26(10), 2356–2369. doi:10.1162/jocn_a_00632

Frauenfelder, U., & Schriefers, H. (1997). A psycholinguistic perspective on simultaneous interpretation. *Interpreting. International Journal of Research and Practice in Interpreting*, 2(1–2), 55–89. doi:10.1075/intp.2.1-2.03fra

Gable, P. A., & Harmon-Jones, E. (2008). Approach-motivated positive affect reduces breadth of attention. *Psychological Science*, 19(5), 476–482. doi:10.1111/j.1467-9280.2008.02112.x

García, A. M. (2014). The interpreter advantage hypothesis: Preliminary data patterns and empirically motivated questions. *Translation and Interpreting Studies*, 9(2), 219–238. doi:10.1075/tis.9.2.04gar

García, A. M., Muñoz, E., & Kogan, B. (2019). Taxing the bilingual mind: Effects of simultaneous interpreting experience on verbal and executive mechanisms. *Bilingualism: Language and Cognition*, 1–11. doi:10.1017/S1366728919000063

Geranpayeh, A. (2003). A quick review of the English quick placement test. *UCLES Research Notes*, 12, 8–10

Gerver, D. (1976). Empirical studies of simultaneous interpretation: A review and a model. In: R. W. Brislin (Ed.), *Translation: Application and Research*. New York: Gardner.

Gile, D. (2009). *Basic Concepts and Models for Interpreter and Translator Training* (2nd ed.). Amsterdam: John Benjamins.

Guo, Y., Li, W., Lu, X., Xu, X., Qiu, F., Shen, M., & Gao, Z. (2019). Emotional states affect the retention of biological motion in working memory. *Emotion*. doi:10.1037/emo0000668

Gürergene, E. (2019). A comparative study on the effect of varied reading input on discourse signaling awareness. *Advances in Language and Literary Studies*, 10(2), 27–37. doi:10.7575/aiac.alls.v.10n.2p.27

Henrard, S., & Van Daele, A. (2017). Different bilingual experiences might modulate executive tasks advantages: Comparative analysis between monolinguals, translators, and interpreters, translators, and interpreters. *Frontiers in Psychology*, 8(1870). doi:10.3389/fpsyg.2017.01870

Hild, A. (2014). The role of self-regulatory processes in the development of interpreting expertise. *Translation and Interpreting Studies*, 9(1), 128–149. https://doi-org.ru.idm.oclc.org/10.1075/tis.9.1.07hil

Jia, H., & Liang, J. (2020). Lexical category bias across interpreting types: Implications for synergy between cognitive constraints and language representations. *Lingua*, 239. doi:10.1016/j.lingua.2020.102809. http://www.ncbi.nlm.nih.gov/pubmed/102809

Köpke, B., & Nespoulous, J.-L. (2006). Working memory performance in expert and novice interpreters. *Interpreting. International Journal of Research and Practice in Interpreting*, 8(1), 1–23. doi:10.1075/intp.8.1.02kop

Liang, J., & Lv, Q. (2020). Converging evidence in empirical interpreting studies: Peculiarities, paradigms, and prospects. In: L. Vandevoorde, J. Daems, & B. Defrancq (Eds.), *New Empirical Perspectives on Translation and Interpreting*. New York: Taylor & Francis/Routledge.

Liang, J., Fang, Y., Lv, Q., & Liu, H. (2017). Dependency distance differences across interpreting types: Implications for cognitive demand. *Frontiers in Psychology*, 8(2132). doi:10.3389/fpsyg.2017.02132

Liang, J., Lv, Q., & Liu, Y. (2018). Interpreting as a mirror for language foundations: Comment on "Rethinking Foundations of Language from a Multidisciplinary Perspective" by T. Gong et al. *Physics of Life Reviews*, 26–27, 139–141. doi:10.1016/j.plrev.2018.06.002

Liang, J., Lv, Q., & Liu, Y. (2019). Quantifying interpreting types: Language sequence mirrors cognitive load minimization in interpreting tasks. *Frontiers in Psychology*, 10(285). doi:10.3389/fpsyg.2019.00285

Lin, Y., Lv, Q., & Liang, J. (2018). Predicting fluency with language proficiency, working memory, and directionality in simultaneous interpreting. *Frontiers in Psychology*, 9(1543). doi:10.3389/fpsyg.2018.01543

Liu, M., Schallert, D. L., & Carroll, P. J. (2004). Working memory and expertise in simultaneous interpreting. *Interpreting. International Journal of Research and Practice in Interpreting*, 6(1), 19–42. doi:10.1075/intp.6.1.04liu

Liu, Y., & Wang, Z. (2014). Positive affect and cognitive control: Approach-motivation intensity influences the balance between cognitive flexibility and stability. *Psychological Science*, 25(5), 1116–1123. doi:10.1177/0956797614525213

Luck, S. J. (2014). *An Introduction to the Event-Related Potential Technique*. Cambridge, MA: MIT Press.

Lv, Q., & Liang, J. (2019). Is consecutive interpreting easier than simultaneous interpreting? – A corpus-based study of lexical simplification in interpretation. *Perspectives*, 27(1), 91–106. doi:10.1080/0907676X.2018.1498531

Ma, T., Chen, R., Dunlap, S., & Chen, B. (2016). The effect of number and presentation order of high-constraint sentences on second language word learning. *Frontiers in Psychology*, 7, 1396. doi:10.3389/fpsyg.2016.01396

Mahdavirad, F. (2015). The impact of form-focused guided strategic planning on oral task performance. *Research Papers in Language Teaching and Learning*, 6(1), 134–143.

Mishra, R. K. (2018). *Bilingualism and Cognitive Control*. Cham, Switzerland: Springer.

Miyake, A., & Friedman, N. P. (2012). The nature and organization of individual differences in executive functions: Four general conclusions. *Current Directions in Psychological Science*, 21(1), 8–14. doi:10.1177/0963721411429458

Morales, J., Padilla, F., Gómez-Ariza, C. J., & Bajo, M. T. (2015). Simultaneous interpretation selectively influences working memory and attentional networks. *Acta Psychologica*, 155, 82–91. doi:10.1016/j.actpsy.2014.12.004

Moser-Mercer, B. (2003). Remote interpreting: Assessment of human factors and performance parameters. https://ecfsapi.fcc.gov/file/7521826425.pdf

Namaziandost, E., Hafezian, M., & Shafiee, S. (2018). Exploring the association among working memory, anxiety and Iranian EFL learners' listening comprehension. *Asian-Pacific Journal of Second and Foreign Language Education*, 3(1), 20. doi:10.1186/s40862-018-0061-3

Paap, K. (2019). The bilingual advantage debate: Quantity and quality of the evidence. In: J. W. Schwieter & M. Paradis (Eds.), *The Handbook of the Neuroscience of Multilingualism* (pp. 701–735). Hoboken: Wiley-Blackwell.

Padilla, P., Bajo, M. T., Ca-as, J. J., & Padilla, F. (1995). Cognitive processes of memory in simultaneous interpretation. In: J. Tommola (Ed.), *Topics in Interpreting Research* (pp. 61–71). Turku: Center for Translation and Interpreting.

Peng, J., Wang, C., & Lu, X. (2020). Effect of the linguistic complexity of the input text on alignment, writing fluency, and writing accuracy in the continuation task. *Language Teaching Research*, 24(3), 364–381. doi:10.1177/1362168818783341

Pöchhacker, F. (2011). Simultaneous interpreting. In: K. Malmkjær & K. Windle (Eds.), *The Oxford Handbook of Translation Studies* (pp. 189–200). New York: Oxford University Press.

Rojo, A. (2017). The role of emotions. In: J. W. Schwieter & F. Aline (Eds.), *The Handbook of Translation and Cognition*. Hoboken: Wiley-Blackwell.

Rojo, A., & Caro, M. R. (2016). Can emotion stir translation skill? Defining the impact of positive and negative emotions on translation performance. In: R. M. Martín (Ed.), *Reembedding Translation Process Research*. Amsterdam: John Benjamins.

Rosiers, A., Woumans, E., Duyck, W., & Eyckmans, J. (2019). Investigating the presumed cognitive advantage of aspiring interpreters. *Interpreting. International Journal of Research and Practice in Interpreting*, 21(1), 115–134. doi:10.1075/intp.00022.ros

Russell, J. A., Weiss, A., & Mendelsohn, G. A. (1989). Affect grid: A single-item scale of pleasure and arousal. *Journal of Personality and Social Psychology*, 57(3), 493–502. doi:10.1037/0022-3514.57.3.493

Santilli, M., Vilas, M. G., Mikulan, E., Martorell Caro, M., MuÑOz, E., SedeÑO, L., & GarcÍA, A. M. (2018). Bilingual memory, to the extreme: Lexical processing in simultaneous interpreters. *Bilingualism: Language and Cognition*, 22(2), 331–348. doi:10.1017/S1366728918000378

Seeber, K. G., & Kerzel, D. (2012). Cognitive load in simultaneous interpreting: Model meets data. *International Journal of Bilingualism*, 16(2), 228–242. doi:10.1177/1367006911402982

Sudevan, P., & Taylor, D. A. (1987). The cuing and priming of cognitive operations. *Journal of Experimental Psychology: Human Perception and Performance*, 13(1), 89–103. doi:10.1037/0096-1523.13.1.89

Timarová, á., Čeňková, I., Meylaerts, R., Hertog, E., Szmalec, A., & Duyck, W. (2014). Simultaneous interpreting and working memory executive control. *Interpreting*, 16(2), 139–168. doi:10.1075/intp.16.2.01tim

Tzou, Y.-Z., Eslami, Z. R., Chen, H.-C., & Vaid, J. (2011). Effect of language proficiency and degree of formal training in simultaneous interpreting on working memory and interpreting performance: Evidence from Mandarin–English speakers. *International Journal of Bilingualism*, 16(2), 213–227. doi:10.1177/1367006911403197

Yudes, C., Macizo, P., & Bajo, T. (2011). The influence of expertise in simultaneous interpreting on non-verbal executive processes. *Frontiers in Psychology*, 2(309). doi:10.3389/fpsyg.2011.00309

12 Flipped Classrooms and Translation Technology Teaching

A Case Study

Piero Toto

Translation Technology Training

Translators are increasingly under pressure to keep up with the technological advances in the world of translation software and to refine their skills in order to be competitive professional translators. As suggested by García (2006, p. 98) in his study on translators' attitudes to technology, translators are often faced with a steep learning curve when trying to use the latest computer-aided translation tools (CAT tools) available on the market or when developing their translator competence (Kiraly, 2013). Traditional forms of translator training, which is commonly understood as being "the creation of skills needed in the labour market for translators" (Pym, 2001, p. 1), include *inter alia* on-site translation technology short courses and webinars. On-site translation technology teaching at both undergraduate and postgraduate levels involves the use of highly sophisticated translation software which speeds up the translator's work by leveraging existing translations in a translation memory (Muegge, 2010), providing terminology suggestions from dedicated databases ("termbases") for consistency. These tools also offer automated quality assurance checks and integrated machine translation engines for post-editing purposes, i.e. reviewing a target-language text translated with the use of automated translation (Quah, 2006). At the level of the universities participating in the European Master's in Translation (EMT) Competence Framework, of which London Metropolitan University (London Met) is a member at the time of writing, translation technology training is embedded within translation courses to promote greater uptake and professionalisation of tools (Rothwell & Svoboda, 2017).

At its core, translation technology teaching aims to ensure that students develop translator competence (Kiraly, 2006) for better marketability and competitiveness in the translation industry once they graduate, and to increase their employability chances. Employability will be understood as "the teaching and learning of a wide range of knowledge, skills and attributes to support continued learning and career development" (Pegg et al., 2012,

p. 7). It is therefore important for students' training to include sufficient in-class practice with translation tools (i.e. machine translation, translation memory systems/translation environment tools, terminology tools) so that they can be more competitive in the market once they complete their studies (Pearse, 2019). However, different learning paces and time constraints may hinder or slow down the in-class learning process, thus creating the impression that the translation technology trainer did not provide enough opportunities for practice or that the newly gained skills remain underdeveloped and unusable. Knight and Yorke (2003, p. 99) suggest that activities which are directly linked with the industry translate into more practical, realistic, and challenging pieces of work which stimulate a "deep approach to learning" (Biggs, 1999, p. 36). Although this statement mainly involves summative assessments and end-of-year assignments, it will be shown in this chapter how weekly activities that centre around student productivity, file processing, efficient execution of tasks, and financial benefits are vital for student employability.

"Flipping" Translation Technology

Flipped learning is a student-centred pedagogical approach in which the conventional notion of classroom-based learning is inverted. Students are introduced to the learning material before class, then classroom time is used predominantly to deepen understanding through discussions with peers facilitated by the teacher ("guide on the side") (HEA, 2018), as well as for assignments, problem-solving, group-learning, and other interactive activities.

Although theorisations of this approach can be traced back to the late 1990s, it was not until 2007 that this pedagogy took centre stage in the instructional education world thanks to Bergmann and Sams (2012), who made PowerPoint slides and online video content for their students in order to allow those living in rural areas to watch YouTube tutorials before going to class. Through this method, students are encouraged to explore a variety of resources. If students go to a class already knowledgeable about its content, responsibility is transferred from the teacher to them (Ozdamli & Asiksoy, 2016); this serves as an empowering educational model for learners. However, this "transfer" may pose problems if students do not carry out the required preliminary studying as expected or if, in the case of differing educational backgrounds coexisting within the same cohort, some students expect the teacher to take a "leading" role rather than act as a moderator. This is one of the drawbacks also highlighted by Evseeva and Solozhenko (2015, p. 208), for whom in this new context the role of the teacher is pivotal in ensuring a friendly environment to allow students to interact with one another and guide them through the new approach. Within the "Traditional Flipped Classroom" model (Bergmann & Sams,

2012), homework is carried out in class and theory is dealt with outside of classroom times. The educator establishes a one-to-one relationship with the student, ensuring ongoing observation and evaluation of their performance through informal or structured feedback.

Translation technology does not usually appear in case studies on flipped learning (Chen & Summers, 2015; Hao, 2016). Although at the time of writing no empirical studies involving the formal introduction of flipped learning in the translation technology classroom have been found, it is certainly possible that similar approaches are being implemented nevertheless and that a variation of the blended learning approach (i.e. involving a combination of materials posted online and contact time in class) is being used to teach technology to budding translators. This pedagogy has been adopted in the context of translation studies as partial flipping (Tsai & Tsai, 2017), where only a few sessions of the module/course are adapted for flipped learning, including sessions on translation technology. It has been found that most students deem the new approach suitable for translation teaching; it has also been employed for foreign language learning (Evseeva & Solozhenko, 2015), a discipline traditionally close to translation in terms of learning styles. The extensive use of education technology conventionally associated with flipped learning allows students to access the required resources remotely and in a flexible manner. As will be seen, the availability of ready-made resources for translation technology teaching on the internet considerably frees up preparation times for tutors. This time can be re-invested in exploring *ad hoc* tools or other materials. It is under these circumstances that the London Met's translation technology tutor decided to try out this new pedagogical approach which, as mentioned earlier, remains mostly unexplored and unmined in the realm of translation technology learning and teaching.

In vocational courses such as the two translation courses referred to below, developing translator competence as part of employability is a key learning outcome. When students are engaged in actively processing information by reconstructing that information in new and personally meaningful ways, they are far more likely to remember it and apply it to new situations (King, 1993, p. 30). Technology in flipped learning, and more specifically in translation technology teaching, is therefore both a means and a topic. In this constructivist view of learning, "students use their own existing knowledge and prior experience to help them understand the new material" (King, 1993, p. 30).

Flipped learning was first introduced as a trial in the teaching of translation technology modules (BA and MA Translation at London Met) in the 2015/2016 academic year as a result of the feedback received in the module evaluation forms (MEFs) for those modules: students predominantly indicated that they would have liked to have had more time for software practice. Initially, only some sessions in the modules in question were "flipped";

conversely, in the 2016/2017 academic year, all sessions for all modules involved were officially "flipped."

Overview of the Undergraduate Module

Module TR5051 (Electronic Tools for Translation) is a core 12-week, semester-based, Level 5 (second year) undergraduate module run as part of the BA Translation course at London Met. The course offers English combined with French, Spanish, Italian, Arabic, Portuguese, German, Polish, or Russian, as well as French, Spanish, and Arabic combined with English. Module TR5051, however, is not language-specific and runs in the first semester only. The size of the module cohort varies from 20 to 40 students and is predominantly made up of white, European female students in the 18–20 age range, followed by a similar group in the 21–29 age range. Black, Asian, and minority ethnic (BAME) students traditionally make up one-third of the cohort. The cohorts usually comprise a mixture of UK-educated and non-UK-educated students.

Module TR5051 focuses on developing students' knowledge of the range of electronic tools available for translation, including post-editing. The assessment strategy consists of ongoing weekly formative feedback and a piece of summative assessment.[1] This involves a timed online translation using translation environment tools (TEnTs) with integrated machine translation (MT), followed by a technical report and an evaluation of MT post-edited outputs according to a set of adapted industry-recommended parameters, i.e. the TAUS Error Typology Guidelines (2013).

Overview of the Postgraduate Module

Module TR7042 (Translation Tools and the Translator) is a core 12-week, semester-based, Level 7 (master's level) postgraduate module run as part of the MA Translation course at London Met. The MA Translation course is offered with Arabic, Mandarin, Dutch, French, German, Greek, Italian, Japanese, Polish, Portuguese, Russian, and Spanish combined with English (either direction). Module TR7042, however, is not language-specific. It runs in the autumn and spring semesters for full-time and part-time students, respectively. The size of the combined cohort varies from 20 to 30 students, predominantly white, European female students in the 21–29 age range. BAME students traditionally make up one-third of the cohort. As in the BA cohort, students are a mixture of UK-educated and non-UK-educated participants.

This module focuses on the TEnTs that the translator is likely to use in their day-to-day work. These include proprietary software for professional terminology management and for translation, as well as machine translation and post-editing. At the end of the module, students are expected to be able to deal with the practicalities of the daily work of translators as regards efficient technology use, meeting deadlines, and software troubleshooting. The assessment strategy consists of ongoing weekly formative feedback and a summative assessment task at the end of the teaching semester. This involves a timed online translation using TEnTs and related built-in features, as well as a report detailing the technical issues encountered and any troubleshooting solutions adopted.

"Flipping" the Translation Technology Classroom

Overview and Implementation

In both modules, students were encouraged from the outset to take a proactive stance in their learning, which can be defined as a predominantly learner-centric teaching approach. Computer literacy is an essential requirement of both modules, which falls in line with what is currently offered by most translation courses across Europe (Graham, 2015). In both modules, students are encouraged to bring their own device to class, so that they can work within their own preferred environment and not have to deal with occasional PC failures at university. By doing so, students simulate working as future freelancers, thus relying on their own technical resources and facing real-life problems should their own laptops fail in any way. As outlined by Rothwell and Svoboda (2017, p. 35), this approach is symptomatic of the greater attention provided by translation courses to the effective inclusion of professional workflows. While online, students connect directly to Weblearn (Blackboard), where they can upload/download materials and communicate with one another through a discussion board and other interactive tools which will be illustrated below.

According to Osman et al. (2017, p. 707), flipped learning is most suited for "themes that require a higher level of understanding," which would imply that flipping the traditional classroom should be reserved to disciplines where student engagement with theory would take up the majority of the class time. They also point out that students who fail to review the relevant materials before the next session feel unprepared to attend the flipped classroom and would much rather miss the class altogether than turn up without having revised the theory.

Traditionally, tutors who "flip" their classroom create content (videos, presentations, instructional content, etc.) to aid students' learning outside of the classroom. At London Met, students are redirected to already existing user-generated content, translation software manufacturers' own instructional materials, blog entries, journal articles, or the tutor's own adaptations of such materials on Weblearn. For example, in Week 2 of TR5051, students are asked to consult specific sections of Andy Walker's SDL Trados Studio manual (Walker, 2014). As will be explained below, SDL Trados Studio is the main software adopted throughout the course, and it is thus crucial that students learn about its features through Walker's manual.

Students are therefore asked to read about sections on editing source segments, merging two or more consecutive segments, and merging segments over hard returns, in order to scaffold their knowledge in preparation for the practical in-class activity scheduled for the following week. In Week 11, before their final online exam, students are asked to read an article on ethics and MT use published by Nimdzi, a US translation and localisation company, concerning the ethical implications of using machine translation. This is in preparation for the report on the use of MT that they will need to write as part of their exam and which will help them further consolidate their knowledge. Although comprehension of this latter reading is not tested in class, previous similar readings are provided on a weekly basis as part of students' self-study activities. This is done to improve their learning experience without significantly affecting the number of resources needed to deliver extra practical/contact hours, whilst taking into account the constraints of the curriculum (i.e. teaching weeks and learning outcomes).

Although in the traditional model of the flipped classroom the tutor is seen to create original content for the lecture videos (e.g. pre-recorded sessions), at London Met the availability of weekly class recordings allows students to catch up on any missed classes and to watch/listen to the recordings wherever they are, provided they have a device available (smartphone, tablet, laptop, PC/Mac). Students can thus learn at their own pace and in their own time. In designing these asynchronous learning modules, it was useful to keep in mind that, as highlighted by Santally and Raverdy (in Byrne, 2008), e-learning is a relatively new technology and should be considered more as a new means of flexible delivery than a totally new paradigm for learning. Technology proficiency is embedded in the curriculum, as advocated by JISC (2013), whereby "embedding technology effectively into learning and assessment activities enhances the delivery of all types of curricula"; however, certain considerations must be taken into account in order to deliver effective flipped learning.

Both modules include a significant e-learning component, which has been designed to incorporate the following main points:

- Cohort size: this is under 25 students per module, which was considered feasible and is recommended as desirable in order to provide each student with feedback on their performance. A large cohort will have an impact on the choice of learning materials due to a greater incidence of different learning styles, diversity of cultural/academic backgrounds, student expectations, etc.
- Learning materials: these are made available as e-books, scanned copies, videos, web articles, blogs, and the like (i.e. content which is freely available and accessible online). Students also have access to the university library e-resources, some of which are not available on the internet.
- Learning activities: these can be accessed at any time via the virtual learning environment (VLE) in the form of questionnaires, writing

exercises, quizzes, and collaborative activities, in order to enhance in-class participation and further stimulate group work.

- Choice of CAT tools: the main tool used is SDL Trados Studio, a market-leading TEnT (SDL, 2020) installed in London Met's IT labs and provided to students for free at home. Other tools used include Memsource Cloud and Wordfast Anywhere, two free cloud-based programs which provide a more economical solution for tackling the budgeting limitations faced by universities (Rothwell & Svoboda, 2017).
- IT literacy: before starting the module, students are provided with supporting material to help them refresh or learn basic IT skills. Given the heterogeneity of students' backgrounds, it is certainly not uncommon for both mature students and younger students to face the same IT-related difficulties. This is addressed by providing dedicated support and materials to ensure equal access to the learning platform and any translation software.

So far, the main approach adopted for teaching the translation technology modules has been a predominantly competency-based approach, which aims to "develop competent performance in the specified roles" (Toohey, 1999, p. 93). These "specified roles" here should be understood as (freelance) translation roles. Despite its obvious downside (its focus on technical skills), assessment of performance is a common trait of vocational courses under which both the BA and MA Translation courses at London Met can be categorised, unlike other translation courses. In actual fact, students are required to perform their final exam completely online, simulating a real-life assignment where they are given a tight deadline to submit their translation to the "client" (the translation tutor) in order to prepare them for the industry. In the weeks leading up to the exam, particular focus is placed on communication (between tutor and learners), collaboration (amongst students), and technology proficiency (Melville et al., 2009). This is to promote a more "holistic" approach which takes into account potential teaching limitations (e.g. lack of use of and interaction with the VLE on the part of the student) and, at the same time, enables students to fully benefit from and to further enhance their independent learning. To this end, Garrison and Anderson's "community of inquiry" model (2003, p. 23) was used as the framework to develop this approach (see Figure 12.1).

This framework consists of a "group of individuals who collaboratively engage in purposeful critical discourse and reflection to construct personal meaning and confirm mutual understanding" (Garrison & Anderson, 2003, p. 2). This promotes "cognitive independence and social interdependence simultaneously" (Garrison & Anderson, 2003, p. 23). The three "presences" on which it relies must be developed in a balanced manner, i.e. each presence needs to have equal relevance in the learning process.

The social presence relates to the way students (re)present themselves within the group. Since all students work towards being professional

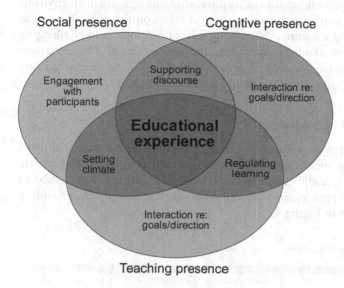

Social presence   Cognitive presence

Engagement with participants

Supporting discourse

Interaction re: goals/direction

Educational experience

Setting climate

Regulating learning

Interaction re: goals/direction

Teaching presence

Figure 12.1 The Community of Inquiry Model.

translators (and some of them already work professionally), their interactions are underpinned by this underlying common trait. This contributes to group identification, group cohesion, and achieving the relevant educational outcomes.

The cognitive presence element focuses, in bare terms, on critical thinking and on the students' validation of knowledge through its conceptualisation (at home) and consequent sharing with the group (in class or online). Within the context of translation technology, this presence is exemplified by the students' troubleshooting efforts – for instance, when facing technical issues with the software – which allows them to contextualise their problems and devise suitable solutions.

In terms of the teaching presence (i.e. the third constitutive element of the community of inquiry model), some of the main aims according to Garrison are "designing experiences that facilitate reflection and discourse, and diagnosing and assessing learning outcomes" (Garrison, 2003, p. 14). This presence moves along three key axes, namely design and organisation, facilitating discourse, and direct instruction. Each axis encapsulates the novel role of the tutor, acting as 1) a facilitator rather than a leader; 2) designing materials/ activities promoting collaboration and self-study in equal measure (*ibid.*), which is an aspect aligned with the flipped approach adopted at London Met and replicated in most flipped courses; and 3) supporting students along their journey. It is therefore evident how the role of the module designer (the translation technology tutor) and their ability to achieve all of this is paramount in such a model, and this needs to be considered when discussing resource availability. Through communities of inquiry, students operate in an environment in which they can be responsible for and take control of their learning "through negotiating meaning, diagnosing misconceptions, and challenging accepted beliefs – essential ingredients for deep and meaningful learning outcomes" (Ramsden in Garrison & Anderson, 2003, p. 27). As mentioned earlier, the tutor acts mainly as a "guide on the side" (HEA, 2018).

Learning Materials and Activities

In class, students engage with and exchange knowledge on practical tasks with one another by means of canvas-style tools, such as Padlet, which are integrated into the weekly VLE materials. On Padlet, students are asked to post questions and problems to which their peers will reply by providing solutions, as shown in Figure 12.2.

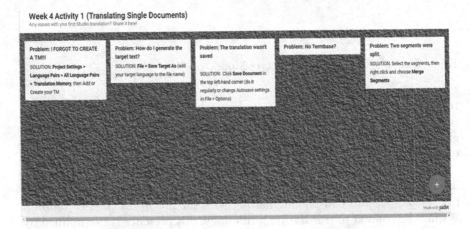

Figure 12.2 Example of In-Class Weblearn-Based Activity Using Padlet.

The tutor monitors the activity in real-time and can ask for clarifications or validate the students' answers (and correct them where necessary). This allows students to share their knowledge in a safe and friendly environment, in which they soon realise that their doubts about using the software are also shared by their peers. Since Padlet is embedded *ad hoc* within the relevant weekly materials, students can go back to those materials whenever they encounter the same problem or need a quick reference solution (especially if practising on their own at home). This reassures students about the availability of support within the module structure.

Additionally, students engage in peer-reviewing activities in which they test their own knowledge of translation tools and self-reflect on their own workflow and practices by evaluating someone else's work, as shown in Figure 12.3, which presents one of the teaching weeks' in-class activities (a consolidation task).

Formative Peer Feedback 🔗

Studio feedback: Pair up with a language partner. **Upload (as a zip folder) any of your currently available and completed projects** (including the TM and the termbase) to this <u>shared folder</u> (use your Londonmet account to access it). Then create a Google doc in the same shared directory and review your allocated peer's project providing them feedback on the basis of the *Feedback Guidelines* below:

- Project Settings
- Allow source editing/Enable merge segments across paragraphs
- Project File location
- TM (name, location, enabled)
- TM settings (minimum match value/concordance)
- Termbase (correct indexes, terms added)
- Report (saved as Excel file)
- Files (all uploaded)
- All segments translated and saved
- F7/F8 (any unresolved errors)
- Target texts (generated and saved)

Figure 12.3 Outline of Peer-Review Activity on Weblearn.

By drawing students' attention to their peers' performance in class, students are encouraged to develop self-awareness around the potential issues that they themselves could come across during the execution of their task. This self-reflection is an important step towards validating students' current knowledge, boosting their confidence, and, at the same time, making them aware of the potential gaps in their experience of the software.

Furthermore, students' experiences and appreciation of flipped learning are checked on an ongoing basis to ensure that the content delivered and the tools made available to them are suitable and effective. To this end, a tool such as Mentimeter is used, since this interactive presentation platform allows users' reactions to be visually represented in real-time in a "word cloud" in which words "grow" the more they are input by the users. This is done to initiate a conversation around on-the-spot feelings and opinions about the topics being covered and has been found to be an effective way of involving students in the learning process, thus making their experiences count.

Evaluating the Flipped Classroom

One of the main advantages of the flipped classroom model is that students feel empowered and accountable for their own learning, which occurs at their own pace, as reflected in the students' own assessment of the modules. Flipped learning allows lecturers to develop more tailored approaches to individual student learning and (depending on class size) more relevant one-to-one relationships, with each student's work being addressed on an individual basis at some point during the lesson. Module TR5051, in its current iteration, relies on three hours of weekly in-class contact time, whereas module TR7042 relies on two hours per week. This means that, throughout the relevant semesters, 100% (or at least 90%) of the time is devoted to providing students with the above-mentioned one-to-one or group feedback, depending on the activity. This has translated into higher satisfaction rates, as documented in the relevant module evaluation forms collected since this new pedagogical style was adopted. Each module evaluation form is an anonymous, mostly Likert scale–style, survey (answers range from *Strongly*

Agree to *Strongly Disagree*), with a mixture of questions and statements (24 in total for the undergraduate module and 13 in total for the postgraduate module) ranging from "I am satisfied with the overall learning experience provided by this module" to "The computer lab was satisfactory," and also includes open-ended questions asking students for their input on what works in the module or what could be improved (see Table 12.1).

Table 12.1 List of Questions and Statements in the MEFs

Questions/Statements in the TR5051 MEF	Questions/Statements in the TR7042 MEF
1. I am satisfied with the overall learning experience provided by this module 2. This module has been helpful in developing my IT, CAT tools and postediting skills 3. The module was well organised 4. The topics studied were interesting 5. The amount of work required is fair and manageable 6. In-class exercises and weekly tasks are useful 7. The lectures were well-presented and delivered at a pace I could follow 8. The module was taught in a way that I could understand 9. The tutor was helpful in terms of giving guidance to students 10. The tutor's office hours were generally scheduled at convenient times 11. Opportunities for student participation were about right and adequate chances were provided to students to ask questions 12. The guidelines on assessment tasks were useful 13. I like submitting assignments via Weblearn 14. The feedback received was helpful in terms of enabling me to understand strengths and areas for improvement 15. The feedback on activities and tasks was received in time for me to benefit from it 16. The online materials posted on Weblearn for this module were useful 17. The in-class mock assessments and drop-in sessions were useful in terms of exchanging ideas with peers and gathering further knowledge in an informal setting 18. The computers' performance was satisfactory 19. Weblearn's performance and usage were satisfactory 20. The computer lab was satisfactory 21. What did you enjoy most about this module? 22. What didn't you enjoy about this module? 23. How did you find the "flipped classroom" format? Did it work for you? If not, how can it be improved? 24. What suggestions would you make for improving this module?	1. Thinking about your learning experience overall, to what extent are you satisfied with this module? 2. How helpful has this module been in developing your IT, CAT tools and research skills? 3. How were the topics studied? 4. Was the amount of work required fair and manageable? 5. Please rate presentation and delivery (Were lectures well-presented and delivered at a pace you could follow?) 6. How helpful was the tutor in terms of giving guidance to students? 7. How helpful were the guidelines on assessment tasks? 8. Do you like submitting assignments via Weblearn? If not, please explain why in the Comments section (at the end of the questionnaire). 9. How useful were the online materials posted on Weblearn for this module? 10. How would you rate computers' performance? 11. What did you enjoy most about this module? 12. What didn't you enjoy about this module? 13. What did you think of the "flipped classroom" format? Did it work for you? If not, how can it be improved?

The questions in both MEFs partly reproduce a standard university-wide MEF, the content of which was adapted to match the specificities of the two modules. For the purposes of this case study, only a specific set of questions from both MEFs was analysed to provide a snapshot of student experience, namely: for TR5051, Questions 1, 9, 21, 22, 23; for TR7042, Questions 1, 6, 11, 13. These questions in particular were deemed to tie in more closely with students' experiences of the flipped approach. Although flipped learning was introduced in the 2016/2017 academic year, the data analysed in this case study relates to the MEFs from the 2017/2018 academic year onwards only. This is due to a technical problem in storing the data for the first academic year, which included responses from an additional 36 students on the BA and MA courses.

A total sample of 78 respondents is included in Figure 12.4, in which the questions about the overall learning experience and the usefulness of the tutor in terms of guidance have been worded in a more chart-friendly manner so as to make the relevant figures easier to read and interpret.

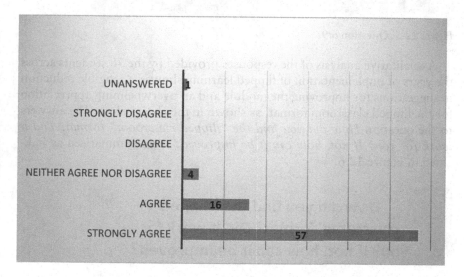

Figure 12.4 Question 1 in Both MEFs.

The overall picture painted by the graph in Figure 12.4 shows that, apart from four students who did not express any nuanced level of satisfaction with their learning experience, all the other students enjoyed the modules, with a large majority strongly agreeing with this statement.

The graph in Figure 12.5 shows that 100% of the students who replied to the questionnaires appreciated the tutor's support and guidance throughout the module, which works in favour of the previously mentioned teaching presence from the community of inquiry framework.

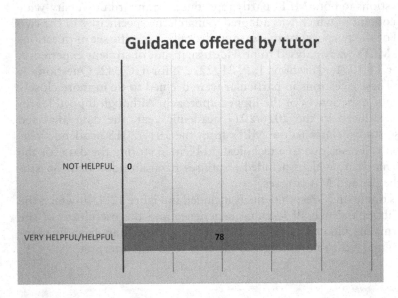

Figure 12.5 Question 6/9.

A qualitative analysis of the responses provided by the 78 students across the years of implementation of flipped learning showed a tangible reduction in suggestions for improving the module and an overwhelming appreciation for the flipped classroom format, as shown in the chart below. The answers to the question *How did you find the "flipped classroom" format? Did it work for you? If not, how can it be improved?* were summarised as indicated in Figure 12.6.

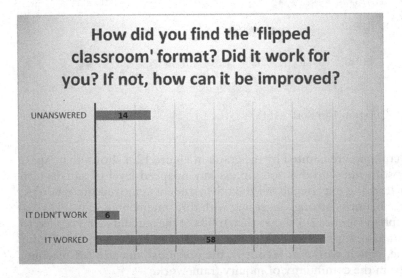

Figure 12.6 Students' Satisfaction with the Flipped Model.

As can be seen in Figure 12.6, only 7.6% of students across the years expressed dissatisfaction with the model, which, according to the analysis of the data, may have been predominantly due to some students' preferences for a more traditional approach or their low levels of IT literacy (despite the support provided), compared to a majority of 74% of students supporting the format.

This question in the MEF allows students to provide feedback on the overall pedagogy of the module and affords the tutor a further opportunity to gauge the successful implementation (or lack thereof) of flipped learning. The qualitative data derived from this particular question suggests that, despite some initial scepticism about the format, students were generally happy with the structure, delivery, and innovative element of the module. They could also appreciate how the pedagogy in question might not be suitable for other modules in the same curriculum, and how it allowed them to study at their own pace and have immediate access to personalised feedback.

Some of the following comments, made by students in response to this particular question, can be considered as being representative of the answers collected:

> I think it was useful, because we do need some practice on our own in order to make mistakes and have them corrected in class.
> It worked for me.
> It helped me to understand certain topics better on my own first.
> It was a great experience. I prefer to study more at home and this format allowed me to work and practice [sic] on my own.
> I enjoyed learning on my own and then practising it in [the] classroom, where I could receive immediate feedback.
> [D]oing exercises in class and asking questions is much easier and useful than doing the exercises at home and then asking all the questions the following week when we meet again. It is a good system and I am happy with it.
> On a regular basis, I appreciated this format. We used our time in class to do practical exercises, which I found very useful.
> I think it is a good idea as it means that any problems encountered can be discussed and shared in class. This allows formative feedback to be given fairly quickly.

Studying from home was seen as a clear benefit, along with an appreciation of the range of software programs offered.

Responses to Question 22/12 ("What didn't you enjoy about this module?") were either a simple "Nothing/I wouldn't change anything" or expressed dissatisfaction with the computer performances in the IT labs; on other occasions, the responses included requests for more in-class time and contact hours. Given the positive outcome of the MEFs, this should be regarded as a confirmation of the success of the model adopted rather than as a failure of the new approach.

In order to accommodate students' ever-changing needs and the dynamic nature of the topics covered, translation technology teaching at London Met has undergone a series of tweaks before arriving at the current model. The original module formats predominantly involved explaining translation technology theory in class, followed by assignments to be completed in preparation for the following week. These assignments, however, were not always completed by the students. Therefore, the tutor had to resort to allocating extra marks (up to five extra marks) to students who performed their weekly homework in order to foster individual engagement outside of the classroom. This was made possible by the marking system in place at the time, i.e. a points-based system. In the 2017/2018 academic year, the university switched to a pegged marking system, which no longer allowed the allocation of points or additional rewards outside of the pegged marks.

As postulated by Hamdan et al. (2013), the flipped classroom can be interpreted as a model that teachers use to meet the demands of students by availing themselves of a variety of tools. In line with previous findings (Hao, 2016), students in both modules found quizzes for testing their knowledge the least likeable feature introduced because they felt put on the spot. However, these drawbacks can be prevented with careful classroom management and activity planning, and by involving students in the creation of content. Hao (2016, p. 91) points out that students' evaluation of their flipped classroom experience may be influenced by the teacher–student relationship when the researcher is also the instructor, which is the case for the modules discussed in this chapter. It is particularly significant that, in many instances, the students' response to the question "What did you enjoy most about this module?" was an appreciation of the tutor's role in facilitating their learning as well as their overall teaching style. It was noted that the "human element" in teaching was a significant contributor to the students' learning experiences. As stated by Li (2018), in order to run a successful flipped classroom "a teacher has to rely on human qualities like high self-discipline, high motivation, initiative and personal charisma," but this may not always be the case for all students and all teachers. The perception that personal charisma was a determinant factor in students' evaluations of the module was particularly felt in the undergraduate responses, which tended to comment on the tutor's impact on the students' learning rather than discuss the module content or format.

The overall level of satisfaction with the implementation of this pedagogical approach appears to fall in line with the current literature (e.g. Blair et al., 2016): the analysis of the qualitative data demonstrates an increased perception of the usefulness of the course in general as well as the students' time-management skills. Mostly in line with Blair et al.'s (2016) findings, no significant performance improvement was registered at the level of summative assessment. Students, however, mentioned that they felt more confident in tackling the final exam. This can also be seen in the tenor of the open-ended responses provided in the MEFs, showing an overall higher perception of self-achievement and satisfaction with the module and its format.

Conclusion

The success of a course/module depends on a series of factors which need to be considered when "flipping" classes. Flipped learning may not be the preferred model or strategy for all students or for all tutors. It is not to be intended as a one-size-fits-all approach, nor can it be deemed as a panacea for all disciplines. The success of the flipped classroom model relies on students being accountable for out-of-class learning and for attending lessons after having revised the relevant materials and theory. When this does not happen, students' unpreparedness can be viewed as a "flipped *flop*," which may adversely affect not only their own progress but also that of the rest of the class, thus further exacerbating the heterogeneity in learning pace within the same cohort. It was observed, however, that peer pressure and the aforementioned tutor–student relationship affect this variable: only a handful of students failed to engage with the theory before class for the two modules in question, and they usually caught up in class or in preparation for the next session.

Collaboration and self-study in such a community of inquiry are possible only through suitable and carefully designed materials, which need to be integrated into the existing VLE, and also through attentive interpersonal relationships (between peers and between students and tutors) that can foster a positive working environment and a relaxed learning space (Gray & Klapper, 2003, p. 331) . The students' perceived need for more in-class practice when learning about new translation software can be addressed by freeing up class time to supervise students individually – where class group size allows – and increase their overall satisfaction with the module/course. The current iterations of the modules in question contain a good balance of theory-inspired and practice-based activities in the form of reflection activities and translation tasks (timed or otherwise), peer-review exercises, readings, videos, and other materials suggested by the tutor. It was useful to provide a theoretical framework (i.e. the community of inquiry approach) to this implementation so as to clearly identify students' and curriculum needs in terms of learning/teaching materials and activities.

It should be noted that one of the ongoing challenges facing translation technology tutors is the speed of technological change affecting the language industry (Pielmeier & O'Mara, 2020) and the consequent focus on professionalisation which guides many of the design decisions taken (Baños-Piñero & Toto, 2015, pp. 202–203). As the technology available to translators becomes increasingly more complex, it may be necessary to reconsider whether to "flip" a whole module or only a few sessions in order to make the trickier underlying theory behind the technology more accessible for students instead of redirecting them to online resources or other available materials. Given the technological nature of the topics, the metalanguage used in the suggested readings or audiovisual materials may pose difficulties to some students, especially non-native speakers. This potential cognitive challenge is a common trait of translation technology teaching, and should be taken into consideration when selecting the relevant supporting materials: in order to foster student engagement, alternative readings or videos on the same topic may need to be provided, thus offering students a choice of customised content based on their individual abilities. This solution may of course increase class preparation times for the tutor instead of reducing them.

On the other hand, though, this approach reinforces the central role of the tutor as facilitator of the overall learning experience and relies on the pivotal "human qualities" discussed earlier, including the tutor's suitability for "flipping." Students coming from a more traditional educational background, where power distance (Hofstede, 1984) scores high, may feel uncomfortable or unprepared to take full ownership of their learning. By acting as "mediator" in the classroom rather than "sage on stage," the lecturer's role and function may be at risk of being devalued. The level of energy and empathy required to run a flipped classroom may also need to be investigated further in order to establish which particular traits are conducive to more successful flipped learning opportunities and identify any other strategies that may need to be adopted in order to make the flipped model more viable and thus more beneficial to both students and educators.

Note

1 Students also sit a mock exam in the weeks prior to the official online exam so as to prepare them for the format and any time constraints they might encounter in their professional life.

References

Baños-Piñero, R. & Toto, P. (2015). Challenges and constraints in designing a localisation module for a multilingual cohort. In: P. Sánchez-Gijón, B. Mesa-Lao & O. Torres-Hostench (Eds.) *Conducting Research in Translation Technologies* (pp. 185–206). Oxford: Peter Lang.

Bergmann, J. & Sams, A. (2012). *Flip Your Classroom: Reach Every Student in Every Class Every Day*. Washington, DC: International Society for Technology in Education.

Biggs, J. (1999). *Teaching for Quality Learning at University*. Maidenhead: Society for Research into Higher Education & Open University Press.

Blair, E., Maharaj, C. & Primus, S. (2016). Performance and perception in the flipped classroom. *Education and Information Technologies*, 21(6), 1465–1482. doi:10.1007/s10639-015-9393-5.

Byrne, J. (2008). Learning technology in the translation classroom. In: *Proceedings of the XVIII Fit World Congress Shanghai*. http://www.jodybyrne.com/769.

Chen, H. L. & Summers, K. L. (2015). Developing, using, and interacting in the flipped learning movement: Gaps among subject areas. *International Review of Research in Open and Distributed Learning*, 16(3), 41–64. doi:10.19173/irrodl. v16i3.1975.

Evseeva, A. & Solozhenko, A. (2015). Use of flipped classroom technology in language learning. *Procedia-Social and Behavioral Sciences*, 206, 205–209. doi:10.1016/j.sbspro.2015.10.006.

García, I. (2006). Translation memories: A blessing or a curse? In: A. Pym, A. Perekrestkenko & B. Starink (Eds.), *Translation Technology and Its Teaching* (pp. 97–105). Tarragona: Universitat Rovira i Virgili.

Garrison, R. & Anderson, T. (2003). *E-Learning in the 21st Century: A Framework for Research and Practice*. London: Routledge/Falmer.

Graham, N. (2015). European MA translation & interpreting courses. https://ni kkigrahamtranix.com/ma-translation-courses/.

Gray, C. & Klapper, J. (2003). Key aspects of learning and teaching in languages. In: H. Fry, S. Ketteridge & S. Marshall (Eds.) *A Handbook for Teaching and Learning in Higher Education. Enhancing Academic Practice* (pp. 323–344). London: Kogan Page.

Hamdan, N., McKnight, P., McKnight, K. & Arfstrom, K. (2013). A review of flipped learning. http://flippedlearning.org/cms/lib07/VA01923112/.

Hao, Y. (2016). Exploring undergraduates' perspectives and flipped learning readiness in their flipped classrooms. *Computers in Human Behavior*, 59, 82–92. doi:10.1016/j.chb.2016.01.032.

Heacademy.ac.uk (2018). Flipped learning. https://www.heacademy.ac.uk/knowled ge-hub/flipped-learning-0.

Hofstede, G. (1984). *Culture's Consequences: International Differences in Work-Related Values* (2nd ed.). Beverly Hills CA: SAGE Publications.

JISC (2013). Enhancing curriculum design with technology. http://www.jisc.ac.uk/ sites/default/files/enhancing-curriculum-design.pdf.

King, A. (1993). From sage on the stage to guide on the side. *College Teaching*, 41(1), 30–35.

Kiraly, D. (2006). Beyond social constructivism: Complexity theory and translator education. *Translation and Interpreting Studies*, 6(1), 68–86. doi:10.1075/ tis.1.1.05kir.

Kiraly, D. (2013). Towards a view of translator competence as an emergent phenomenon: Thinking outside the box(es) in translator education. In: D. Kiraly, S. Hansen-Schirra & K. Maksymski (Eds.) *New Prospects and Perspectives for Educating Language Mediators* (pp. 197–224). Tübingen: Gunter Narr Verlag.

Knight, P. & Yorke, M. (2003). *Assessment, Learning and Employability*. Maidenhead: Society for Research into Higher Education & Open University Press.

Li, Y. (2018). Current problems with the prerequisites for flipped classroom teaching: A case study in a university in Northwest China. *Smart Learning Environments*, 5(1), 1–23. doi:10.1186/s40561-018-0051-4.

Melville, D., Allan, C. et al. (2009). Higher education in a web 2.0 world. http:// www.jisc.ac.uk/publications/generalpublications/2009/heweb2.aspx.

Muegge, U. (2010). Ten good reasons for using a translation memory. *Tcworld Magazine*. https://works.bepress.com/uwe_muegge/9/.

Osman, A., Jalal, S. R. & Azizi, S. (2017). Flipped learning: Should it replace didactic learning? *Advances in Medical Education and Practice*, 8, 707–708. doi:10.2147/AMEP.S149533.

Ozdamli, F. & Asiksoy, G. (2016). Flipped classroom approach. *World Journal on Educational Technology: Current Issues*, 8(2), 98–105. https://files.eric.ed.gov/fulltext/EJ1141886.pdf.

Pearse, B. (2019). How to become a professional translator in 2019. https://www.smartcat.ai/blog/what-it-takes-to-become-a-translator/.

Pegg, A., Waldock, J., Hendy-Isaac, S. & Lawton, R. (2012). *Pedagogy for Employability*. York: Higher Education Academy. http://www.heacademy.ac.uk/assets/documents/employability/pedagogy_for_employability_update_2012.pdf.

Pielmeier, H. & O'Mara, P. D. (2020). *The State of the Linguist Supply Chain*. CSA Research. https://insights.csa-research.com/reportaction/305013106/Toc.

Pym, A. (2001). *E-learning and Translator Training. Translator Training and E-Learning. An Online Symposium*. Intercultural Studies Group. https://www.researchgate.net/publication/237666540_E-Learning_and_Translator_Training.

Quah, C. K. (2006). *Translation and Technology*. Houndmills: Palgrave Macmillan.

Rothwell, A. & Svoboda, T. (2017). Tracking translator training in tools and technologies: Findings of the EMT survey 2017. *The Journal of Specialised Translation*, 32. https://jostrans.org/issue32/art_rothwell.php.

SDL plc (2020). *SDL Trados Studio*. http://www.translationzone.com/products/sdl-trados-studio/.

Taus.net (2013). *Error Typology Guidelines – TAUS – The Language Data Network*. https://www.taus.net/academy/best-practices/evaluate-best-practices/error-typology-guidelines.

Toohey, S. (1999). *Designing Courses for Higher Education*. Maidenhead: The Society for Research into Higher Education & Open University Press.

Tsai, Y. & Tsai, A. (2017). Flipped translation training: The student perception. *Studies in English Language and Literature*, 39, 187–206. https://ctld.ntu.edu.tw/rp/report/103_08_.pdf.

Walker, A. (2014). *SDL Trados Studio – A Practical Guide (E-Book)*. Birmingham: Packt Publishing Ltd Online.

13 An Empirical Study on Distance Interpreter Training in China Before the COVID-19 Pandemic

A Mixed-Methods Approach

Mianjun Xu, Tianyuan Zhao, and Juntao Deng

Introduction

Professional interpreter training in China only started with the launch of Bachelor of Translation and Interpreting (BTI) programmes in 2006 and Master of Translation and Interpreting (MTI) programmes in 2007. As of 2019, there were respectively 281 and 253 universities and colleges offering BTI and MTI programmes ("BTI institutions" and "MTI institutions" for short). However, not all BTI and MTI institutions have sufficient numbers of competent interpreting teachers who have rich experience in both interpreting teaching and practice, which greatly hinders the sound development of BTI and MTI education and the quality of interpreting graduates (Zhong, 2019).

One way to solve the problem is to rely on distance interpreter training (DIT) (Deng & Xu, 2013; Deng & Zhong, 2019). Compared with traditional face-to-face instruction, DIT has a number of advantages, such as flexibility, convenience, and cost-effectiveness (Güven, 2014, p. 119) as well as capacity to cope with the increasing number of students and to prepare students for the changing professional world (Jiménez-Crespo, 2015, p. 35). DIT can be interpreted in two different ways: first, the teaching of distance or technology-assisted interpreting, such as telephone interpreting or videoconference interpreting (e.g. Braun et al., 2011); second, teaching interpreting by the distance mode (e.g. Ko, 2004, 2006, 2008; Ko & Chen, 2011). In this chapter, the focus will be on the second one.

In China, the most common forms of distance education include massive open online courses (MOOCs), small private online courses (SPOCs), flipped classrooms, micro-lectures, video open courses, and live webcast courses, all of which have been included in the national strategies to share high-quality education resources, to bridge the inter-collegial and inter-regional disparities, and to boost education equity. However, DIT, as a new form of instruction, is yet to receive more practical or scholarly attention in China, because both teachers and students seem to take face-to-face instruction for granted and consider DIT a daunting task. In view of this, it is necessary to carry out empirical studies on the current status quo, including the actual use and perceptions of DIT by major stakeholders such as interpreting teachers, to reveal merits and demerits so that more well-targeted courses can be designed and implemented.

Background

DIT started in the late 1990s and has seen rapid development in the new millennium (Sandrelli & de Manuel Jerez, 2007; Ko & Chen, 2011). For example, Cervato and De Ferra (1995) reported a computerised self-study course for students of Italian in their final year to practice liaison interpreting. Ko (1996, 1999, 2004, 2006, 2008), Ko and Chen (2011), Sandrelli (2001, 2002, 2003a, 2003b, 2007, 2011, 2015), Sandrelli and de Manuel Jerez (2007), Chan (2013, 2014), Degueldre and Angelelli (2014), Kajzerwietrzny and Tymczyńska (2014), and Sachtleben and Crezee (2015) all tried to conduct interpreter training by the distance mode or to integrate technology into interpreter training at their respective institutions. Ehrlich and Napier (2015) discussed the digital evolution in interpreter education. Tymczyńska (2009) and Güven (2014) also reported DIT used in subject-specific interpreting courses such as in the medical field. As reported by the scholars, all these experiments of DIT have proved successful in that they can either supplement or replace offline interpreting training to some extent.

Scholars also try to evaluate different DIT courses, for example, Carr and Steyn (2000) briefly discussed the challenges of the DIT project developed between Vancouver Community College and the Open Learning Agency, but they did not offer details of the project. Moser-Mercer et al. (2005) reported the first assessment of an online and offline blended interpreting course offered by the University of Geneva to train interpreter trainers and found that learners thought highly of such a mode of learning, especially in terms of the learning environment and human resource organisation. Mayer and Ivars (2007) thought the advantages of DIT projects included benefits for students who could not physically attend classes, greater autonomy on the part of students, and teachers as learning facilitators. Şahin (2013) discussed how virtual worlds such as Second Life could be used by interpreter trainers, including offering a quasi-authentic environment, facilitating teacher–student communication and interactions, recording everything on screen for feedback and self-evaluation, and following up on interpreting lessons.

Lee and Huh (2018) found that a 20-week online interpreting course for beginners was received generally positively by the trainees, who listed logistical convenience, self-paced learning, and one-to-one trainer feedback as advantages, while it was received by the trainers with mixed views. On the one hand, they agreed with the trainees to some extent, but on the other hand, they preferred the synchronous mode and emphasised the importance of teacher–student interactions; they also thought that teaching presence was not strongly established, thus affecting social presence and cognitive presence.

This brief review shows that DIT has been discussed and practised extensively, with both advantages and challenges acknowledged, such as flexibility, convenience, and cost-effectiveness for the former, and lack of teacher–student interactions, difficulty in assessing the learning outcome, and technology constraints for the latter.

In China, because professional interpreter training only has a history of a dozen years or so and mostly takes place within BTI and MTI institutions, the varieties and numbers of DIT courses offered are limited (Xu et al., 2020). Up till now, there have not been any empirical studies on the overall situation of DIT in China or the specific use and perceptions of it from the interpreting teachers' perspectives. For this reason, the authors of this study try to answer the following research questions in the hope of having a closer examination of DIT in China and further developing it:

1) What is the status quo of DIT in China?
2) How do interpreting teachers perceive DIT?
3) What are the motivating and/or demotivating factors for interpreting teachers to engage in DIT?

Coincidentally, the data collection and writing processes of this paper were closely followed by the COVID-19 pandemic, which has changed the entire world. DIT, which used to be considered formidable, became a reality instead of a potential choice for all teachers, because all teaching activities in China, ranging from primary to tertiary education, were moved from the brick-and-mortar classrooms to the internet.

At the beginning of the pandemic, the decision for mandatory distance education was negatively received by most teachers, because, with little or no such experience, they were quite at a loss for what to do. Some even wished that they could postpone their teaching until after students could go back to school. As a result of the pandemic, interpreting teachers' perceptions and predictions of DIT have greatly altered.

Research Methods

This study adopts a mixed-methods approach, involving both a questionnaire survey and in-depth semi-structured interviews of interpreting teachers. The combination of the two research methods has enabled the authors to take advantage of each of them. On the one hand, a well-designed questionnaire distributed to the right respondents can generate a large amount of quantifiable data. On the other hand, interviews enable researchers to pay attention to facts and ideas that cannot be revealed by questionnaires. As a result, the two methods can supplement and triangulate each other, enabling the authors to present a more objective and comprehensive picture of the research topic.

The Questionnaire

The questionnaire consists of 30 questions, including single-answer and multiple-answer questions. Questions 1–7 concern the respondents' personal information, while the remaining 23 deal with their experience and perceptions of DIT.

The questionnaire was designed using the free online questionnaire website wenjuan.com, and was distributed to a number of WeChat (the most popular social media app in China) groups consisting of translation and interpreting teachers, professional translators and interpreters, and administrators of language service companies between 30 September and 31 December 2019. A total of 75 responses (see Table 13.1 for a summary of the respondents' demographic information) were collected, all of them valid, i.e. all of them were filled out by interpreting teachers and with no unanswered items. The respondents came from different age groups and different types of universities and, with varying research fields, years of interpreting teaching and professional titles, so they are representative of the greater interpreting teacher population in China to some extent. Though the sample size was smaller than expected, it still sufficed to present a rough picture of DIT used and perceived by interpreting teachers. The collected data were initially analysed by the questionnaire website and further processed by the authors.

The Interviews

Apart from the questionnaire survey, a total of 14 interpreting teachers were interviewed by the authors either face-to-face or through WeChat voice calls between December 2019 and January 2020. The interviewees were recruited by snowball sampling with the intention of including the greatest possible number of interpreting teachers with different backgrounds and from different types of universities and geographical locations within the writing period. The interviews were done by the first and second authors by following the same interview guide, with follow-up questions according to the interviewees' answers. Before each interview, the potential interviewees were briefed on the content and nature of the research project and their rights to quit, to remain anonymous, and to know the research results.

Table 13.1 Summary of Respondents' Demographic Information

Item		Nos.			Nos.
No. of respondents		75	Type of university	Comprehensive	29
Gender	M	28		Foreign languages	19
	F	47		Science and technology	14
Age	20s	9		Teacher education	10
	30s	44		Medicine	1
	40s	19		Higher vocational college	1
	50s	3		Independent college with special focus on science and technology	1
Years of teaching	≤ 5 years	36	Types of students taught	Undergraduate English majors	43
	6–10 years	20		MTI students	32
	11–15 years	12		BTI students	25
	16–20 years	6		MA in Translation Studies	13
	> 20 years	1		Higher vocational college students	8
Professional title	Teaching assistant	9		Undergraduate non-English majors	7
	Lecturer	31		Masters of other majors	4
	Associate professor	27	Types of interpreting courses taught	Consecutive interpreting	55
	Professor	8		Thematic interpreting	30
Research fields of academic degrees	Translation studies	62		Simultaneous interpreting	28
	Linguistics	37		Liaison interpreting	22
	Literature	16		Sight interpreting	22
	Education	16		Basic interpreting	1
	Others	5		Conference interpreting	1

To protect their privacy, they were referred to by numbers instead of their real names (see Table 13.2 for interviewees' profile). With the consent of the interviewees, all the interviews were recorded and transcribed on iflyrec .com mechanically and proofread by the authors. The draft version of the paper was sent to some interviewees for member checks.

Before analysing the transcripts, the authors discussed the coding system together. If there were any disagreements, they went back to the transcriptions for a second and even a third reading and consulted the interviewees to ensure accurate interpretations.

Table 13.2 Interviewees' Profile

Item		Nos.	Item		Nos.
No. of interviewees		14	Type of	Foreign languages	4
Gender	M	3	university	Comprehensive	3
	F	11		Translation and interpreting	2
Years of	≤ 5 years	2		Economics	1
teaching	6–10 years	7		Ethnic minorities	1
interpreting	> 10 years	5		Teacher education	1
Professional	Lecturer	7		Engineering	1
titles	Associate professor	7		Science and technology	1
Experience of	Yes	7	Forms of DIT	MOOCs	4
DIT	No	7		Live webcast courses	2
				Flipped classrooms	1
				Online feedback	1

Data, Data Analysis, and Analysis Results

This section reports the findings from both the questionnaire survey and the in-depth semi-structured interviews. As all the interviews were conducted in Chinese, all direct quotations were translations by the authors.

Use of DIT

Experience of DIT

Only 17 (22.7%) respondents had experience of DIT while 58 (77.3%) had none. Of the former group, 11 were engaged in MOOCs, seven in open video courses, five in micro-lectures, five in live webcast courses, and three in SPOCs.

Half of the 14 interviewees had DIT experience. Teacher 1 had the experience of co-teaching with another colleague in the form of a live webcast. He stayed in the classroom to answer students' questions while his colleague was lecturing in the distance mode. Teacher 3 was the only one who had the experience of both consecutive interpreting MOOC and live-webcast courses. Teachers 4 and 5 took part in recording interpreting MOOCs. Teacher 9 was engaged in a provincial interpreting teaching reform project of flipped classrooms, so she made a lot of short videos, which were uploaded to Douyin, the Chinese version of TikTok, a short video and music video app most popular among young people in China. She required her students to watch them before each lesson. In addition, she also ran an interpreting WeChat public account with her students, where they shared interpreting resources. Teacher 13 had made a public speaking MOOC.

Teacher 14 used the distance mode for feedback and formative assessment of students' after-class performance.

Use of DIT Resources

Table 13.3 shows respondents' (potential) use of domestic and international DIT resources. As some respondents used or intended to use more than one type of DIT resources, the total numbers far exceeded those of the respective respondents.

For the interviewees, interpreting MOOCs also came out on top. For example, Teacher 13 mentioned that she would use DIT courses such as MOOCs from some prestigious universities when she was preparing lessons. She could learn from their teaching methods and the way they presented the lessons, but she would not recommend her students to watch those MOOCs. In her opinion, interpreter training is highly personalised. Different teachers have their own ideas about the teaching process, such as how to teach the principles, methods, and thinking process of interpreting. If she let her students watch the DIT courses of other teachers, she was afraid that their teaching systems would contradict with her own.

Apart from MOOCs, the interviewees also made use of various online resources at home and abroad. The Speech Repository of the European

Table 13.3 Respondents' Use of Domestic and International DIT Resources

Item		Nos.	Item		Nos.
Use of DIT resources	Yes	29			
	No	46			
Types of DIT resources used	Interpreting MOOCs	18	Types of DIT resources to be used	Interpreting MOOCs	52
	Open video interpreting courses	15		Interpreting corpora	51
	Interpreting teaching resource libraries	13		Open video interpreting courses	49
	Interpreting micro-courses	12		Interpreting teaching resource libraries	49
	Interpreting corpora	9		Interpreting SPOCs	36
	Online course management systems	8		Online course management systems	28
	Interpreting SPOCs	7			

Commission was the most frequently mentioned resource library by the interviewees. Apart from that, TED Talks and websites of the UN, the White House, and *China Daily* were also frequently used. Some domestic English learning websites such as putclub.com, kekenet.com, and En84.com also offered numerous verbal, audio, and video materials for interpreting teaching and practice.

Knowledge and Use of Online Interpreting Course Management Systems

Again, only 29 respondents had heard of online interpreting course management systems, of whom 14 had used Moodle, nine Blackboard, and two PostNuke.

Though the majority of the interviewees' universities were equipped with online course management systems, such as ChaoXing, Rain Classroom, Smart Class, and Blackboard, they were hardly used by the interviewees. Instead, some openly accessible social media were more popular among them, such as QQ groups, WeChat groups, or the Baidu Cloud, which were used for teacher–student and student–student communications and for uploading and downloading course materials.

Perceptions of DIT

General Comments on DIT Resources

Only seven (9.3%) respondents thought the existing DIT resources abundant in variety and quantity. Another 40 (53.3%) thought them insufficient and 28 (37.7%) thought them scarce.

When asked to comment on the existing DIT courses, some interviewees expressed their concern about the current assessment mechanism of elite online courses in China. At the moment, whether a course can be appraised as a National Elite Online Course depends largely on the number of registrations. Though this can reveal to some extent the popularity of a certain course, it is not the only criterion for assessing the course and the teacher(s).

Suitability of Interpreting Courses for DIT

Concerning whether and which interpreting courses were suitable for DIT, 70 (93.3%) respondents were positive, while only five thought none suitable. But when it came to specific interpreting courses, they were not as affirmative, with no interpreting courses winning over 50% of respondents' support. Table 13.4 shows respondents' ideas about the suitability of different types of interpreting courses for DIT.

The majority of the interviewees thought interpreting history, introduction to interpreting skills and coping tactics, and interpreting theories,

Table 13.4 Suitability of Interpreting Courses for DIT

Types of Interpreting Courses	Nos. (%)
Thematic interpreting	36 (48.0%)
Consecutive interpreting	34 (45.3%)
Sight interpreting	33 (44.0%)
Interpreting studies	31 (41.3%)
Interpreting workshop	25 (33.3%)
Liaison interpreting	23 (30.7%)
Simultaneous interpreting	17 (22.7%)

Table 13.5 Advantages of DIT over Face-to-Face Instruction

Potential Advantages	Nos. (%)
Breaking spatial and temporal constraints	64 (85.3%)
Breaking the number constraint	58 (77.3%)
Learning advanced teaching methods and philosophy from prestigious universities	58 (77.3%)
Repeatability of courses	50 (66.7%)
Useful supplement to offline teaching	49 (65.3%)
Effectively bridging the inter-collegial and inter-regional disparities and promoting education equity	46 (61.3%)
No advantage	5 (6.7%)

which did not require a lot of teacher–student interactions, were suitable for DIT, but they did not think DIT a good choice for training professional interpreters.

Advantages of DIT Over Face-to-Face Instruction

On the whole, the majority of the respondents were positive about the provided potential advantages of DIT, while only five were totally negative (see Table 13.5 for details).

The interviewees held similar opinions concerning the advantages of DIT. All of them regarded "breaking spatial, temporal and number constraints" the biggest advantage. In the DIT mode, students could enjoy greater flexibility and make use of fragmented time. The second advantage was that it offered teachers whose universities were not so well positioned in interpreter training the chance to learn from the more prestigious ones. Teacher 5 said she not only studied interpreting MOOCs of other universities herself but also recommended excellent ones to her students. Teacher 13 acknowledged that she benefited a lot from excellent DIT courses and thought them useful teaching resources for teachers in smaller and less developed cities.

Teacher 2 thought DIT could increase the revenues of the course-offering institutions and boost their popularity if their courses were taken by huge numbers of learners. But this is dubious because, in China, most DIT courses offered by universities are free of charge.

Teacher 3 thought there might be the occasional advantage of bringing convenience to the interpreting teachers if they happened to be busy and could not teach the lessons in person, but this was not a long-term advantage. Though convenience was generally considered as an advantage of DIT, no other interviewees mentioned this as an advantage to themselves.

Teacher 9 mentioned an advantage overlooked by others, that is, in the distance mode, students were more willing to express themselves so that teachers could know them better. She requested her students to leave their comments after watching her short videos on Douyin, but she did not demand them to use their real names. She was surprised to know that her students were much more willing to express themselves, quite different from how they appeared in the offline classrooms.

Disadvantages of DIT Over Face-to-Face Instruction

On the other hand, DIT had some disadvantages over face-to-face instruction as perceived by the respondents (see Table 13.6).

To the interviewees, the disadvantages of DIT included the following. First, there was no screening for the students enrolled. In the DIT mode, students' competencies, educational background, and personal traits could not be predicted and screened, so it was impossible to carry out well-targeted and individualised teaching. Take interpreting MOOCs as an example. Anyone can register as a student with a QQ or WeChat account without revealing their real identity, so the teachers may have no idea who their students are in the online classrooms.

Second, there was a lack of teacher–student and student–student interactions. The interviewees all agreed that most interpreting courses were practice-oriented and it was highly necessary for teachers to give instantaneous

Table 13.6 Disadvantages of DIT over Face-to-Face Instruction

Potential Disadvantages	Nos. (%)
Lack of sense of presence	63 (84.0%)
Not conducive to teacher–student and student–student interactions	59 (78.7%)
Restricted by hardware and software conditions	53 (70.7%)
Failure to offer students individualised guidance	50 (66.7%)
Teachers under greater pressure	26 (34.7%)
Increasing teachers' workload	23 (30.7%)
No disadvantage	0 (0.0%)

feedback to students' performance. The distance mode prevented teachers from close observations of students' interpreting process and products, their notes, or even their facial expressions and other paralinguistic features. "In my classes, I readjusted my teaching according to the students' responses. But if the lessons have been recorded in advance, it will be quite boring" (Teacher 2, 19 December 2020).

Third, the shooting process of recorded DIT courses also made teachers uncomfortable. Teacher 4 recalled her experience of shooting the interpreting MOOC:

> I took part in shooting an interpreting MOOC, but I didn't quite like it. You had to write the scripts, you had to get used to the limelight. You didn't have much freedom as in real classrooms. In addition, it felt rigid. You stood there. Your gestures were different from what you did in the classroom. It felt like acting. I was not quite used to it.
>
> (31 December 2019)

Fourth, objective and comprehensive assessment of students' performance was difficult if not impossible. Though the capacity of distance courses to enrol unlimited numbers of students could be regarded as an advantage, it was considered a disadvantage by the interviewees. Teacher 3 explained:

> In the online mode, if 200,000 students register for my course, it is impossible for me to listen to their recordings one by one. I think this is the biggest restriction of DIT. Before [an] automatic scoring system is put into use, I don't think there is any good way to quickly know whether the students have learned the interpreting skills well and to assess them scientifically.
>
> (30 December 2019)

Another closely related disadvantage is the lack of monitoring of students' learning activities. As students were learning online, the teachers did not know whether they had spent the time learning or idling.

Knowledge and Competencies Suitable to be Taught by DIT

Respondents' opinions on the suitability of various knowledge and competencies to be taught by DIT were more diverse, with only encyclopedic knowledge acknowledged by over half of them (see Table 13.7).

The interviewees agreed that the DIT mode was suitable for imparting declarative knowledge or declarative parts of procedural knowledge. Teacher 9 explained:

> Declarative knowledge, such as interpreters' professional ethics, procedures of interpreting, and basic requirements of interpreters can be

Table 13.7 Knowledge and Competencies Suitable to be Taught by DIT

Knowledge or Competency	Nos. (%)
Encyclopedic knowledge	48 (64.0%)
Bilingual competence	37 (49.3%)
Strategic competence	37 (49.3%)
Bilingual transfer competence	35 (46.7%)
Cross-cultural competence	29 (38.7%)
Interpersonal competence	18 (24.0%)
Psychological competence	17 (22.7%)
Others	3 (4.0%)

imparted by online courses. In addition, declarative part[s] of procedural knowledge, such as the concept of information listening, methods and suggestions for practices, as well as how to find reference materials can all be taught online. But when it comes to procedural knowledge such as how to practice their listening and how to handle difficulties in the process of practice, I still think it more effective for teachers to have targeted feedback and guidance in real classrooms.

(5 January 2020)

Perceptions of the Most Effective DIT Modes

Blended online and offline teaching was recognized by 54 (72.0%) of the respondents as the most effective mode of teaching while other DIT modes were much less positively received, namely, MOOCs by 11 respondents (14.7%), micro-lectures by five (6.7%), and SPOCs by four (5.3%). One respondent acknowledged being unable to answer the question.

Teacher 3 argued that the main purpose of DIT courses, such as MOOCs, was not to teach students any knowledge or skills of interpreting but to inform them that certain courses were offered by certain universities. If they really wanted to learn how to become professional interpreters, they had to go to the physical classrooms and receive formal interpreter training (30 December 2019).

Perceptions of Intrinsic Factors Affecting DIT Effects

The most important intrinsic factors affecting DIT effects perceived by the respondents showed great disparities, the top three factors being "course presentation forms" with 61 responses (81.3%), "teacher–student and student–student interactions" with 47 responses (62.7%), and "course content" with 44 responses (58.7%). Other factors were much less recognised, with none exceeding 50% of the responses (see Table 13.8).

Table 13.8 Intrinsic Factors Affecting DIT Effects

Intrinsic Factors	Nos. (%)
Course presentation forms	61 (81.3%)
Teacher–student and student–student interactions	47 (62.7%)
Course content	44 (58.7%)
Teachers' feedback on students' performance	30 (40.0%)
Teachers' belief in DIT	17 (22.7%)
Number of students	15 (20.0%)
Students' belief in DIT	11 (14.7%)

Class size

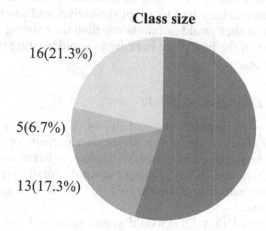

16(21.3%)

5(6.7%)

13(17.3%)

■ ≤20 ■ 21-40 ■ 41-60 ■ Number of students does not matter

Figure 13.1 Perceived Ideal Class Size for DIT.

The interviewees thought course design a major intrinsic factor affecting DIT effects. If a course was not well designed, it was impossible to achieve the expected effects. In addition, the absence of students in the distance mode affected the teaching effects.

Perceptions of Ideal Class Size for DIT

As in offline interpreting classes, smaller class sizes were preferred by the majority of respondents (see Figure 13.1).

The interviewees held the opinion that the class size should vary in accordance with the different types of courses offered. If they focused on imparting declarative knowledge, the class size could be larger, but if they were skill-based and demanded a lot of teacher–student interactions, the smaller the better.

Willingness to Engage in DIT

The respondents' predictions of their own and students' willingness to engage in DIT were similar. Only 11 respondents (14.7%) clearly expressed their reluctance to engage in DIT while the others were either "very willing" (33 responses, 44.0%) or "so-so" (31 responses, 41.3%). Similarly, 33 respondents (44.0%) thought students did not care; 29 (38.7%) thought them very willing, and 13 (17.3%) thought them unwilling.

The interviewees were split about half and half in their willingness to engage in DIT. Some thought that DIT would be a natural trend with the advancement of technologies so they had to adapt themselves and catch up with it. The others thought if they could not do better than the existing DIT courses, they would not try in the first place in order to avoid wasting time, money, and human resources.

Perceptions of the Future Development of DIT

The overwhelming majority of respondents, namely, 64 (85.3%) were neither too positive nor too negative about the future development of DIT, maintaining that it would be a useful and essential supplement to traditional face-to-face instruction. Only five (6.7%) thought it would totally replace traditional face-to-face instruction and another six (8.0%) were negative about its future development.

All the interviewees agreed that DIT would supplement and enhance offline interpreting education. No one thought it would replace traditional face-to-face instruction in the near future. At the moment, technology remained a major problem hindering the further development and popularisation of DIT.

The necessity of developing DIT courses was questioned by some interviewees. Teacher 5 and Teacher 7 doubted, as there were already 253 MTI and 281 BTI institutions nationwide, who else would take the DIT courses. Was it possible that after certain DIT courses had been created, few students would actually take them? Teacher 8 had similar concerns: "If the courses fail to achieve the expected results after so many efforts have been spent, isn't it a waste of time and resources?" (5 January 2020).

Some interviewees were more positive in that they held the opinion that interpreting teachers should embrace technologies and make them serve the classrooms, the teachers, and the students. As there were so many online teaching resources, teachers could be spared repetitive work. They could use 5G and virtual reality (VR) to make their classes more interesting to the tech-savvy generation. For example, Teacher 4 allowed her students to take their tablets instead of the traditional paper notebooks to her interpreting lessons.

Motivating or Demotivating Factors for DIT

Motivating Factors

The motivating factors are listed in Table 13.9 from top to bottom.

The answers of the interviewees somewhat differed from the questionnaire results. Teacher 3 cited curiosity as a major motivator.

> At the very beginning, we had no presumptions. We just wanted to know what DIT courses could do, whether they could teach students the same skills as offline ones. We had the platform and the funding, so we simply started.
>
> (30 December 2019)

Apart from curiosity, Teacher 3 also mentioned self-retrospection and self-perfection:

> After the first version of our MOOC came out, I found some defects, so I wanted to improve them in the second and third rounds. We tried to revise the course according to the suggestions of students, colleagues and our own reflections. It is a good chance for us to sort out our ideas in the process of designing the course, writing up the scripts and actually presenting it.
>
> (30 December 2019)

Another important motivator is preferential treatment by the university authorities in professional title appraisal and performance evaluation. "These are practical reasons for interpreting teachers to engage in DIT. Otherwise, few teachers would do it out of their noble sentiments" (Teacher 8).

Demotivating Factors

Figure 13.2 lists the demotivating factors that might prevent respondents from engaging in DIT in the first place, with "no technological support" ranking the top. The interviewees revealed similar demotivating factors for

Table 13.9 Motivating Factors for DIT

Motivating Factors	Nos. (%)
Having strong support for educational technology	54 (72%)
Having a teaching team and avoiding solitary operations	53 (70.7%)
Raising the pay of DIT	43 (57.3%)
Reducing the workload of offline teaching	43 (57.3%)
Preferential treatment for DIT in professional title appraisal and performance evaluation	42 (56.0%)

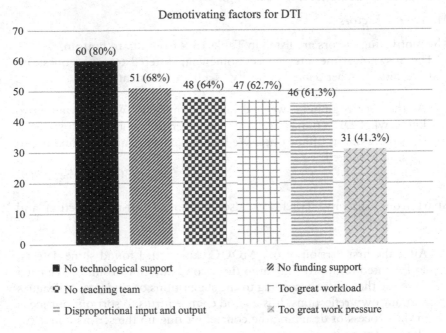

Figure 13.2 Demotivating Factors for DIT.

engaging in DIT. The objectives for DIT courses were not clear. "I have no idea who the students will be and what the courses intend to achieve" (Teacher 7).

Funding could be a major problem that prevents teachers from applying in the first place. "The application process was so complicated that it was enough to intimidate any teacher from applying" (Teacher 3). The making of an online course could take hundreds of thousands of RMB. If the university did not sponsor the teachers, nobody would start running any DIT course.

A number of interviewees expressed their reluctance to try any DIT courses because they were not confident they would improve upon the existing ones, such as the consecutive interpreting MOOC offered by Guangdong University of Foreign Studies, which won high recognition among the interviewees.

Discussion

This study confirms earlier research findings that DIT is a useful supplement to face-to-face instruction (e.g. Mayer & Ivars, 2007). The majority of both questionnaire respondents and interviewees agreed that the blended online and offline teaching mode can achieve better teaching effects than the solely online or offline modes. Compared with its western counterparts, DIT in China still has much room for improvement. In the following section, problems and suggestions, as well as the latest developments, will be discussed.

Problems with DIT in China

First, the interpreting teachers' motivations to engage in DIT are not strong enough, despite the efforts of the Ministry of Education and their respective universities to develop it, because conditions for successful DIT such as strong teaching teams, technological support, funding support, and preferential treatment for those engaged in DIT are devoid or inadequate.

Second, there are insufficient types and numbers of existing DIT courses. For the time being, the most common are MOOCs, especially those on consecutive interpreting. Other interpreting courses, such as liaison interpreting, thematic interpreting, simultaneous interpreting, or interpreting theories are not offered online.

Third, there are no integrated DIT resources available, be they distance courses, resource libraries, or others. When interpreting teachers prepare their lessons, they have to spend large amounts of time searching the internet for suitable teaching and practising materials.

Fourth, interactions with and assessment of DIT learners are not satisfactorily handled. Because of the large numbers of registrations, it is impossible to have instantaneous teacher–student interactions, individualised feedback, or objective and comprehensive assessments of students.

Fifth, few interpreting teachers use any online course management systems, though, as reported by the interviewees, their universities are equipped with such systems. This may affect their course management and teacher–student interactions.

Suggestions for Improvement

Because of the COVID-19 pandemic and the nationwide online education in the first half of 2020, some problems discussed above have been fully or partially solved while some more deep-rooted ones are still waiting for joint efforts of all parties concerned. The experience during COVID-19 has proven that DIT has a much greater role in education and should be developed more vigorously so that regular education activities can continue in times of crisis. The following are some suggestions for the future development of DIT.

First, universities should offer more incentive measures, especially in terms of funding, technological support, and most importantly, preferential treatment for interpreting teachers who engage in DIT courses in professional title appraisal and performance evaluation so that interpreting teachers will be better motivated to engage in DIT. Because making DIT courses demand much extra time and energy on the part of interpreting teachers, if the rewards are not worth their while, few will have the motivations for such teaching reforms or innovations. Of course, in extreme cases such as the COVID-19 pandemic, administrative mandates can make seemingly impossible things possible.

Second, before large-scale DIT courses are launched, it is necessary to carry out need analyses of the potential learners, including their identity, language proficiency, objectives for taking the DIT courses, and expectations from these courses. The more details the course designers know about the potential course-takers, the better targeted the courses will be. Apart from the existing consecutive interpreting MOOCs, more varieties and greater numbers of DIT courses can be offered to cater to the needs of different learners. Admittedly, interpreting teachers' perceptions of DIT have been much broadened or altered by their own DIT experience during the pandemic. Instead of engaging in pre-recorded courses for some unknown number of unknown students, most of them have been engaged in live webcasts for their offline classes.

Third, greater supervision and coordination of education authorities and closer inter-collegial cooperation and collaboration should be enhanced to avoid further waste of educational resources and to encourage BTI and MTI institutions to offer characteristic DIT courses in line with their respective disciplinary advantages. If there are sufficient numbers of quality DIT courses available, both interpreting teachers and students can benefit from them.

In addition, the education authorities should also try to construct or entrust certain universities to construct a national DIT resource library or libraries to cater to the needs of different universities and learners. Universities concerned can learn from successful examples abroad, such as the Speech Repository of the European Commission.

Fourth, more advanced technologies, such as automatic scoring systems, VR, and artificial intelligence (AI) should be introduced to the interpreting classrooms. Though VR and AI have played increasingly greater roles in interpreting education (Şahin, 2013), they have not been effectively used in China. It is essential to explore ways to further integrate them into DIT for more vivid presentation of interpreting scenarios and teacher–student and student–student interactions. Once automatic scoring systems are developed, the problem of assessing students comprehensively and objectively can be solved accordingly. The pandemic has greatly boosted the popularity and reputation of a large number of social media and online education platforms, such as Tencent Classroom, Tencent Meeting, QQ Classroom, Zoom, Rain Classroom, and Dingding, to name just a few. Such new developments have greatly improved the technology competence of interpreting teachers and students and offered a good chance to further integrate and upgrade them to facilitate DIT.

Fifth, course management systems should be made more user-friendly to attract more interpreting teachers to use them for more efficient resource sharing and teacher–student interactions. With improved interaction and storage functions of DIT platforms and software, DIT will surely be more popular among interpreting teachers even in normal times.

Conclusion

This study has attempted to explore DIT in China from the interpreting teachers' perspectives with both quantitative and qualitative data collected from a questionnaire survey and in-depth semi-structured interviews of 14 interpreting teachers. Being the first of its type in China, this study enables readers to better understand DIT in China, especially its status quo, including interpreting teachers' use and perceptions of it, and the motivating and demotivating factors for it. Its findings can serve as a reference for policymakers of DIT and as a window to understanding it in China. Its latest developments in China and in the rest of the world since 2020 and a comparative study of the same group of interpreting teachers before and after the COVID-19 outbreak will be the topics of our next studies.

References

Braun, S., Taylor, J., Miler-Cassino, J., Rybińska, Z., Balogh, K., Hertog, E., van den Bosch, Y., & Rombouts, D. (2011). Training in video-mediated interpreting in legal proceedings: Modules for interpreting students, legal interpreters and legal practitioners. In: S. Braun, & J. Taylor (Eds.), *Videoconference and Remote Interpreting in Criminal Proceedings* (pp. 205–254). Guildford: University of Surrey.

Carr, S., & Steyn, D. G. (2000). Distance education training for interpreters. An insurmountable oxymoron? In: R. P. Roberts et al. (Eds.), *The Critical Link 2: Interpreters in the Community* (pp. 83–88). Amsterdam: John Benjamins.

Cervato, E., & de Ferra, D. (1995). Interpr-It: A computerised self-access course for beginners in interpreting. *Perspectives*, 2, 191–204.

Chan, C. H. (2013). From self-interpreting to real interpreting: A new web-based exercise to launch effective interpreting training. *Perspectives*, 21(3), 358–377. doi:10.1080/0907676X.2012.657654.

Chan, C. H. (2014). Building an online library for interpretation training: Explorations into an effective blended-learning mode. *Computer Assisted Language Learning*, 27(5), 454–479. doi:10.1080/09588221.2013.770034.

Degueldre, C., & Angelelli, C. V. (2014). Implementing new technologies in the teaching of interpreting. *Cuadernos de ALDEEU*, 25, 253–278.

Deng, J., & Xu, M. (2013). Interpreting teaching in the context of information technology—International experience and domestic exploration (in Chinese). *Modern Educational Technology*, 23(1), 55–58.

Deng, J., & Zhong, W. (2019). Integrating information technology into interpreting teaching: Levels, mechanisms and prospect (in Chinese). *Chinese Translators Journal*, 6, 88–95+192.

Ehrlich, S., & Napier, J. (2015). Introduction: Digital evolution: Contextualizing a volume on digital education in interpreter education. In: S. Ehrlich, & J. Napier

(Eds.), *Interpreter Education in the Digital Age: Innovation, Access, and Change* (pp. xv–xxi). Washington, DC: Gallaudet University Press.

Güven, M. (2014). Distance learning as an effective tool for medical interpreting training in Turkey. *Open Learning: The Journal of Open, Distance and e-Learning,* 29(2), 116–130. doi:10.1080/02680513.2014.964196.

Jiménez-Crespo, M. A. (2015). The Internet in translation education: Two decades later. *Translation and Interpreting Studies,* 10 (1), 33–57. doi:10.1075/tis.10.1.03jim.

Kajzer-Wietrzny, M., Tymczynska, M. (2014). Intergrating technology into interpreter training course: A Blended learning approach. *inTRAlinea* Special Issue: Challenges in Translation Pedagogy, http://www.intralinea.org/archive/article/2101.

Ko, L. (1996). Teaching dialogue interpreting. In: C. Dollerup, & V. Appel (Eds.), *Teaching Translation and Interpreting 3 - New Horizons* (pp. 119–128). Amsterdam: John Benjamins.

Ko, L. (1999). To be or not to be: Prospects of interpreting and translation education in Australia. In: U. Ozolins (Ed.), *Interpreting/Translating Education in the Age of Economic Rationalism, Proceedings of the XVII Conference of the Interpreter/ Translator/Educators' Association of Australia* (pp. 61–79). Centre for Research and Development in Interpreting and Translating. Australia: Deakin University.

Ko, L. (2004), *Teaching Interpreting by Distance Mode.* PhD thesis. University of Queensland. (Unpublished).

Ko, L. (2006). Teaching interpreting by distance mode: Possibilities and constraints. *Interpreting. International Journal of Research and Practice in Interpreting,* 8(1), 67–96.

Ko, L. (2008). Teaching interpreting by distance mode: An empirical study. *Meta,* 53(4), 814–840.

Ko, L., & Chen, N. S. (2011). Online-interpreting in synchronous cyber classrooms. *Babel. Revue Internationale de la Traduction / International Journal of Translation,* 57(2), 123–143. doi:10.1075/babel.57.2.01ko.

Lee, J., & Huh, J. (2018). Why not go online?: A case study of blended mode business interpreting and translation certificate program. *The Interpreter and Translator Trainer.* doi:10.1080/1750399X.2018.1540227.

Mayor, M. J. B., & Ivars, A. J. (2007). E-learning for interpreting. *Babel. Revue Internationale de la Traduction / International Journal of Translation,* 53(4), 292–302.

Moser-Mercer, B., Class, B., & Seeber, K. G. (2005). Leveraging virtual learning environments for training interpreter trainers. In: *Proceedings of the 50th Anniversary Conference of Meta, Montreal, April 7-9, 2005. Meta,* 50(2) (CD-ROM).

Sachtleben, A., & Crezee, I. (2015). Digital innovation serving interpreter education in New Zealand. In: S. Ehrlich, & J. Napier (Eds.), *Interpreter Education in the Digital Age: Innovation, Access, and Change* (pp. 18–38). Washington, DC: Gallaudet University Press.

Şahin, M. (2013). Virtual worlds in interpreter training. *The Interpreter and Translator Trainer,* 7(1), 91–106. doi:10.1080/13556509.2013.798845.

Sandrelli, A. (2001). Teaching liaison interpreting: Combining tradition and innovation. In: I. Mason (Ed.), *Triadic Exchanges* (pp. 173–196). Manchester: St Jerome.

Sandrelli, A. (2002). Computers in the training of interpreters: Curriculum design issues. In: G. Garzone, M. Viezzi, & P. Mead (Eds.), *Perspectives on Interpreting* (pp. 189–204). Bologna: CLUEB.

Sandrelli, A. (2003a). New technologies in interpreter training: CAIT. In: H. Gerzymisch-Arbogast et al. (Eds.), *Textologie und Translation* (pp. 261–293). Tübingen: Gunter Narr.

Sandrelli, A. (2003b). New technologies in interpreter training: The state-of-the-art. In: C. Greensmith (Ed.), *New Challenges for the European Year of Language*, Proceedings of the ITI/IALB Annual Conference, University of Hull (pp. 22–25). November (2001) (CD-ROM).

Sandrelli, A. (2007). Designing CAIT (Computer-Assisted Interpreter Training) tools: Black box. In: H. Gerzymisch-Arbogast, & S. Nauert (Eds.), *Challenges of Multidimensional Translation: Proceedings of the Marie Curie Euroconferences MuTra: Challenges of Multidimensional Translation, Saarbrücken, 2-6 May 2005*. http://www.euroconferences.info/proceedings/2005_Proceedings/2005_p roceedings.html

Sandrelli, A. (2011). Computer assisted interpreter training (CAIT) for legal interpreters and translators (LITs). In: B. Townsley (Ed.), *Building Mutual Trust: A Framework Project for Implementing EU Common Standards in Legal Interpreting and Translation* (pp. 234–268). London: Middlesex University. http://www.lr.mdx.ac.uk/mutual-trust/mtdocs/BMT%20Report.pdf

Sandrelli, A. (2015). Becoming an interpreter: The role of computer technology. *MonthTI*, Special Issue, 2, 111–138. doi: 10.6035/MonTI.2015.ne2.4

Sandrelli, A., & de Manuel Jerez, J. (2007). The impact of information and communication technology on interpreter training: The state-of-the-art and future prospects. *The Interpreter and Translator Trainer*, 1(2), 269–303. doi:10.1080/1750399X.2007.10798761

Tymczyńska, M. (2009). Integrating in-class and online learning activities in a healthcare interpreting course using Moodle. *The Journal of Specialised Translation*, 12, 148–164.

Xu, M., Deng, J., & Zhao, T. (2020). On status quo, problems, and future development of translation and interpreting MOOCs in China – A mixed methods approach. *Journal of Interactive Media in Education*, 1(13), 1–10.

Zhong, W. (2019). Translator and interpreter education in China in the four decades of reform and opening up: Achievements, challenges and developments (in Chinese). *Chinese Translators Journal*, 40(1), 68–75.

Index

Printed in the United States
by Baker & Taylor Publisher Services